THE OCEAN CLASS

THE OCEAN CLASS of the Second World War

Malcolm Cooper

Seaforth
PUBLISHING

First page: *Ocean Verity* leaving New York for Halifax on 23 August 1942, her battered paintwork concealing the fact that she was still on the first leg of her maiden voyage from the west coast of North America and had yet to make the North Atlantic convoy crossing to Britain.
(US Coast Guard/Mariners' Museum & Park)

Previous spread: *Ocean Viceroy*, photographed passing under the Sydney Harbour Bridge in the livery of the Clan Line, would be renamed *Clan Kenneth* when Clan bought all seven of its chartered Oceans at the end of 1947 and *Omonia II* when resold to Greek owners in 1958, serving the latter until she was broken up at Hamburg in 1966 after damage from a dockside fire.
(V H Young and L A Sawyer)

First published in Great Britain in 2022 by
Seaforth Publishing,
A division of Pen & Sword Books Ltd,
47 Church Street,
Barnsley S70 2AS

www.seaforthpublishing.com

British Library Cataloguing in Publication Data

A catalogue record for this book is available from the British Library

ISBN 978 1 3990 1553 0 (HARDBACK)

ISBN 978 1 3990 1554 7 (EPUB)

ISBN 978 1 3990 1555 4 (KINDLE)

Pen & Sword Books Limited incorporates the imprints of Atlas, Archaeology, Aviation, Discovery, Family History, Fiction, History, Maritime, Military, Military Classics, Politics, Select, Transport, True Crime, Air World, Frontline Publishing, Leo Cooper, Remember When, Seaforth Publishing, The Praetorian Press, Wharncliffe Local History, Wharncliffe Transport, Wharncliffe True Crime, White Owl and After the Battle.

Typeset and designed by David Rose

Printed and bound in India by Replika Press Pvt Ltd

FSC www.fsc.org MIX Paper from responsible sources FSC® C016779

CONTENTS

ACKNOWLEDGEMENTS

Much of my research on the Ocean class merchant ships of the Second World War was carried out at The National Archives of the UK (TNA) at Kew. This publication contains public sector information licensed under the Open Government Licence v3.0. I would like to express my thanks to the research and reading room support staff at TNA for their unfailing professionalism and helpfulness, not just while I was working on this project, but also over my entire career as an historian, stretching back to my first doctoral research visits soon after the Kew reading rooms opened in 1978. I think it fitting also to register here my admiration for the ongoing enhancement of facilities, systems and services which have maintained TNA's position as a world-class and reader-friendly archival resource throughout this period.

I completed my research for this project through visits to other repositories around the UK and extend my thanks to the staff at the following institutions for their cheerful assistance dealing with my document requests: The National Records of Scotland, Register House, Edinburgh; the Caird Library, National Maritime Museum, Greenwich; the Imperial War Museum, London; the Glasgow City Archives, Mitchell Library, Glasgow; the Glasgow University Archives, Glasgow; the Maritime Archives & Library, National Museums & Galleries on Merseyside, Liverpool; the Manchester Archives & Local Studies Centre, Manchester Central Library, Manchester; the Teeside Archives, Middlesbrough; and the Glamorgan Archives, Cardiff.

While I was lucky enough to finish the archival research for this book before Covid-19 pandemic related closures interfered with access to sources, the same was not true of the collection of photographs, and the completion of the extensive portfolio of images in this book is testament to the dedication of archivists and technical specialists in institutions in three different countries who continued to work through partial shutdowns, remote access and other challenging operating conditions. In this regard, I would like to thank staff at the National Maritime Museum and the Imperial War Museum, London; the Nova Scotia Archives, Halifax; the City of Vancouver Archives, the Vancouver Maritime Museum, and the Museum and Archives of North Vancouver in Canada; the Library of Congress, and the Naval History and Heritage Command, Washington, DC; the Mariners' Museum and Park, Newport News, Virginia; the Hoover Institution Library and Archives at Stanford University; the Richmond Museum of History, and the San Francisco Maritime National Historical Park Research Centre in California; and Old Oregon Photos, Portland, Oregon.

I have benefitted throughout from the help of friends and colleagues in the international maritime history research community and fellow members of the World Ship Society. I owe special thanks to my good friend Roy Fenton who has supported the project throughout, providing generous access to research materials in his own collection, searching for images on my behalf in his own extensive collection of photographs and those of Ships in Focus and the World Ship Society, answering many of my questions on points of detail, reading through and commenting on the draft manuscript, and ultimately introducing me to my publisher. I am also grateful to Bill Schell, not just for providing me with photographs from his splendid collection, but also for deploying his immense expertise on vessel ownership histories to help me navigate through the often-complex peacetime careers of the Ocean class ships. I am similarly indebted to Richard Osborne for providing detailed answers to my questions on naval issues which would otherwise have been beyond my power to resolve. I would also like to thank Ian Buxton, Bill Harvey, and Patricia Richardson for their help on individual issues along the way.

The same international community of maritime historians provided generous assistance in providing me with photographs from their collections of the Oceans in war and in peace, in which regard I would like to thank Roy Fenton, John and Marion Clarkson, Malcolm Cranfield, John D Hill, George Robinson, Ships in Focus, the World Ship Society archives, and Comunn Eachdraidh Nis/Ness Historical Society in the UK; Bill Schell and Peter J Marsh in the United States; Howard Dick, Russell Priest and the Nautical Association of Australia in Australia; and Vic Young in New Zealand. I would also like to acknowledge the use of photos from Fotoflite incorporating Skyfotos, Archivi C N R Palermo, the Valles Steamship Co Ltd, and C C Hsu – Eddie Steamship Co Ltd accessed through intermediate collectors.

Finally, I am grateful to Julian Mannering, my editor at Seaforth Publishing, for providing me with the opportunity to publish with his imprint and for his guideness during the completion of the project. My greatest debt, as always, is to my wife Xingyan, whose unflagging love, support and understanding has sustained me throughout.

Malcolm Cooper
Thames Ditton, May 2021

INTRODUCTION

Ocean Traveller arriving at New York on 5 September 1943 in ballast from the Mediterranean with convoy GUS 12. After loading a military cargo, she would sail from Hampton Roads for Port Said in UGS 19 on 25 September. *(US Coast Guard/Mariners' Museum & Park)*

When Britain went to war in 1939, her merchant marine and the shipbuilding industry that supported it were ill-equipped to meet the demands of a titanic battle of attrition on her trade routes. As early as the summer of 1940, it was clear that meeting the mushrooming demands of supplying both the home islands and the wider war effort was beyond the capacity of shipping companies seriously weakened by depressed pre-war trading conditions. Similarly, it was already obvious that the British shipbuilding industry, its capacity seriously reduced by interwar yard closures, would struggle not only to support the expansion of the merchant marine, but even to replace its spiralling losses. While additions from Allied merchant fleets whose home countries had been overrun and purchases of redundant First World War era tonnage from the USA went some way to meeting immediate demands, an effective long-term response could only be achieved if the British government could tap the shipbuilding capacity of North America.

It was a measure of just how desperate the situation was perceived to be that a British shipbuilding mission arrived in the United States as early as the first week of October 1940 and that a contract to build sixty vessels in US shipyards was signed before the year was out. The same mission also visited Canada, placing orders for vessels with yards on both the east and west coasts. Canada, however, was an ally and had sufficient building capacity at least to commence its Fort-class ship construction programme as soon as orders were received. The situation in the United States was totally different. Not only was the country neutral, but the provisions of the Neutrality Acts meant that combatants had to buy goods on a 'cash and carry' basis, paying in hard currency and undertaking their own shipments. In addition, the US government had embarked on an ambitious programme of shipbuilding aimed at the modernisation and expansion of both the US Navy and the merchant marine, a programme which by

Photographed here steaming through the English Channel, *Clan Macbean* (ex-*Ocean Courier*) was one of seven Oceans purchased by the Clan Line at the end of 1947.
(Fotoflite incorporating Skyfotos)

1940 was absorbing all the country's peacetime shipbuilding resources.

The British decision to build sixty 10,000dwt steam tramps in the US was significant for three reasons. In the first case, the size of the order was equivalent to roughly half of the UK annual average output of all types of sea-going merchant ships. In addition, it was a purely commercial contract, settled entirely from the government's US dollar reserves at a time when neutrality legislation and isolationist popular sentiment blocked any overt support from the Roosevelt administration. Finally, it was part of a larger transaction which also involved the British-financed construction of two completely new yards, one in California on the west coast and one in Maine on the east coast, designed specifically to undertake the entire sixty-vessel order. All of this was undertaken at a time when Allied war fortunes were at a low ebb, and when there were many competing demands on strained British public finances.

The new ships were all given two-word names beginning with 'Ocean'. The first, *Ocean Vanguard*, was delivered at Richmond, California, in late October 1941, and the last, *Ocean Glory*, at South Portland, Maine, in November 1942. They all arrived in the combat zone in 1942, the darkest year of the trade war, when the number of vessels sunk by submarines exceeded the combined total for 1939–41. As with other modern, war-built tonnage, the vessels were heavily deployed in the most demanding assignments in the most dangerous waters. Just under one-third of the Oceans, nineteen out of sixty, would be lost between February 1942 and January 1944, of which four were lost in the Atlantic before they reached Britain, two on Arctic convoy duties, six to submarines in distant waters, and seven supporting amphibious and military operations in the Mediterranean.

The impact of the Oceans on the Allied war effort stretched far beyond the direct contribution of the ships themselves. The new yards constructed to build the ships would be sold to the US while the British order was still completing and would move seamlessly to the production of Liberty cargo ships for the US War Shipping Administration. These same yards would also serve as models for a series of new US shipyards, designed to assemble vessels on mass production principles: shipyards which would produce ships with such speed and in such volume as to completely reverse the mathematics of attrition, which had run so badly against the Allies into 1942. As British-financed yards contributed to the expansion of shipbuilding, so British-managed ship design played an important role in the design of the standard cargo vessel which would become the symbol of victory in the war at sea. The US Liberty ship was directly modelled on its Ocean design predecessor. While an undoubted improvement in some areas, particularly its composite superstructure design and oil-fired, water-tube boilers, basic hull design was almost identical, while its triple expansion steam engine was a standardised version of a British model which was fitted in all Ocean and Liberty ships, as well as in the similar Fort and Park merchant ships built in Canada.

History has not been particularly generous to the Oceans, which have tended to be pushed into the background by other larger classes. Canadian production of Forts and Parks, which stretched from 1941 to 1945, passed the 300 mark, five times the Ocean level. Even this was dwarfed by the output of American shipyards, which included just over 2,700 Liberty ships, to say nothing of 530 faster, steam turbine-driven Victory ships, and large numbers of other, generally higher-specification types. The name of the first of the class, *Ocean Vanguard*, was nonetheless well chosen. She and her sisters were in the vanguard of the Allied shipbuilding effort in North America, all the ships arriving at a time when the German U-boat threat was at its most dangerous, and British shipping resources were stretched to the limit. The ships were heavily deployed on the key long-distance supply routes, the Russian convoys, operations in support of the invasions of North Africa and Sicily, ongoing support of the campaigns in Tunisia, Sicily and the Italian mainland, the D-Day landings, and later amphibious operations against the South of France. The last vessels to be deployed on a combat mission were in an invasion force making its way to the west coast of Malaya when Japan surrendered in August 1945.

Finally, the Oceans played an important peacetime role in the recovery of the world's merchant marine from its wartime mauling. All thirty-six vessels still in British government ownership in 1945 were sold to British commercial shipowners, helping fill gaps in their depleted fleets which would be beyond the capacity of the domestic shipbuilding industry to fill for years to come. Most of these vessels served their new owners for at least a decade, and the majority would go on to operate under a variety of foreign flags well into the 1960s. Their experience was broadly matched by those of the five other vessels that had been sold to foreign governments during the war, all of which were still in operation in the new decade. They were joined by three further vessels which returned to service with Italian operators after post-war salvage and repair in the Mediterranean. As late as 1967, there were still nineteen former Oceans in service. The extent to which these ageing war-built veterans were still a global shipping resource can be measured by their ownership profile: five flew a Panamanian flag of convenience for a collection of Italian, Swiss, Taiwanese and Greek companies; five flew either Cypriot or domestic colours for Greek owners; four others operated under the Italian flag, and two more plied eastern waters in the ownership of the People's Republic of China, while there were single representatives flying the flags of Poland, Hong Kong and the Bahamas. The British civil servants responsible first for building and then selling off government-owned tonnage showed little regard for their wartime creations, generally considering them to be poor quality substitutes with little long-term value – they could not have been more wrong.

— 1 —

GENESIS

Torpedoed on 17 October 1940, the Whitby tramp steamer *Scoresby* (3,843g/1923) was just one of seven ships sunk by *U 48* on a single patrol at a time when British shipping losses were threatening to outstrip the country's capacity to replace them.
(R M Scott/Roy Fenton collection)

The Origins of the Shipbuilding Crisis

The British government's decision to order new merchant ship tonnage in the United States was born of a series of developments in the summer of 1940 which, together, made it clear that domestic new-building and the acquisition of existing tonnage from other sources would fall well short of meeting the expanding requirements of the war. The picture here was complex. Overall, the shrinkage of the domestic shipbuilding industry in the inter-war period had left it poorly placed to face the challenge of hostilities. The two basic components of this challenge were the industry's increasingly obvious inability to produce enough new tonnage to replace growing losses; and the geo-political and logistic developments associated with the war which had greatly increased the amount of tonnage required to supply the home islands and support the war effort.

The shortage of shipbuilding capacity was the product of both long-term and war-related factors. In the first of these cases, the inter-war period had witnessed a significant reduction in the number of large British shipyards. One group of long-established concerns went under after the implosion of the post-Great War shipping boom in the early 1920s. Another failed to survive the near-complete cessation of orders during the Great Depression. Finally, one last group of yards were purchased and closed in the 1930s by the National Shipbuilders Security Ltd (NSS), a government-sponsored and industry-financed scheme created to eliminate what was then perceived as over-capacity to improve the competitiveness and profitability of the remaining yards. To give an idea of the extent of the shrinkage, the hitherto well-established cluster of shipyards in the Tees–West Hartlepool area (which had been particularly strong in the construction of deep sea tramp tonnage) saw the disappearance of five long-established firms: Craig, Taylor & Co; Richardson, Duck & Co; Ropner & Sons; Sir Raylton Dixon & Co; and Irvine's Shipbuilding. Significant casualties elsewhere included Workman, Clark & Co in Belfast; D & W Henderson on the Clyde; Palmers' Shipbuilding & Iron on the Tyne; and Earle's Shipbuilding & Engineering in Hull.

Merchant shipbuilding also suffered from a progressive switch of surviving berths to warship construction. Naval rearmament had seen an ongoing increase in warship orders from the mid-1930s. In the short term, this had not impacted significantly on mercantile output as many commercial owners were reluctant to undertake significant fleet renewal or expansion in the uncertain market conditions then prevalent. Naval demand, however, accelerated as war approached, and continued to grow after hostilities began, the calls on yard capacity rising further as war damage and increased service wear and tear produced ever-expanding repair and refit requirements. It rapidly became clear that conflicting demands on berths could only be managed effectively if responsibility were placed in the hands of a single government ministry. Of the two possible candidates, the Admiralty, and the newly created Ministry of Shipping, it is perhaps not surprising that it was the former, always likely to emerge as the senior partner, which was given controlling powers when the decision was taken to unify procurement decision making at the end of January 1940.

Turning from shipbuilding capacity to the wartime demand for merchant shipping, this expanded in two clear stages during the first year of the war. The first of these was triggered by the outbreak of hostilities. The UK was heavily dependent on sea-borne imports of both foodstuffs and many industrial commodities. These demands increased rapidly as the British Government searched overseas for war-related materials, and as merchant shipping was deployed to supply the British Expeditionary Force in France. The immediate introduction of convoys decreased the productivity of shipping itself as it increased not only voyage durations, but also time spent in port, both assembling the convoys at one end, and dealing with increased port congestion at the other. Finally, Admiralty requisition for naval service removed a growing number of vessels from commercial service, including a disproportionate percentage of fast modern tonnage.

If the developments of the early months of the war were burdensome, those of the spring and summer of 1940 were exponentially more severe. They largely stemmed from the German invasion and conquest of Denmark, Norway, the Netherlands, Belgium, and France, and from the entry of Italy into the war as a German ally. The major consequences of this series of disasters can be summarised as follows:

- The closure of the Baltic and the consequent loss of imports, particularly wood products and iron ore (the latter loss compounded by the loss of the Norwegian outlet for Swedish iron ore exports at Narvik)
- The loss of manufacturing capacity (particularly for the heavy forgings essential for marine engineering) in the industrial areas of north Europe in France and the Low Countries, and across the region of shipbuilding berths (foreign yards being particularly prominent in the production of tankers and motor ships)
- The closure of the Mediterranean as a result of the Italian declaration of war with another regional loss of imports, and, more seriously, the forced diversion of Allied shipping around South Africa, producing much longer voyage times both for imports from India and the Far East, and the carriage of supplies to support the increasingly important military campaign in North Africa's Western Desert
- The displacement of sources of imported goods to more distant ports, for example wood products and iron ore to eastern Canada, and the increasing requirement to supplement home production of strategic resources such as steel with heavy imports, primarily from the United States
- The general squeeze on the import of foodstuffs from distant markets in North and South America, and Australasia as a result of competing requirements from other trades, and the need for convoying in the final stage of the inward voyage
- The partial closure of the English Channel and ports in the south of the country, and consequent increases in the length and number of coasting voyages, and of levels of congestion in northern ports.

A victim of the widening U-Boat offensive, Reardon Smith's *Jersey City* (6,332g/1920), seen here at Vancouver, succumbed to a torpedo from *U 99* northwest of Ireland on 31 July 1940.
(Walter E Frost/City of Vancouver Archives CVA 447-2339)

Thus, the demand for tonnage was increasing as the output of tonnage was decreasing, which in turn was further increasing demand. This was taking place at a time when merchant shipping losses appeared to be spiralling upwards, and domestic shipbuilding output seemed increasingly likely to fall short of expectations. As early as the beginning of June 1940, the Admiralty was telling the War Cabinet that the target for annual production of mercantile tonnage to be achieved by the first half of 1941, which had been established as 1.5 million tons as recently as 1 February 1940, would need to be reduced to 1.1 million tons. In making the case for the lower target, Sir James Lithgow, the Controller of Merchant Shipbuilding and Repairs at the Admiralty, cited the main causes as bottlenecks in the supply of heavy forgings and castings required for propelling machinery, and of rolled steel for boilers and hulls, as well as shortages of trained manpower in engineering and shipbuilding establishments. Responding on 7 June 1940 to the Admiralty's suggestion that the output target be reduced, the Minister of Shipping rehearsed the problems the British were facing, highlighting 'the losses incurred in recent operations, the additional demands on merchant shipping for direct naval and military purposes, the reduction in importing capacity due to diversion from the Mediterranean, the possible further reduction arising from the accentuated risks of interruption to the working of our ports, the necessity of resorting to more distant sources of supply for iron ore, timber and other commodities and the greatly increased demands of the French due to the effect on their production of the German invasion.'

The situation would get much worse over the next few weeks. By the end of June, the Allies had lost the campaign in Norway, and France had surrendered, leaving Britain alone in Europe to face not only Germany but its new Axis ally Italy. The entire western coastline of the continent, from North Cape to the Pyrenees, was now in enemy hands, while the Mediterranean had been closed to any merchant shipping not supported by a heavy naval escort. This gloomy picture was made darker still by a sharp increase in mercantile losses from enemy action. Reviewing the situation in mid-July, the Minister of Shipping noted that the average weekly loss rate due to enemy submarines of British-flagged vessels was 40,000 tons over the five-week period ending 14 July, and that the figure rose to 70,000 tons per week when allied and neutral losses were added. When losses due to all other causes (of which those from air attack were particularly severe) were added, the total weekly loss rate over the five weeks in question reached 116,000 tons, a level which, if sustained, would result in annual losses of roughly six million tons. A follow-up War Cabinet memorandum by the First Lord of the Admiralty and the Minister without Portfolio dated 16

August suggested that a continuation of current casualty rates would result in annual losses (exclusive of marine causes) of between 4.5 and 6 million tons, adding: 'whether or not our losses reach these dimensions, there can be no doubt that our shipping position is likely to be one of considerable difficulty by the winter of 1941–42.'

The Emergence of the American Solution

The British government responded to the progressive deterioration of the strategic situation through the spring and early summer of 1940 with a series of different measures to improve its shipping capacity. As the Netherlands and Belgium fell to the German invaders in May, so their surviving merchant fleets were chartered to operate under British control, with responsibility for manning and day-to-day management being retained by shipping missions established in London by their respective governments-in-exile. A similar arrangement brought part of the large Norwegian merchant fleet into the fold in June, although in this instance roughly one-third of the ships controlled by the Norwegian Shipping and Trade Mission (Nortraship) were managed by a second office in New York and would not come under British charter and control until early 1942. The governments of the other two countries to fall in 1940, Denmark and France, remained in place at home under varying degrees of German influence, and in both cases Britain responded by seizing all ships found in port or intercepted at sea and operating them under the British flag.

Even while these measures were still underway, the Ministry of Shipping began to restock Britain's own shipping inventory by direct purchases from the neutral world's largest pool of surplus tonnage, the United States merchant marine. When America entered the First World War in April 1917, the newly established US Shipping Board and its associated Emergency Fleet Corporation requisitioned all ships building in American yards, including 150 vessels of 869,000dwt on order for the British Shipping Controller, and launched a massive building programme which by October 1919 would complete just under 1,500 vessels aggregating another 8.1 million dwt. This armada far exceeded the peacetime needs of the US economy, and much of it went straight into long-term layup. This surplus fleet was further swelled in the winter of 1939–40 as commercial operators withdrew vessels from transatlantic services suspended under the provisions of the Neutrality Acts.

The first British purchases, all from commercial operators of ships built in 1919–20, were completed in February 1940, the biggest single transaction eventually including five ships

Empire Hawksbill (ex-*Delawarean*, 5,724g/1920), the first of the Ministry of Shipping's American acquisitions to reach the UK, photographed in the Cape Cod Canal on 22 September 1940. *(Wm Schell collection)*

National Government which came to power in 1931, led by Ramsay MacDonald but dominated by the Conservative Party, repeatedly averred that the industry had been left free to seek its own salvation. Showing little interest in determining what capacity might best support the national interest, it even allowed two of the eight yards capable of building large warships for the Royal Navy, Beardmore on the Clyde, and Palmers on the Tyne, to be dismantled.

In the absence of any other guidelines, the determinant of candidacy for NSS sterilisation became the relative financial strength of potential targets rather than any assessment of their long-term viability. While many of the smaller, low value-added tramp ship builders had little prospect of recovery in the face of increasing foreign competition, some of the larger yards, particularly vertically integrated concerns with their own engineering works, were arguably candidates for financial restructuring rather than closure. One example of the latter was the Meadowside yard of D & W Henderson on the north bank of the Clyde at Partick, Glasgow, which had been in business since the mid-nineteenth century building vessels for a range of established clients ranging from the Liverpool cargo liner operator T & J Harrison to the large Glasgow tramp owner Maclay & McIntyre. Henderson had been taken over by Harland & Wolff of Belfast in 1916, but was left exposed, like several of the latter's other Clydeside acquisitions, when its parent's over-stretched finances left it unable to maintain working capital investment through the Depression. Henderson managed to launch nine ocean-going merchant ships for long-term clients between August 1933 and July 1935, a time when many of its competitors had no orders at all. The last of these, however, went down the ways after the banks had declined to provide further bridge funding and the receivers had been called in, and the NSS acquired the yard for dismantling late in the following year. There is no doubt that the business was in financial extremis, but its candidacy for sterilisation took no account of its long-term business fundamentals, or, indeed, even of the immediate impact of recovery in the global shipping industry, a recovery which had in fact begun before D & W Henderson closed its gates. National Shipbuilders Security Ltd paid just under £175,000 for the yard on 11 November 1936 and subsequently dismantled everything but its ship repair facilities. It is arguable that British interests might have been better served if a similar level of funding had been invested in saving the business. Set in an international context, the closure was in stark contrast to developments across the Atlantic, where on 26 October, three weeks before the Meadowside sale, the US Government had set up the United States Maritime Commission with an explicit mandate to re-build and expand the US merchant marine to meet the twin challenges of supporting a recovering national economy and modernising the mercantile marine in the face of growing international competition.

Overall, the yard closures of the early 1930s meant that the 1.5 million-ton wartime output target was never realistic, and it is hard to understand why it was ever set that high in the first place. The lost yards had been deliberately put beyond redemption by the sale or destruction of their entire plant,

One of the last ships built by D & W Henderson, *Loch Lomond* (5,452g/1934), owned by Maclay & McIntyre of Glasgow, was sunk by *U 100* on 20 October 1940 after losing contact with convoy HX 79 on a voyage from Montreal for Immingham with a cargo of lumber and steel.
(Roy Fenton collection)

and most of the survivors occupied crowded river fronts and could not be easily expanded. Merchant ship output in 1939–40 averaged only 790,000 tons. This performance improved in 1941, from when an average output of 1.1 million tons was maintained through to the end of 1944. The 'reduction' of the shipping output target in the summer of 1940 might better be termed a tacit admission that the original target had been set too high. Set against the background of increasing losses and expanding shipping requirements, British shipping policy would have been forced eventually to embrace a move to finance vessel construction abroad. Without the trigger of the abandonment of the 1.5 million-ton target, however, the policy itself might have taken longer to mature.

The Dynamics of Wartime Decision Making

Before discussing the final developments leading to the despatch of a mission to the United States empowered to order new tonnage, it is necessary to consider the structure of British governmental decision making on shipbuilding. The overall direction of the war rested with the War Cabinet, a much smaller but more powerful body than the main cabinet. Of the four ministers most directly involved in the decision to press ahead with ordering new ships overseas, the Chancellor of the Exchequer, Sir Kingsley Wood, the First Lord of the Admiralty, A V Alexander, the Minister of Shipping, Ronald Cross, and the Minister without Portfolio, Arthur Greenwood, only the last-named was a member of the War Cabinet (although he would be joined there by Wood in October 1940).

Ronald Cross (1896–1968), whose portfolio might suggest a deep involvement in mercantile marine procurement, was very much the junior of the four. He was, in fact, the third man to serve as Minister of Shipping since the post's re-creation in mid-September 1939, the first having died in post, and the second moved to another portfolio on Churchill's elevation to Prime Minister in May 1940. Cross did, however, have the support of two very experienced policy makers: his parliamentary under-secretary Sir Arthur Salter (1881–1975), who was one of the most respected transport economists of the day, and the departmental permanent under-secretary Sir Cyril Hurcomb (1883–1975), who would become the first Chairman of the British Transport Commission after the war. Sir Kingsley Wood (1881–1943) as Chancellor of the Exchequer, controlled the purse strings, a particularly important consideration when it came to the use of US dollar funds for purchases in the United States, which made him key to obtaining consensus on procurement abroad. He was, however, hard-pressed to resist demands from the war spending departments couched in terms of strategic necessity. At the Admiralty, A V Alexander (1885–1965) exercised control over merchant shipbuilding, and effectively the entire war at sea, placing him at the centre of the decision-making process. This position was strengthened first by Alexander's earlier experience in the post (he had also occupied it in the coalition government of the early 1930s), and second by the prestige of the shipping industry leaders seconded to fill the senior shipbuilding control posts beneath him. The surviving documents suggest that Arthur Greenwood (1880–1954), first as a member of the War Cabinet, and second as the honest broker between the conflicting objectives of the other three, played a central role in formulating the procurement proposals which would form the basis of the overseas building effort.

By early September, Greenwood had succeeded in reaching agreement with the Admiralty and Ministry of Shipping on a proposal to order sixty new ships in the United States. Before this proposal could be taken forward to the War Cabinet, it was necessary to obtain the agreement of the Chancellor. Given the scale of the project, it was inevitable that Wood would seek to scale it back. Writing to Greenwood on 7 September, he stated that while he recognised the gravity of the situation and did not wish to contest the necessity of increasing merchant shipping resources on the scale proposed, he was not satisfied that it was necessary to place a contract in the USA as large as that proposed at once. Pointing out that an order for sixty ships would represent 'a serious addition to the burden of dollar expenditure', and that American-built ships would cost at least twice as much as those constructed at home, he concluded that in these circumstances the acceptance of the view that the target for home construction must be reduced from 1.5 to 1.1 million tons or less per annum seemed 'tragic', and went on to say that he was not satisfied that it was not possible to obtain a substantial part of the increased tonnage required by additional building at home. On these grounds, he stated that he could only support an initial order for thirty new ships, with the proviso that he would be prepared to reconsider the remaining thirty ships afresh if circumstances required.

It was an indication of the speed at which matters were proceeding that Greenwood agreed immediately with the Admiralty that Wood's suggested compromise should be accepted in the meantime, and that Sir James Lithgow should make arrangements for the immediate despatch of a mission to the United States with a mandate to negotiate the building order. On 9 September, a joint memorandum was submitted to the War Cabinet under the names of Alexander, Wood, Greenwood and Cross. The central recommendation of this document is worth quoting in full, as it laid the foundations for the shipbuilding programme to follow.

> We consider it essential that our programme of home construction should be supplemented by the immediate placing in the United States of as substantial an order for new tonnage as can be laid down in the near future, and preliminary enquiries have been made as to the possibilities. It may be practicable to place orders for, say, sixty ships of 10,000 tons deadweight with United States yards for delivery at the end of 1941. The Controller of Merchant Shipbuilding thinks that it would be unduly optimistic to look for any earlier date of delivery. We recognise that the cost of this tonnage must be high, but our wastage of shipping must be made good. An expenditure of £20 million of which not more than £5 million would be required before the 31st March would be necessary for the acquisition of this tonnage. The Chancellor of the Exchequer has definitely agreed to orders being placed for thirty ships, in order that the immediate negotiations may be undertaken.

The War Cabinet accepted the recommendations of the memorandum at its meeting on 19 September, by which time the Admiralty had already come to broad conclusions on the way forward. Even before the recommendations above were framed, it had become clear that acquiring new tonnage in the United States would not simply be a matter of ordering completely new vessels from established yards, or buying new ships approaching completion. Preliminary enquiries concerning the current state of US shipbuilding, made both through the American Embassy in London and British officials already based in Washington, DC and New York, established that there was little, if any, spare building capacity. Most of the new yards responsible for the huge increase in shipping output during and immediately after the First World War had been closed in the early 1920s, and the Great Depression had produced another round of closures. While remaining shipbuilding capacity was substantial, it was heavily deployed on both a large expansion of the US Navy to make it fit to fight a 'Two Ocean War', and on the programme of the United States Maritime Commission to build a modern new fleet of cargo vessels for the American mercantile marine. During the initial phase of investigations, the possibility of either chartering new tonnage as it completed or purchasing it while still under construction was also discounted as being politically impossible, such measures being likely to aggravate domestic sentiment on many fronts, not least widely held non-interventionist sentiments in the delicate run-up to the US presidential elections.

As early as 1 September, more than two weeks before the War Cabinet approved the building of ships in the USA, contradictory, but generally negative intelligence regarding the possibility of accessing tonnage had led the Admiralty to conclude that it was possible it would not know what the exact position was 'until someone has been sent to the United States to find out.' Events moved rapidly thereafter, and as early as 5 September, several days before agreement had been reached with Wood at the Exchequer, and two weeks before War Cabinet approval was obtained, the Admiralty had decided that it would send a mission to the United States, Sir James Lithgow telling British government representatives already overseas that the First Lord had given him authority to send two shipbuilders to America to work with officials already in place 'to make contact with the Maritime Commission, the Shipbuilding Association, and the individual shipbuilders recommended by them, with a view to developing (a) precise programme for the ordering of the said sixty ships, that is, yards to undertake them, deliveries to be achieved and terms of payment to be demanded.'

Two men within the Admiralty, both very experienced commercial shipbuilders with previous exposure to public service departments, dominated the entire decision-making process for merchant ship construction. Sir James Lithgow (1883–1952), who was co-chairman of the large Clyde shipbuilder Lithgows Ltd of Port Glasgow, and the former Chairman of National Shipbuilders Securities, had been appointed Controller of Merchant Shipbuilding and Repair, and a Lord Commissioner of the Admiralty early in the war. His prestige and influence were immense, not least because of his direct access to the First Lord, and the quick decision to send a dedicated mission to the USA to pursue the acquisition of US-built merchant tonnage was very much a result of his initiative. While Lithgow provided overall strategic guidance and impetus, responsibility for the day-to-day execution of building plans rested with an equally formidable industry figure, Sir Amos Ayre (1885–1952), former chairman of the Burntisland Shipbuilding Co Ltd, which he had founded with his brother in 1918, and Chairman of the British Shipbuilding Conference since 1936. Ayre had been appointed Director of Shipbuilding and Repairs for the Ministry of Shipping at its inception in mid-September 1939 and had moved to the Admiralty with the same title to work under Lithgow in February 1940 when responsibility for all ship construction was concentrated with the latter body. In 1941 he would be promoted to Deputy Controller and Director of Shipbuilding, with responsibility for repairs moved elsewhere.

Given that much of the initial motivation to build merchant tonnage in the USA came from shortfalls in British domestic production, it is ironic that Lithgow at National Shipbuilders Securities, and Ayre with the Shipbuilding Conference, had worked together, albeit within a widely agreed brief, to eliminate what was then considered to be excess yard capacity in the 1930s. Both men, however, brought strong track records as successful builders to their new posts. Lithgow had kept his yard well employed through the Depression when most others were closed, while Ayre had helped pioneer the 'economy ship' concept which would transform British tramp ship design in the 1930s. Lithgow would remain a strong supporter of the new-building scheme throughout, retaining the influence to be able to iron out a host of departmental and governmental difficulties. Ayre, who had been born in South Shields and apprenticed at Wood, Skinner & Co Ltd on the Tyne before moving north to Burntisland, brought to bear strongly held views on marine architecture and building practice, together with what seems to have been an aggressive personality on co-ordinating the building programme itself. Surviving correspondence gives evidence of strong drive and no small appetite for work. It does, however, also suggest that his relationship with those negotiating and then running the programme in America was sometimes difficult, due in part to what appears at times to have been a tendency to micro-manage.

The Admiralty decision to send a special mission to the United States, empowered to expedite the proposed construction of new vessels, was followed rapidly by the appointment of its two senior members, one a shipbuilder and one a marine engineer. Surviving records suggest that there was little if any internal discussion regarding the selection of these individuals, and it is almost certain that the appointments were decided by Lithgow and Ayre, based on their extensive knowledge of and contacts within the industry. The shipbuilder appointed was R Cyril Thompson (1907–67), managing director of the long-established Sunderland firm of Joseph L Thompson & Sons Ltd, and a director of another Wearside shipbuilder, Sir James Laing & Sons Ltd. The marine engineer was Harry Hunt, Technical Director of North Eastern Marine Engineering Co. (1938) Ltd. of Wallsend-on-Tyne. Thompson was appointed head of the mission 'with power to make all decisions on behalf of the Controller of Merchant Shipbuilding', and his influence, underpinned by his own drive and forceful personality, was to prove immense. Of the three other members of the mission, two, William Bennett, principal surveyor of Lloyd's Register of Shipping for the United States & Canada, and J S Heck, principal engineer surveyor of Lloyd's Register of Shipping, New York, were effectively technical consultants. The other, Richard R Powell, an assistant secretary in the Admiralty, already in North America with the British Admiralty Technical Mission, was a senior civil servant who would provide the secretariat.

R Cyril Thompson officiating with Mrs W Kippen, the wife of his client's Marine Superintendent, at the 11 September 1946 launch of *Ionian*, the second of four sisters built at his North Sands shipyard for the Mediterranean service of Ellerman & Papayanni Lines Ltd.
(Sunderland Echo/author's collection)

British Tramp Ship Design

The appointments of Thompson and Hunt were to prove particularly significant, as with the mission's brief providing only outline specifications for the new vessels it was hoped to build, the blueprints for the vessels and their propulsion machinery were to be derived from those of ships and engines currently in production at their respective firms. These early choices were to exercise a strong influence over the long-term design, not only of the sixty Ocean-class vessels which would be built in the United States as a direct result of the Thompson mission, but also of over 300 Canadian-built Fort- and Park-class near-sisters, the first of which were also ordered by the mission, and ultimately of more than 2,700 Liberty ships whose design was derived directly from Ocean blueprints.

The origins of the vessel itself have been the subject of much comment, and in some cases somewhat uninformed speculation, by historians. The three most favoured ancestors for the Oceans, and thence for the Forts, Parks, and ultimately the Liberty ships, were all products of the Joseph L Thompson & Sons North Sands yard. The earliest of these was *Embassage* (Yard No 572) which had been launched for Hall Bros of Newcastle in July 1935, the result of the first order received since the shipyard's closure in 1930 due to the Depression. The second candidate was *Dorington Court* (Yard No 592) launched in May 1939 for the Court Line of London, and Thompson's last delivery before the outbreak of the Second World War. The final candidate, whose very name seems to have influenced some commentators in her favour, was *Empire Liberty* (Yard No 611), which would be launched on 23 August 1941, exactly a week after the first of the sixty ships contracted for in the USA, *Ocean Vanguard*, had been launched into San Francisco Bay.

A balanced judgement on the real conceptual process behind the development of the Ocean prototype requires an understanding of three overlapping processes: the evolution of British deep-sea tramp design over the period 1935–9, the Government's distillation of existing practice to arrive at an outline blueprint for the vessel it was hoped to order, and finally the brief which Thompson and Hunt were given on their departure for the USA and the preparations they made to fulfil it.

British tramp ship design, which had only been evolving slowly in the opening decades of the twentieth century, entered a period of more rapid change in the second half of the 1930s. The main impetus was the difficult trading conditions prevailing in the wake of the Great Depression. Shipowners needed to operate their vessels more economically to make profits at a time of low freight rates, while shipbuilders had to compete more strongly for a reduced order flow for new vessels. The result of these reinforcing influences was an increased focus on scientific vessel design,

Embassage (4,954g/1935), built for Hall Brothers of Newcastle-on-Tyne, was the first ship launched by J L Thompson & Sons after the yard's Great Depression closure – she was torpedoed by *U 557* west of Ireland on 27 August 1941, with only three of her crew surviving to be rescued by a Canadian destroyer after four days in a lifeboat.
(Ships in Focus)

Burntisland Shipbuilding's 'Economy' ship *Byrnymor* (4,258g/1929), built for Ambrose, Davies & Mathews of Swansea, and renamed *Pensilva* after sale to the Chellew Navigation Co Ltd, was an early victim of the U-boat offensive, sunk by *U 49* on 19 November 1939 northwest of Cape Ortegal. ***(Nautical Photo Agency)***

much of it the product of the testing of hull forms in specially designed tanks; more focus on hull structures to provide strength while achieving economies in steel consumption; and more fuel-efficient engines, be they of traditional coal-fired reciprocating design, or oil-burning marine diesels.

The first shipbuilders to design and market an explicitly labelled 'economy' ship were Amos and Wilfred Ayre and their team at Burntisland Shipbuilding on the north shore of the Forth Estuary in Scotland. The prototype design was first marketed in January 1929, attended with the offer of a guaranteed saving in fuel of 35 per cent in fully loaded condition during an extended six-hour trial trip. Success was immediate, the Ayre brothers receiving orders for seven of the new vessels from four different shipowners before the Depression choked off the flow of new business. Although mercantile shipbuilding came to an almost complete stop in Britain between 1930 and 1934, most of the industry leaders retained their core design staff and undertook extended research and tank-testing on new models. These were then marketed explicitly under the 'economy' ship label, when builders began to compete for the new orders which started to trickle through in 1935.

The basic hull structure of the new generation of tramps moved away from past practice in three important ways. As mentioned above, the contours of the hull itself were modified to improve its movement through the water. Additionally, the structure of the stern was modified to eliminate loss of propeller efficiency from turbulence created by non-streamlined design. Finally, the single-decked designs common in most vessels designed and built over the previous decades gave way to shelter-deck layouts with continuous upper and second decks, about 7ft 6in to 9ft 6in apart, forming a 'tween deck. Under peacetime conditions, the 'open' shelter-deck type was generally considered the most economical, complying as it did with contemporary regulations which exempted most of the 'tween deck from tonnage measurement calculations. As freeboard was measured from the second deck in the 'open' configuration, however, this arrangement did carry the penalty of reduced draught and thus lower deadweight capacity.

Ayre's firm, Burntisland, which like most of its competitors had been forced to close doors over the early 1930s, returned to business with a modified version of its earlier 'economy' ships. The two firms more commonly associated with the new design concept, however, were both based at Sunderland on the River Wear. William Doxford & Sons at Pallion was perhaps the better known of the two, not least because it was able to capitalise on expertise with diesel-powered tramps gained in the 1920s, but it is their rival, Joseph L. Thompson & Sons of North Sands, which is more relevant to our story. As already noted, Thompson had built no ships in the period 1931–4, but had returned to business with *Embassage* in 1935. The vessel was a commercial success, and the yard built on its basic design to meet a stream of new orders, of which the twentieth was *Dorington Court*, the last vessel completed before the outbreak of war.

Given the range of opinions on the parentage of what were to become the Ocean-class ships, it is important to be clear about the development of the Thompson steam tramp between 1935 and 1940. There was a strong developmental

Royal Sceptre (4,853g/1937), another J L Thompson completion for Hall Brothers, photographed at Vancouver 12 March 1939 less than six months before she was sunk in the North Atlantic by *U 48*, Captain James Gair dying on his bridge to become the first master of a British merchant ship killed in war. *(Walter E Frost/City of Vancouver Archives CVA 447-2637)*

line between *Embassage* and the ships which followed. These latter were not, however, built to the same exact model; rather they evolved to offer greater cargo-carrying efficiency as the builder sought to compete for new orders in a demanding marketplace. Thus, *Dorington Court* was neither the hull nor the engineering sister of *Embassage* (she was, for example, 20ft longer and had a larger engine). *Dorington Court* was used, in turn, as the basis for the ships which Thompsons began to build for Government account after it had completed another eight already-contracted-for ships for commercial owners to a range of different specifications around the same basic model (the one exception was *Port Quebec*, Yard No 593, which was a diesel-powered cargo liner). One of the most obvious variations among the ships was between the conventional split-superstructure design (with a hatch between the bridge and the rest of the midships superstructure) and a more cost-effective composite design with everything in one central structure.

The first two vessels built to Admiralty order, *Empire Wind* and *Empire Meteor*, were in many ways close to being sisters of the Court Line vessel. Superficially, they varied due to wartime building practice, such as limiting funnel diameter to reduce visible profile. More fundamentally, they moved from 'open' to 'closed' shelter-deck design. This was a reaction to the requirements of war, which gave carrying capacity priority over economy. The revised design, whose ships were often described as full scantling vessels, allowed freeboard to be measured from the upper deck, which in turn allowed more cargo to be carried. In terms of gross registered tonnage, the rough order of change was from 5,280 to 7,460 tons between *Dorington Court* and the *Empire Wind*/*Empire Meteor* pair. Externally, the latter were near hull sisters to the Court Line vessel with the same length and beam, the difference in tonnage being entirely accounted for by the move to 'closed'/full scantling shelter-deck design, which moved the upper deck up one for measurement purposes and resulted in an increase of 9ft 6in in registered depth. The design of the latter was then altered slightly for the next eight vessels (Yard Nos 603 to 610), which were all built to the same modified design. There would be another change of specification for *Empire Liberty* (Yard No 611), which would then provide the template for further tramp ship production. We will return to *Empire Liberty* later, but to summarise the position regarding the other two candidates for prototypes of the ships to be built in North America, it would be more accurate to identify *Embassage* and *Dorington Court* (and

Scottish Trader (4,016g/1938), a Thompson composite superstructure design, became yet another victim of the U-boat war, sharing the fate of many convoy stragglers when she went down with all hands in the Atlantic 300 miles south of Iceland after being torpedoed by *U 131* on 6 December 1941.
(Roy Fenton collection)

indeed their early Empire successors) as important markers in an ongoing development process rather than isolate any one ship as the sole ancestor of the ships to follow.

As was the case with the other successful participants in the 'economy' ship building surge, the Thompson model was based on a marriage between a new hull design and a fuel-efficient engine, in this case the 're-heater' design of the North Eastern Marine Engineering Co Ltd of Wallsend-on-Tyne. The latter was an updated version of the triple-expansion reciprocating engine, which had been the power plant of choice for tramp ships since its introduction in the 1880s. Up until the 1920s, the main impetus behind

Empire Meteor (7,457g/1940), the second Thompson wartime completion for the Ministry of Shipping, survived the war to serve the Court Line for a decade as *Dorington Court*, replacing her half-sister of the same name which had been sunk in 1942.
(Roy Fenton collection)

evolving engine design was the need to provide more powerful plant to propel larger and larger vessels. The focus shifted in the inter-war period to designing more efficient power plant that would reduce fuel expenditure, and thus the largest item of variable cost, to allow vessel operators to remain competitive and profitable in an era of generally low freight rates. The 're-heater', introduced by North Eastern Marine Engineering in 1934, improved efficiency by passing steam through a heat exchanger (the 're-heater') between the boiler and the engine's high-pressure cylinder and then again between the intermediate and low-pressure cylinders. This kept the steam drier and, because steam loses efficiency as it loses its heat content and becomes progressively wetter or saturated, improved the power to fuel consumption ratio, the 're-heater' being advertised as being 10 per cent more efficient than the previous superheating technology. Speeds remained in the basic ten to eleven knot range, with the system continuing to be designed to burn coal, which would produce steam from relatively simple Scotch Type boilers.

From the outset, the Admiralty and the Ministry of Shipping had been pursuing a shared vision of a shelter-decked vessel of roughly 10,000dwt, with reciprocating engines capable of 10.5 to 11 knots. Indeed, as early as 22 August, it had asked British delegates already in the USA to explore the possibilities of obtaining vessels of this specification, going as far as to mention dimensions of 'about 425 feet by 56 feet.' This basic ideal was one matched by most of the tramp ships then being built around the UK and was one which both Lithgow and Ayre had been building at their own yards. The intended design achieved firmer shape at a meeting of the joint Admiralty/Ministry of Shipping Advisory Committee held on 18 September, the minutes of which recorded '... the type of vessel which the Committee would like was about 9,300 tons deadweight "open" on twenty-five feet, three inches (10,000 tons deadweight "closed"), speed not less than ten-and-a-half knots loaded, with reciprocating engines and Scotch boilers if obtainable.' Two days later, Ayre wrote to the Ministry of Shipping stating explicitly that in establishing the overall design of the ship that they hoped could be ordered in the United States they had 'taken into account the particular builder who is leading the mission (Mr Cyril Thompson of Messrs J L Thompson & Sons Ltd)' and explaining that Thompson was taking with him 'the plans of his firm's vessel.' The vessel was defined simply as being of the shelter-deck type, 'carrying about 9,900 tons on twenty-five feet, six inches "open" or 10,800 on twenty-seven feet "closed."'

Although Thompson made two visits to London for meetings with Lithgow and Ayre before his departure, there appears to have been no attempt to take the proposed specifications for North American-built vessels beyond the outline stage. When he sailed for the United States, he simply took

The immediate predecessor to *Empire Wave*, Thompson's *Empire Sky* (7,455g/1941), seen here at New York on 6 December 1941, was sunk by *U 625* in the Barents Sea exactly eleven months later while on solo voyage to north Russia, her entire crew of sixty dying when the cargo of ammunition blew up.
(US Coast Guard/Roy Fenton collection)

with him the plans of the vessel most recently designed for the government account. This was Yard No.607, which would be launched in March 1941 as *Empire Wave*. Although this vessel does not feature in most accounts of the design process, it was to be her plans on which a series of modifications would be made to produce the blueprint used for the construction of the US and Canadian-built ships.

Whitehall policy makers were more optimistic about finding builders for their ships than they were about securing supplies of either reciprocating engines or Scotch boilers. There was a fundamental difference in the requirements of the British and American merchant marines. The former included a large tramp fleet that, while it traded heavily in the cross-trades, was critical to Britain's import economy with its heavy dependence on bulk cargoes such as grain and metal ores. By contrast, the United States was largely self-sufficient in food and industrial raw materials, and its merchant marine was almost entirely made up of cargo liners carrying export and import cargoes of finished goods. In the inter-war period, this translated into a clear divergence in marine engineering practice, with the US fleet being powered largely by steam turbines fed by water-tube boilers burning oil. Those ships not powered by steam turbines were diesel-powered motor ships, and there was a widely held view that coal-driven propulsion, Scotch boilers and triple-expansion engines were all out of date. The preliminary assumption of the British mission was that neither existing engineering facilities nor expertise would support supply of the optimal power plant, and that it might be necessary to accept another type of machinery to secure quick delivery. This notwithstanding, Hunt, like Thompson, left for America with his firm's current blueprints, in this case those for the latest version of its 're-heater' triple-expansion engine.

It should be stressed here how important the choice of Thompson and Hunt as the mission's principals was to the design of the entire stream of vessels, from the Oceans, to the Forts, Parks and Liberties that flowed from them. There were several good designs for both vessels and engines available. In the former case, even a smaller Sunderland builder like Bartram & Sons had designed and sold its own 'economy' ship, while the Pallion yard of William Doxford & Sons was the biggest producer of new generation tramp tonnage in Britain, its 'economy' ships attracting particular attention from more progressive owners because they were built around a modern diesel engine, which Doxford built to its own design at its own engineering works. The Ocean-class ships could have been designed around any of these or other available models. In this sense, it was the selection of Cyril Thompson as the man with the best mix of experience and drive, rather than the selection of one of his ships as the model for the future, which really determined where the design process would start.

One of William Doxford & Sons' commercially successful series of diesel-powered 'Economy' ships, *Riley* (4,993g/1936) served Stephens, Sutton & Co for two decades and was finally broken up in Japan in 1966 as the Panama-flagged, Hong Kong-owned *Kien Ping*.
(Roy Fenton collection)

— 2 —

MISSION TO AMERICA

The Cunard–White Star liner *Scythia* (19,730g/1921), which took Cyril Thompson's Shipbuilding Mission to New York, was requisitioned for service as a troopship in October 1940 after returning from the voyage, survived serious aerial torpedo damage in 1942 during Operation Torch, and was finally broken up in 1958. *(John & Marion Clarkson collection)*

The Merchant Shipbuilding Mission

With the Admiralty having completed preliminary arrangements before final War Cabinet approval was received, the shipbuilding mission got off to a fast start. Thompson and Hunt sailed from Liverpool for New York in Cunard's *Scythia* on 26 September 1940, just a week after the War Cabinet decision. As a 17kt vessel, *Scythia* made the passage independently and arrived safely at her destination on 3 October. Considerable preparatory work had been done before their arrival, and the two men were briefed the next day by Sir Walter Layton, Director of Programmes at the Ministry of Supply, who was on a visit to the United States, and Arthur Purvis, Head of the British Purchasing Commission (BPC). On the same evening, the delegation, which had now been joined by its other three members, flew to Washington, DC, where Thompson had dinner with the British Ambassador, Lord Lothian. On the next day, Saturday, 5 October, the mission met with the US Maritime Commission, the effective arbiters of merchant shipbuilding policy in America.

Established by the Merchant Marine Act of 1936, the US Maritime Commission (USMC) was an independent executive agency of the federal government, briefed to upgrade yard capacity, and to design and build modern merchant ships to replace the existing merchant fleet, almost all of which had

The C1, C2 and C3 cargo liners, the three main classes at the heart of the US Maritime Commission's building programme, were all high-specification vessels unsuited to British requirements.

Top: Seen here in neutrality markings at New York in 1941, Grace Line's C1 turbine steamer *Santa Cruz* (6,761g/1941) had been laid down as *Cape San Martin* for the USMC and would return to government ownership in 1946 after wartime service as a troopship.
(R Scozzafava/Wm Schell collection)

Middle: Another Grace Line vessel, the C2 type turbine cargo vessel *Santa Rita* (8,379g/1941), seen here leaving New York on 3 February 1942, would fall victim to *U 172* just five months later, succumbing to a combination of torpedo and shellfire in the Atlantic 700 miles northeast of Puerto Rico on 9 July while homebound from Port Sudan and Lourenço Marques with a cargo of chrome ore.
(US Coast Guard/Wm Schell collection)

Bottom: *Mormacpenn* (7,886g/1940), a diesel version of the C3 type cargo vessel, photographed on Moore-McCormack Lines service at Buenos Aires on 11 August 1940. Like many of her sisters, she was taken over soon after completion for US naval service and spent the remainder of her life as the submarine tender *Griffin (AS-13)*.
(R Maya/Wm Schell collection)

been built in 1918–20 and was reaching the end of its effective life. At the time of the Commission's creation, there were only ten shipyards with a total of forty-six slipways capable of building vessels more than 400ft in length. The new body thus turned its hand to both increasing yard capacity and putting in place a programme of new building which would see fifty modern merchant ships completed each year for the next decade. By the end of 1939, it had already ordered 145 ships of 1.15 million tons, and the new-building programme had accelerated further away from its original targets when the Thompson mission arrived. With yard expansion only just beginning, and with US naval rearmament absorbing more and more capacity, there was now little scope for placing a large British order for new ships with existing builders.

Apart from the lack of yard capacity, the scope for an easy solution was further narrowed by the concentration of such resources on building ships of different specifications to those the British sought. The USMC building programme prioritised the development of a range of standard cargo liners with an expected life of twenty years designed to be competitive on the routes served by the established national carriers and to offer scope for conversion for auxiliary naval purposes. These vessels were larger, faster, and more complex than the British 'economy' tramp, and they were equipped far more lavishly, particularly with regard to power plant, cargo-handling gear, and accommodation. They were also oil-fired and powered by steam turbines or diesels, double-reduction geared to one or two shafts. The three main models, labelled C1, C2, and C3, ranged in length from 396ft through 441ft to 469ft, with service speeds of 14kts, 15.5kts, and 16.5kts, respectively. Highly capable and efficient though these vessels would have been for cargo liner operations, they were beyond the reach of the intended British building programme, not least due to their high unit cost and to Britain's tenuous wartime oil supply situation, which rendered dependence on coal-firing a strategic imperative for most new building.

The two key decision makers in the Maritime Commission were retired naval officer, Rear-Admiral Emory S Land, former Chief of the US Navy Bureau of Construction and Repair, and since February 1938 chairman of the Commission, and his deputy, a serving naval officer, Commander (later Vice-Admiral) Howard L Vickery. Land proved very willing to be helpful and suggested that while existing yards were working at full capacity, it might be possible to 're-habilitate' yards which had been closed after the First World War, initially suggesting sites at Baltimore, Maryland, on the east coast, and Portland, Oregon, on the west. He also said that he believed that supplies of reciprocating engines and Scotch boilers could be obtained without interfering with existing marine engineering output, and that delivery of such machinery would probably be quicker than would be the case for turbines.

More meetings followed quickly, the most important of which was held on 7 October with John D Reilly of the Todd Shipyard Corporation, the firm which Admiral Land had indicated would be best placed to satisfy the British requirement for new yard space. In its current manifestation, Todd was predominantly a large multi-site ship repair concern, but its proposal involved it working with an even more powerful civil engineering syndicate known as the Six Companies Inc (sometimes referred to as Six Services). The latter comprised a group of western states contractors which had built the Hoover Dam on the Colorado River and the Grand Coulee and Bonneville Dams on the Columbia River. The largest partner in the engineering consortium, with a stake of 30 per cent, was a joint venture between two California firms: the Henry J Kaiser Co of Oakland and the Bechtel Corporation of San Francisco.

It became immediately clear that Todd executives had done a considerable amount of groundwork on a possible building scheme. Reilly further convinced the British delegates that his company 'had the money and technical experience to put through a very large scheme for mass production of a simple type of merchant ship.' Potential sites mentioned for the construction of new yards included Tacoma, Washington; Portland, Oregon, and San Francisco, Oakland, and Los Angeles, California, on the west coast; and Baltimore, Maryland, and Portland, Maine on the east. At this stage Todd was thinking in terms of seven building berths per yard, capable of turning out approximately forty-five ships each in 1941 on a five-day-a-week basis, or fifty-seven on a seven-day-a-week basis.

While initial discussions were led by the Todd Corporation, the driving force behind the proposed project, with regard to both the building of the necessary shipyard facilities, and to the adoption of pre-fabrication and mass production techniques, came from within the engineering consortium. Henry J Kaiser (1882–1967), the son of German immigrants, was a self-made man who had formed his own construction company in Washington State before the First World War. After successful participation in the large 1930s dam construction projects, he had begun to diversify into shipbuilding. Without any previous experience in the industry, he nonetheless became a leader in both technical and organisational fields. He combined welded construction (for which new workers could more easily be trained than was the case with traditional riveting), out-sourced component pre-fabrication, and yard-based assembly, following mass production principles to achieve rapid large-scale production. A ferociously hard worker who combined a flair for innovation with ruthless self-promotion, Kaiser would become synonymous with US wartime mercantile shipbuilding and the Liberty ship. He cut his teeth, however, within the Todd consortium and with what was to become the British Ocean-class building programme.

After its initial round of meetings, the mission embarked on a rapid round of yard visits on both the east and west coasts. Its remit also took it north of the border to visit Canadian yards in Quebec and British Columbia, which would subsequently be given separate orders for new vessels. Back in the United States, a rapid consensus emerged that it should work out a proposal with the Todd consortium. On 14 October, Powell told Lithgow in London: 'Things seem to be crystallising out and I think that our general feeling is that we shall have to rely on one big concern to give us practically the whole of the annual output required. The Todd Shipbuilding Corporation Syndicate is the one towards which Washington obviously wants to guide us.' The same communication gave an early indication that one of the anticipated stumbling blocks, the supply of reciprocating engines and Scotch boilers, might not prove to be an issue. It appeared that there might, in fact, be a better chance of getting this machinery mix than any other, for the simple reason that 'the capacity which exists for building this type of machinery is of no interest either to the Navy Department or the Maritime Commission!'

Thompson, at least, was an early convert to the need to standardise design for the new order, cabling Lithgow on 15 October 'our investigations so far have convinced us that it is essential to standardise one type of vessel for production in both US and Canada.' He went on to state that no progress was possible without vessel plans, and that he had, therefore, proceeded on the assumption that they would standardise 'our 9,900 tons open vessel' with reciprocating machinery and coal-fired Scotch boilers. His cable, one of the seminal documents relating to the design process, requested that machinery tracings be completed in the greatest possible detail, but stated that hull drawings were 'entirely suitable as already completed', and could be adapted to suit welding construction in the United States (with the work in question to be carried out by the large New York firm of marine architects, Gibbs & Cox). He asserted that there was a reasonable possibility of placing orders in the USA and Canada for sixty vessels to be delivered between the autumn of 1941 and the end of 1942 but requested that orders for all vessels required should be placed as soon as possible to secure building berths and machinery output. Finally, he put forward the tentative estimate that the cost of sixty vessels built to one design would likely be about £25 million.

A second telegram from Thompson to Lithgow, on 29 October, completed the picture. Explaining that they had been impressed by the quality of work being done at Todd's Tacoma yard, one of the many they had visited in a hurricane schedule of yard visits, he reiterated the view that the company had 'been practically allocated to us by the Maritime Commission in fulfilment of their promise to me to hold off and let us in provided we act quickly.' By this stage, events were moving quickly, with firm proposals on price, based on the outline plans the mission had placed before them, expected on about 3 November. Thompson cautioned that it would be imperative to give Todd definite answers very soon thereafter as the latter had 'other irons in the fire', and that if the British did not take their chance 'the Maritime Commission will certainly give them orders.' He concluded: 'Todds are the only source of ships in quantity and we shall have to make best bargain we can with them on price. The larger the original order the lower the price will be and the better the delivery. Moreover, placing a large order is the only way of securing capacity for as long as we are likely to want it. We therefore press most strongly that we be allowed to place orders now for as many vessels as are likely to be required in (the) future if we are satisfied as to price and delivery.' Thompson's insistence on the need to press ahead before the window of opportunity closed was quite justified, as preliminary work on the United States' own emergency shipbuilding programme was already underway, and Admiral Land would submit a detailed memorandum listing recommended sites for new US yards to build a new generation of cargo vessels in early November.

The New Building Programme Takes Shape

Although the Thompson mission had fulfilled the first part of its brief by matching the British requirement for US-built tonnage with that part of American shipbuilding capacity

before orders were placed, the result of a basic acceptance that the decision to build ships in the United States implied embracing American building techniques.

The War Cabinet met on 6 November and approved the order for sixty vessels at the cost of £25 million, subject only to future Treasury consultation if there was any likelihood of the cost estimate being exceeded. While requesting this caveat, the Chancellor added his voice to the case for standardisation of a 'simple type', a request which in his case might have been motivated more by parsimony than an idea of design parameters. Although the leaders of the war effort might be agreed on this fundamental point, some of those responsible for implementing policy were still engaged in an ongoing debate on what standardisation would mean in terms of vessel design. Thus, while Britain was committed to the order of sixty ships, there was still some way to go in terms of both modifying the Thompson design to take account of the use of American shipbuilding techniques and of finalising the specifications to which the ships would be built.

Finalising Overall Design and Yard Arrangements

Three broad requirements impacted on the adaptation of the North Sands vessel for production in US yards. First, the use of complex machined hull plates, particularly in the bow and stern sections, had to be minimised to reduce the need for furnacing and power-pressing, in the interests of speeding up building times and minimising the strain on war-built emergency yards with limited engineering facilities and shallow pools of skilled labour. Second, blueprints had to be adjusted to take account of the shift from riveted to welded construction, the latter being not only the norm in the United States but also a less demanding skill to be taught to workers with no previous shipbuilding experience. Finally, the entire design had to be modified to give maximum scope for component fabrication and assembly without the need for modification or fine-tuning at the yard itself.

Thompson approached the re-design challenge by simplifying the hull specifications. While retaining the general shape and dimensions of the latest version of the economy ship hull, he introduced gentle curvature to the overall form, eliminating most of the double curves, and reducing the need for furnacing and power pressing design to two plates on either side of the forefoot. The general effect of this was to make the hull fuller at each end, something which made the bow section in particular look much blunter but had no significant impact on vessel performance. The burden of the other work fell not just on Thompson but also on Gibbs & Cox, the US firm of naval architects retained to produce the detailed blueprints to send to the new shipyards. The biggest single change was the alteration of the complete set of hull plans to take account of the move from riveted construction, in which hull plates overlapped, to welded construction in which they fitted against each other. While this challenge had been anticipated, a second challenge came with the more surprising discovery that the British drawings were not detailed enough for US shipbuilders. British design practice generally involved issuing only about 30 per cent of the drawings required by American yards, largely because the more highly skilled British workmen were accustomed to doing more benchwork such as hand fitting and filing. As a result, the British drawings had first to be systematically interpreted and amplified, and then reissued as a comprehensive set of templates which would allow the complete vessel to be built without modification or design intervention at the US builder's yard.

Most of this work could only be progressed when the final specifications for the vessel had been agreed between the shipping mission and its masters at the Admiralty. Unfortunately, this proved to be far from straightforward. Thompson's initial cable of 15 October, stating that he was proceeding with the 9,900dwt. vessel whose plans he had brought with him, appears to have triggered a bout of second-guessing at the Admiralty and Ministry of Shipping. This proposal was first accepted by Ayre at the Admiralty, but following discussions with the Ministry of Shipping, he cabled Thompson that his proposal to standardise at 9,900dwt. was 'not acceptable as too large for so many vessels.' The counter proposal was that standardisation should be at 9,300dwt. There was no explanation as to why a relatively minor difference in specification was so important, and it is difficult to understand what the reasoning was behind it. Towards the end of the month, Thompson cabled back that he could reduce the dimensions of the ship to obtain the newly specified deadweight. Ayre then replied on the last day of October that he assumed existing hull plans could be used as guidance, for 'reducing beam to about fifty-six feet ten inches moulded to produce 9,300dwt on twenty feet six inches', but that the preference was for 9,300dwt. on 25ft 'which would involve alteration of two dimensions.'

At this stage, the design discussion appears to have become decidedly disjointed. On 9 November, Thompson sent a telegram to Ayre which he must have assumed would finalise the outline design question saying that he had ascertained that all dimensions could be adjusted simultaneously with adapting the plans for welded construction, and proposing length between perpendiculars of 410ft, moulded breadth of 58ft 1.5in and depth of 36ft 6in to carry 9,300dwt on 25ft draft open with scantlings for 26ft 6in closed. Ayre, however, replied immediately to the effect that it was preferable to keep the length constant at 416ft, making all the reduction on the beam. Thompson, who was clearly feeling the pressure of being the lead negotiator on the spot while simultaneously facing a procession of design changes from across the Atlantic, responded that he could not agree to retaining the original 416ft length, as this would involve new model forms 'for which we could not be responsible.' He also pointed out that new general arrangement and classification plans suitable for welding were already well advanced based on the revised 410ft length and the original model form. He concluded with understandable frustration that he felt he 'must stress that continued alterations are causing consternation here to all concerned, and they will inevitably cause eventual delay' and that he therefore trusted that Ayre would be able 'to agree with our proposals.'

Ayre's 14 November response gave no ground at all, and there was never any acknowledgement of the fact that the shorter hull form with which Thompson was working was the product of the Admiralty's request for a smaller vessel issued only a few weeks before. Ayre informed Thompson that increased length was essential to allow hatches long enough to accommodate cased aircraft, and that accepting a narrower beam was necessary to reduced potential strain on UK dry docks when servicing the new fleet of sixty vessels. He went on to deliver a mini lecture on marine architecture, stating that the desired beam could be achieved by the 'proportionate reduction of waterplane ordinates without impairing model form' and that such a change was 'considered to be an improvement.' If this assertion shook Thompson, the next must have been even more startling, as Ayre breezily stated that Thompson's own shipyard at North Sands 'have redesigned for 9,300 on 425 feet six inches with fifty-six feet ten inches moulded beam' and that it would build to this in future! He then concluded: 'Please accept assurance that fullest regard has been given to alterations relative your difficult position but new strategic developments concerning the trading of the vessels and the needs of Ministry of Shipping and other War Departments in this respect made alterations essential to latest war requirements … It is not contemplated that further alterations will be required our effort having been made to complete these before sending you our final instructions.'

An internal Admiralty memorandum dated 15 November, sent to Ayre but undoubtedly drawn up for the record at his request, summarised the position after the round of design alterations. It is quoted here in full, as it sheds considerable light on the debate over the Ocean class's design antecedents, and hence those of its Fort- and Park-class sisters and Liberty ship cousins.

> The Merchant Shipbuilding Mission in the USA have been authorised by you to contract with the Todd Shipbuilding Corporation to build at Seattle sixty open shelter deck type vessels of 9,300 tons deadweight on twenty-five feet draft, with a service speed (loaded) of ten- and one-half knots and 2,500ihp with reciprocating engines, and three Scotch boilers of fourteen feet nine inches by eleven feet nine inches and about 7,000ft^2 heating surface, with superheat. The scantlings to be such that the vessels can, if so desired later, be loaded one foot six inches deeper as 'closed' shelter deck vessels. The vessels will have a block co-efficient of 0.75, and, in addition to facilitate for carrying ample bunkers, will have a deep tank. The vessels will be all welded and will be built to the 100 A1 classification of Lloyd's Register of Shipping, whose surveyors will supervise the work throughout. The length of the vessels will be 416 feet and it is understood that the beam will be about fifty-seven feet. The four main hatches will be thirty-five feet long, and the height of the 'tween deck a minimum of eight feet nine inches, it being understood that this gives a clearance between coamings for cases from the hatchways into the 'tween decks of seven feet two inches minimum, and in number one hold about three feet more than this, resulting from the straight second deck. Special importance is attached to suitability for stowing cased aircraft in the 'tween decks. You are also stipulating that the crew accommodation shall be up to our best standard for such vessels.

Given the confusing progression of alternative length specifications, it is important to clarify the difference between several of the quoted dimensions. The figure of 416ft was the length measured 'between perpendiculars.' This was a different figure from the registered length of 425ft 6in, which was the measurement quoted in registration documents. The 416ft vessel which Ayre requested from Thompson, and the 425ft 6in vessel he said had been re-designed at North Sands were, in fact of the same length, the difference in figures being a product of the methods of calculation.

The one detail in this document which did not prove accurate was the identification of Seattle as the location of the builder's yard. While Todd did have a yard there, the company proposed to construct new facilities elsewhere to carry out the British building programme. The first definite news on this front arrived on 19 November, when Thompson informed the Admiralty that Todd proposed to build the ships at three places: Richmond, California; Mobile, Alabama; and Portland, Maine. There may well have been an internal company or overarching political imperative for spreading capacity increases along America's three major seaboards, the Pacific, Gulf and Atlantic coasts. Beyond geographical location, there was one important difference between the proposed sites. Both Richmond and Portland would be completely new facilities, built on empty shore land. In the case of Mobile, however, the company was already operating a yard there, and was simply proposing to expand it.

The proposal envisaged six building ways at Richmond and Portland, with total production of forty-eight ships, divided evenly between the two yards. Two slipways would be added to the existing yard at Mobile, which would be used to build the remaining twelve vessels. Before final negotiations could proceed and contracts signed, it was necessary to obtain American governmental approval. A 'Report on Preliminary Purchase Negotiation' (commonly referred to as RPN) was required for anything purchased with a value of more than $150,000. The RPN for the construction of the sixty vessels was submitted via the British Purchasing Commission on 13 November to the President's Liaison Committee (PLC) of the US Treasury.

On 20 November, the PLC granted the British permission to negotiate with Todd Shipyards Corporation and its associates for production of sixty cargo vessels, subject to the submission of further details as to the locations of the new shipyards and their approval by the Navy Department and the US Maritime Commission. The detailed proposal in question had already been drawn up and was sent to the PLC the same day, giving broad specifications for the six-berth new yards at Portland, Maine, and Richmond, California, to be built at a combined cost of $7.121 million, and for the two-berth extension of the Alabama Dry Docks Company facility at Mobile, Alabama, at a cost of $1.150 million. The proposal also gave outline specifications of the sixty ships to be constructed, which were described as cargo ships of approximately 10,000dwt, fitted with reciprocating engines of 2,500ihp and Scotch boilers, the hull dimensions to be 416ft length, 56ft 10in beam, and 25ft 6in draft.

The PLC responded on 6 December, giving the green light for the construction of the Portland and Richmond yards. The Mobile extension proposal, however, was not approved due to 'the expected interference that would result in existing and prospective shipbuilding, repair and conversion programs for the Navy and the Maritime Commission.' The Alabama decision caused little surprise or disappointment, Powell going as far as to tell the BPC that the mission 'knew some time ago' that permission to build at Mobile was likely to be refused. A fall-back scheme had already been prepared, and, rather than seek an alternative third site (as the PLC expected), it was decided to add an extra way at each of the two new shipyards and to build thirty ships at each, Thompson telling the Admiralty that 'we regard this development as an improvement and likely to lead to economy.' The revised plan received quick American approval, and the way was finally clear to proceed. By this time, arrangements to start work on what would become the first of three waves of capacity expansion in the US emergency programme were also nearing completion, which would result in the British yards being just two of nine new yards – three each on the Atlantic, Gulf and Pacific coasts – with a total of sixty-five building berths being constructed around the country.

At this stage, the combined cost of the two new yards was estimated at $8.5 million. In the early weeks of the mission's explorations, vague hopes had been entertained that either the contractors would provide funds for the yard, or the US government's Reconstruction Finance Corporation (RFC) would finance them as part of its industrial capacity building programme. Neither hope was realistic, and the estimated cost of building the yards was also to prove optimistic. For the moment, however, the anticipated yard construction cost was rolled into the estimated $87.5 million cost of the ships to produce a total expenditure figure equivalent, at the then current rate of exchange of approximately £24 million, a figure within the £25 million expenditure figure which had been approved at the beginning of November.

The contract with Todd was finally signed by the British Purchasing Commission on 21 December 1940. By this stage,

Thompson had left America, his job apparently complete. His homeward voyage, however, was not destined to be as trouble free as the outward leg. He sailed from New York on the Prince Line motor ship *Western Prince* on 6 December. Like *Scythia*, *Western Prince* was fast enough to sail as an independent, but on this occasion, speed did not prove a guarantee of safety. On the morning of 14 December, she was sighted south of Iceland by the German submarine *U 96* and

Below: *Western Prince*, (10,926g/1929), one of a quartet of twin-screw cargo-passenger motor ships built on the Clyde for the Prince Line service between New York and Brazil and the River Plate, was sunk by *U 96* on 14 December 1940 while sailing for Britain as an independent with Cyril Thompson aboard.
(Eric Johnson/ Roy Fenton collection)

Bottom: *Baron Kinnaird* (3,355g/1927), saviour of *Western Prince*'s survivors, would herself become a victim of the Battle of the Atlantic, being sunk with all hands by *U 621* on 10 March 1943 after straggling from a westbound convoy.
(Ships in Focus)

US Emergency Shipyards – First Wave of Expansion

Shipyard	Location	State	Coast	Building Berths	
Todd-Bath Iron Shipbuilding	South Portland	Maine	Atlantic	7	
Bethlehem-Fairfield Shipyard	Baltimore	Maryland	Atlantic	13	
North Carolina Shipbuilding	Wilmington	North Carolina	Atlantic	6	= 26
Alabama Dry Dock & Shipbuilding	Mobile	Alabama	Gulf	4	
Delta Shipbuilding	New Orleans	Louisiana	Gulf	6	
Houston Shipbuilding	Houston	Texas	Gulf	6	= 16
California Shipbuilding	Los Angeles	California	Pacific	8	
Todd-California Shipbuilding	Richmond	California	Pacific	7	
Oregon Shipbuilding	Portland	Oregon	Pacific	8	= 23

sunk with two torpedoes. Fifteen men were lost, including the master, but the remainder were rescued after spending most of the day in the lifeboats, most of them, including Thompson, by the Ardrossan-registered tramp ship *Baron Kinnaird*. Carrying just over 150 survivors, the rescue ship turned back from her westbound passage to North America and landed her charges on the Clyde on 18 December.

Before turning from this description of the process through which the sixty new ships were designed and ordered to an analysis of how they were built and delivered, it is worth pausing first to summarise the Ocean design's antecedents, second to explain how the same design came to be employed as a basis for the Liberty ship programme, and third to establish the relative position of the Fort building programme in Canada to its British and American equivalents south of the border.

As far as design antecedents are concerned, there was no simple copying of any existing design. Rather, a series of changes were made to the plans of the most recent set of drawings for a ship being constructed at the J L Thompson & Sons North Sands Yard (Yard No 607, later launched as *Empire Wave*). While Cyril Thompson was continuously updating his set of plans to meet changing Admiralty requirements, Ayre's cable of 14 November appears to indicate that a similar set of changes had been put through to blueprints at the Sunderland shipbuilding yard. Thompson spent the winter months at Sunderland overseeing the completion of a final set of plans which would serve, with one major exception (the alteration of the design to allow for welded construction in the US), as the blueprints for both the sixty US-built ships, and the soon to be laid down *Empire Liberty* and her sisters. Completed plans were then flown back to the United States, where they were completely re-worked by Gibbs & Cox to allow for welded construction. Simultaneously, the same plans were sent to the Canadian shipbuilders who had signed contracts to build twenty-six ships for the British government account, also the result of the activities of the British shipping mission. The Canadian ships, the first of what were to become a much larger group of Forts and Parks, were built to the same general specifications as the ships ordered in the USA but were riveted rather than welded. In confirmation of their antecedents, the first group of these ships were referred to as the 'North Sands' type. While *Empire Liberty* and the Oceans are often portrayed as mother and daughters, it would be more accurate to describe them and the Canadian Forts as sisters, sisters which were the product of wartime adaption of the Thompson 'economy ship' model, which had itself been evolving since 1935. The decision to name Thompson's Yard No 611 *Empire Liberty* was taken deliberately to align her with the US building programme, producing a one-vessel break in a series of names derived from British historical figures (Yard Nos 609 and 610 had been named *Empire Lawrence* and *Empire Cranmer*, while Yard Nos 612 and 613 would be launched as *Empire Halley* and *Empire Johnson*).

The Liberty Ship Trail

A full description of the evolution of the Liberty ship is beyond the scope of this work, but an examination of the files of the British shipbuilding mission does offer some valuable insights. The pressure on Britain's merchant shipping resources had continued to build while Thompson and his colleagues had been pursuing the original sixty-ship order in October–December 1940. A follow-on order for a second batch of sixty ships had been hovering in the background for some time, but at the beginning of December, the

Empire Liberty, seen here anchored at New York on 24 July 1942 carrying a cargo of phosphate rock for the UK which she had loaded the week before at Tampa, Florida, was the first vessel completed by J L Thompson's Sunderland yard to the same basic design as the US-built Oceans.
(US Coast Guard/Mariners' Museum & Park)

Chancellor made it clear not only that there were insufficient dollar resources to spend any more on shipbuilding in the United States, but also that gold and dollar reserves would be 'entirely exhausted in a limited number of weeks.' Enquiries were made in Washington, DC as to whether the US would be prepared to build the ships itself and then 'rent' them to Britain. Initial indications were far from positive, and even when the restrictions imposed by the Neutrality Act were lifted, it was clear that there was little appetite for building British-style tramps. The US Navy objected to the vessels in terms of speed, as it had no wish to convoy such slow ships should war occur. The US Treasury objected to the vessels as they would be of little use if the United States had to take them over, the country only requiring vessels of the cargo liner type as it did not share Britain's reliance on bulk carriers for the carriage of essential raw materials and food stuffs such as coal, ore, and grain, which it was not economical to carry in faster vessels with higher operating costs.

Against this background, a cable from the shipping mission on 24 January 1941 must have been a bolt from the blue. It stated that the United States Maritime Commission had asked for and been given all plans and specifications of the British cargo vessels recently contracted for and reported that plans and specifications had also been sent to Bethlehem, Newport News, in connection with a US programme of 200 cargo ships. The communication ended: 'this may indicate adoption of our hull design for United States ships which we understand will be oil-burning and have water tube boilers.' On the face of things, this marked a complete reversal of American shipbuilding policy, which had revolved around building high-specification cargo ships designed to remain competitive for twenty years. Admiral Land at the USMC had been particularly opposed to going down the British route, writing on 18 November 1940: 'in my judgement we are not interested in the type of ship proposed by the British, which type is for emergency use only… we should build ships for twenty-year life and have an eye on the future.' On 29 November, he had repeated this message in a letter to the President, but with one major rider: 'the last thing I want to do is repeat the mistakes of the last war and have a lot of obsolete vessels on our hands unless the emergency is so great as to make this an absolute necessity.'

The USMC's apparently Damascene conversion was, in fact, related to the conviction of President Roosevelt that Axis aggression and ongoing military success meant that such an 'emergency' already existed. On 3 January 1941 he announced plans to build 200 emergency merchant ships in addition to the ships already planned or under construction as part of the USMC's Long-Range Programme (he had already instructed the USMC to begin negotiations to build the necessary shipyards on 26 December 1940). Even in November, Land had realised that large-scale emergency building would only be possible with 'a simple type of cargo ship with reciprocating engines' and the USMC now had to work very quickly to produce just such a design. The initial appreciation of the existing British design was that its hull form was not best suited for rapid mass production. Instead, the Commission sought to design a new vessel with a straight-line hull form that would facilitate fabrication and assembly and simultaneously investigated the feasibility of reviving one of the more successful designs built for the US Shipping Board during the First World War. While the second option soon proved impracticable, USMC naval architects did produce a fresh design with a considerably simplified hull form, a full plating model of which was then produced by Bethlehem Steel. While the Commission formed the preliminary view that the new design would offer superior capacity to the British vessel and could more easily be mass produced, there were no model basin tests to assess the impact of the hull form on speed and power requirements, and no clear estimation of

A trials photograph of *Patrick Henry*, the first Liberty ship to enter service, taken just before she was delivered at Baltimore by Bethlehem-Fairfield on 30 December 1941.
(John & Marion Clarkson collection)

the lead time required to bring the new ship into production. Gibbs & Cox, who would have been responsible for completing the final design, argued that starting from scratch would cause a significant delay in beginning construction, and that it made more sense to adapt the existing Thompson template. Tellingly, the American shipbuilders consulted at the same time echoed this view and expressed total confidence in their ability to build copies of the British vessel. Under increasing pressure of time, Admiral Land came around to the latter view, concluding that the British design could be adapted for mass production on a much shorter time horizon and with only a slight increase in building man-hours. On this basis, he took a proposal to a congressional committee which accepted it and authorised funding, reporting that 'the design is the best that can be devised for an emergency product to be quickly, cheaply and simply built.'

The as yet unnamed Liberty type and its British-designed counterpart would be near hull sisters, the American substitution of bulwarks for deck rails simply giving the former a flush-decked appearance. The most fundamental external change was the replacement of the traditional British split-superstructure design with one integrated central bridge, funnel and accommodation block and the consequent transfer of number three hold forward of this structure, which in turn allowed the fitting of a second forward mast and set of cargo derricks between the second and third holds. Additionally, the weather deck was modified to eliminate camber between the hatches and use straight camber lines from the sides of the hatches to the sides of the ship, while beneath the waterline, the newly designed 'contra-rudder' delivered small improvements in speed and manoeuvrability at decreased cost. Internally, the most significant change involved the machinery for steam production, the US ships being oil rather than coal-fired and fitted with water-tube rather than Scotch boilers. The Liberties would, however, be powered by the same triple-expansion reciprocating engines taken from the North Eastern Marine Engineering Co plans. The engines themselves were interchangeable between American and Canadian yards, and there would be cases when engines originally ordered for vessels building in one country ended up being diverted to vessels building in the other.

The American ships were ordered under the USMC classification EC2–S–C1, the sobriquet Liberty ship being derived from the subsequent decision to brand the new ships 'the Liberty Fleet'. This term gained further resonance from the choice of the name of Patrick Henry, the Revolutionary era orator famous for his 1775 declaration 'Give me liberty or give me death', for one of the first ships. *Patrick Henry* was launched by the Bethlehem-Fairfield yard at Baltimore, Maryland on 27 September 1941, some five weeks after *Ocean Vanguard* went down the ways at Richmond, but more than two months before Pearl Harbor. Celebrated as the first Liberty ship, *Patrick Henry* would be the first to enter service, but was launched as part of the first 'Liberty Fleet Day' which included two other Liberty ships, *Star of Oregon* built at Portland, Oregon, and *John C Fremont* built at Los Angeles, California, and two British ships, *Ocean Voice* and *Ocean Venture*, launched together at Richmond.

Postscript – The Canadian Connection

An initial order for twenty-six ships based on Thompson's North Sands design was placed in Canada as a direct result of and within the same timeframe as the sixty-vessel Ocean order. The Canadian building programme differed from its Ocean equivalent in four significant ways. Canadian building practice still revolved around the same riveting techniques employed in the UK, with the result that British blueprints did not have to be adapted for welding and the Fort- and Park- class ships that emerged were closer copies of the British original. Initial Canadian orders were placed with established shipbuilders, and although some of these yards had to undertake significant equipment and capacity upgrades, it was not necessary to build new facilities on greenfield sites to get the building programme underway. While Ocean construction came to an end after the initial order was complete, the Canadian programme was extended all the way through to the end of the war. Finally, the British government only purchased the first two Forts completed, *Fort Ville Marie* on the east coast and *Fort St James* on the west. Ownership of the next ninety vessels passed to the United States under the provisions of the Hyde Park Declaration of 20 April 1941, whereby the US government financed their construction and then bareboat chartered them to the UK within the terms of the wider Lend-Lease agreement. The remaining ships were financed in Canada, the final Fort-class vessels also being chartered to Britain, and the overlapping Park class operated under the ownership of a Canadian crown corporation.

Canadian yards would build 200 ships of the original North Sands type, and an additional 120 improved Victory and Canadian variants (the former an oil-burning vessel with two water-tube boilers substituted for the original three coal-fired Scotch boilers, and the latter a compromise between the other two types, with alternate coal/oil capacity and three Scotch boilers), as well as thirty-three vessels modified for service as supply, support, or depot vessels for the Royal Navy and the Royal Fleet Auxiliary. This production, however, was spread between seven different yards on the west coast and four on the east, with completions starting slowly in the first half of 1942 before accelerating as expanded facilities came online later in the year. Only two of the east coast shipyards, Canadian Vickers and Davie, were fully established in 1941, while Burrard on the west coast started with just one slipway. All the other yards required varying degrees of work before they were fully capable of completing the entire building process (the Burrard Dry Docks south yard was never brought up to this standard, the hulls it built being towed across the harbour for fitting out at the parent yard in North Vancouver). On the west coast, North Vancouver Dry Docks did not complete its first Fort until late May, while Prince Rupert finished its first on the last day of July. *Fort Ville Marie* was the only east coast ship delivered in 1941 before the St Lawrence River froze for the winter, and the next completions from the two established yards did not take place until the following April. At this stage, neither Marine Industries nor United Shipyards, which together would account for three-quarters of total Quebec output, were fully operational, and both yards would not make their first delivery until December 1942.

Fort St James, the first member of her class built on the west coast, is shown here leaving Vancouver for sea trials on 29 January 1942 just after completion by Burrard Dry Docks.
(North Vancouver Museum & Archives 27-2401)

Britain's Oceans and Forts, and America's Liberty ships shared a common hull form as evidenced here in representative photographs of new-built members of each class.

Above: *Ocean Volga* photographed on 15 May 1942 in San Francisco Bay, the twentieth vessel completed by the Todd-California shipyard. *(Richmond Museum of History)*

Left: *Fort Chilcotin* framed by the Burrard Bridge on 5 June 1942, the first completion by West Coast Shipbuilders, Vancouver. *(W J Moore/City of Vancouver Archives CVA 195-3)*

Opposite page: *William Blount* leaving Delta Shipbuilding at New Orleans on 26 September 1942, the twenty-seventh Liberty ship built by the yard. *(Naval History & Heritage Command)*

The critical growth phase was underwritten by the overlapping provisions of Lend-Lease and the Hyde Park Declaration, which freed it from dependence on Britain's overstretched foreign currency reserves. The timing differential here was critical, the Ocean contract being signed two-and-a-half months before the Lend-Lease Act became law on 11 March 1941 and almost four months before Canadian output was leveraged at Hyde Park. Britain did, however, achieve one solid advantage from the early start made in building the Oceans. The Todd-California thirty-ship building programme delivery was completed on 22 July 1942 with the delivery of *Ocean Victory*, at which time the total output

of the British Columbia yards had only reached eighteen, ten of these having arrived in June–July. The delivery differential was even more pronounced on the east coast, where total output of the Quebec yards had only reached eleven when the arrival of *Ocean Glory* concluded the thirty-vessel Todd-Bath order on 18 November 1942. While the Canadian ships would play a proportionately larger role in the war effort when their numbers began to swell in 1943, the Oceans made a more important contribution to the critical campaigns of 1942. To take just two examples, *Fort Augustus* was the only ship of its class committed to the North African invasion convoys of November 1942, which included no fewer than fifteen Oceans, while the first Forts deployed on the Russian convoys sailed in JW 54B on 22 November 1943 a year and a half after *Ocean Voice* made her class's debut on the route when she left Reykjavik as commodore ship for PQ 16 on 21 May 1942.

Output of Fort and Park Deep Sea Cargo Vessels from Canadian Yards

Yard	Location	N Sands	Victory	Canadian	Naval	Total	First Completion
West coast	**British Columbia**						
Burrard DD, North	North Vancouver	25	17	3	10	55	29.1.1942
Burrard DD, South	Vancouver	25	17	3	9	54	21.3.1942
North Vancouver/Pacific DD	North Vancouver	26	21	3	5	55	27.5.1942
Prince Rupert DD & Shipyard	Prince Rupert	6	5	2	-	13	31.7.1942
Victoria Machinery Depot	Victoria	9	8	2	1	20	2.6.1942
West Coast SB	Vancouver	22	24	3	5	54	6.6.1942
Yarrows	Esquimalt	2	-	-	-	2	30.6.1942
West coast total	115	92	16	30	253		
East coast	**Quebec**						
Canadian Vickers	Montreal	6	-	-	-	6	21.12.1941
Davie SB & Repairs	Lauzon	19	-	-	-	19	18.4.1942
Marine Industries	Sorel	27	-	3	-	30	25.12.1942
United Shipyards	Montreal	33	-	9	3	45	8.12.1942
East coast total	85	-	12	3	100		
Canada total	200	92	28	33	353		

Aerial views of the Todd-California yard under construction taken at monthly intervals between 31 March and 30 June 1941, with work beginning progressively on each of its seven building berths.
(World War II pictorial collection, Box 2, Hoover Institution Library & Archives)

Top: Aerial view of the Todd-California yard under construction looking south, 31 March 1941.

Above: Aerial view of the Todd-California yard under construction looking south, 30 April 1941.

Top: Aerial view of the Todd-California yard under construction looking north, 29 May 1941.

Above: Aerial view of the Todd-California yard under construction looking south, 30 June 1941.

Aerial view of the partially completed Todd-Bath yard taken on 1 August 1941, with work proceeding slowly on the vessels already laid down in the building basins at the right, and the fitting out berth and much of the yard infrastructure still under construction.
(©National Maritime Museum, Greenwich, London)

located in the East Bay area of San Francisco Bay, was described as 'mostly marsh land and partly tidal flats.' The winter of 1940–41 was very wet in the area, and almost immediately after ground-breaking the site became 'a sea of mud.' The weather remained a problem as construction progressed, the shipyard's in-house magazine reporting fifty consecutive days of rain in February and March. The entire shipyard facility, stretching over 100 acres with a water frontage of nearly 4,000ft, was constructed on 70ft long concrete piles. No fewer than 25,000 of these piles were driven in, and seven slipways erected upon them, with a large pre-assembly facility constructed at their head from where prefabricated hull and superstructure components could be moved to the slipways by large cranes. Each slipway was 425ft long and 90ft wide. In addition, fitting out wharves were constructed, with a total area of 72,000sq ft. The shareholding split among the US managers of what became the Todd-California Shipbuilding Corporation was 65 per cent to the Kaiser-led consortium and 35 per cent to Todd.

An entirely different type of shipyard was constructed at South Portland on Casco Bay in Maine. Here the shoreline had a rock foundation, and the yard to be built on it had to be able to handle a wide tidal range. The solution adopted was to blast basins out of the rock behind a 1,500ft cofferdam. Three basins were excavated, and concrete and steel building berths constructed within them, two each in two of the basins, and three in the third. The berths were each 425ft long and some 95ft wide. Once again, pre-assembly facilities were constructed at the head of each berth. The three basins were fitted with sluices for filling and pumping out the basins, and gates through which completed hulls could be floated out. There was one immense fitting out pier, 1,000ft long and 90ft wide, capable of handling five vessels simultaneously. The management company of what became the Todd-Bath Iron Shipbuilding Corporation, was divided between three participants, the Kaiser consortium and Todd each taking 35 per cent, and the long-established Bath Iron Works the remaining 30 per cent.

Above: Aerial view taken on 15 July 1941 of the first Oceans under construction at Richmond, California, showing (from the top) *Ocean Venture* and *Ocean Voice*, which would be launched together on 27 September; *Ocean Vanguard*, launched as the lead ship of the class on 16 August; *Ocean Vigil*, launched on 31 August, and *Ocean Viking*, launched on 23 October; and work only just beginning on *Ocean Vesper* and *Ocean Valley* on the nearest two berths.
(World War II pictorial collection, Box 2, Hoover Institution Library & Archives)

Below: The first seven east coast Oceans under construction at South Portland, Maine. *Ocean Liberty* is on the far left, with *Ocean Freedom* beside her, both due to be launched on 20 December. *Ocean Peace* and *Ocean Justice* (launched on 8 February 1942), with *Ocean Honour*, *Ocean Faith*, and *Ocean Hope* (launched together on 23 March), are on the right.
(National Maritime Museum)

Construction Company Holdings in Todd-California and Todd-Bath Shipyards

Construction Companies	Todd-California, Richmond	Todd-Bath, South Portland
	(%)	(%)
Todd Shipyards Corp	35.0	35.0
Bath Iron Works	-	30.0
Henry J Kaiser Co	8.125	4.375
Kaiser Co	8.125	4.375
W A Bechtel & Co	8.125	4.375
Bechtel, McCone & Parsons	8.125	4.375
MacDonald & Kahn Inc	6.5	3.5
Utah Construction Co	6.5	3.5
General Construction Co	6.5	3.5
Morrison-Knudsen Co	6.5	3.5
J F Shea Co	6.5	3.5

In both cases, the yards proved considerably more expensive to construct than had been estimated at the time the contracts were first signed. The point was made in a British Merchant Shipping Mission review in July 1942, that the British 'had led the field in the creation of emergency shipbuilding facilities' and that there had been little experience available in the United States to fall back on. The same review, however, admitted that the estimates themselves 'were worked out in a great hurry on quite inadequate study as time was of the essence.' The total cost of the two yards finally came in at $17.3 million, just over double the $8.5 million projected at the end of 1940. This cost was unevenly spread, with Todd-California costing $7,147,121 compared to $10,147,160 for Todd-Bath, a reflection of the much greater burden of civil engineering expenditure on the latter site.

Building the Ships

On both coasts, the first new vessels were laid down before the whole yard was complete. At Richmond, the first keel was laid on 14 April 1941. The first Portland keel was laid six weeks later, on 24 May 1941, the longer lead-time being largely a result of the scale of the engineering challenge confronting the east coast yard builders. As late as May, anticipated output of completed vessels from the two yards, based on contractors' estimates, was almost identical, with both yards expecting to complete their first fifteen vessels by the end of July 1942, and the remaining fifteen by the end of the same year. From this point on, however, the performance of the two yards quickly diverged.

The construction of the Richmond yard benefitted from the direct participation of the Kaiser/Bechtel consortium, which was a joint majority stakeholder in the California venture, but more of a sleeping partner at Portland. In the second week of September, with two vessels already launched, the managers were estimating the completion of eight vessels by the end of the year. By the first week of November, this number had been scaled back to five, with the yard meeting 'considerable difficulty' over a 'large number of small items' needed to complete the first ship. The revised target of five was met, and thereafter yard output accelerated as the last slipways came into service and the fitting-out facilities were completed.

As the west coast shipyard moved ahead, so its twin on the east coast fell behind. On 11 September, after the first two Richmond vessels had been launched, Powell reported on a visit to Portland that 'progress generally is disappointing, and the management does not appear to have that drive and efficiency which is so noticeable at Richmond.' Representatives of the Todd consortium left the visit 'much shaken' and 'fully conscious of the need for greater effort and drive at Portland.' New management was installed at the yard, and steps taken to address the biggest bottleneck, the delivery of the large cranes for the building berths and fitting-out facilities. A follow-up visit on 6 November revealed 'encouraging progress on hulls one and two and generally improved atmosphere in yard.' Six berth cranes were now working, although it was clear by this stage that no deliveries could be expected until early 1942. Although the South Portland yard would make large steps forward in the new year, it would never match Todd-California's performance, not least because the east coast management team, while experienced warship builders, could not match the west coast shipbuilders' expertise in what Admiral Vickery would later characterise as a 'production construction job where they can move a lot of mass material and move it quickly.'

The launch of *Ocean Vanguard* at Richmond took place on 16 August 1941, three months and four days after the keel had been laid – a good performance by any standards for a new yard with some of its facilities still under construction. The launch itself was attended by much ceremony. Both official and public sentiment in the United States had become

Top opposite: The scale of the launch ceremonies for *Ocean Vanguard* is clear from this photograph of the invited audience of shipyard workers and local dignitaries taken from the bow of the vessel before she went down the building way.
(Courtesy of San Francisco Maritime National Historical Park)

Bottom opposite: The launch of *Ocean Vanguard* on 16 August 1941.
(The Log – Organ of the West Coast Marine Industry, August 1941)

Vessels Launched on Liberty Fleet Day, 27 September 1941

Vessel	Type	Customer	Builder	Yard Location and State
Adabelle Lykes	C1	Lykes Bros	Pusey & Jones	Wilmington Delaware
African Planet	C3	American South African Line	Ingalls SB	Pascagoula, Mississippi
Alcoa Polaris	C1	Alcoa SS Co	Consolidated Steel	Long Beach, California
Frederick Funston	C3	US Army	Seattle-Tacoma SB	Tacoma, Washington
James McKay	C1	Lykes Bros	Bethlehem Steel	Sparrow Point, Maryland
John C Fremont	EC2	USMC	California SB	Long Beach, California
Louise Lykes	C2	Lykes Bros	Federal SB	Kearny, New Jersey
Ocean Venture	Ocean	UK Min of War Transport	Todd-California	Richmond, California
Ocean Voice	Ocean	UK Min of War Transport	Todd-California	Richmond, California
Patrick Henry	EC2	USMC	Bethlehem-Fairfield	Baltimore, Maryland
Sinclair Superflame	Tanker	Sinclair Refining	Bethlehem Steel	Quincy, Massachusetts
Star of Oregon	EC2	USMC	Oregon SB	Portland, Oregon
Steel Artisan	C3	Isthmian SS Co	Western Pipe & Steel	San Francisco, California
Surprise	C2	United States Lines	Sun SB & Dry Dock	Chester, Pennsylvania
USS Cowie (DD-632)	Gleaves	US Navy	Boston Navy Yard	Boston, Massachusetts
USS Knight (DD-633)	Gleaves	US Navy	Boston Navy Yard	Boston, Massachusetts

Preparations underway for the double launch of *Ocean Liberty* and *Ocean Freedom* by floating out from their building basins at the Todd-Bath yard on 20 December 1941
(©National Maritime Museum, Greenwich, London)

the building basins bow first. The first pair of vessels, *Ocean Liberty* and *Ocean Freedom*, left basin one on 20 December 1941. At almost seven months, construction time was more than double what had been achieved with the first vessels launched on the west coast. At this stage, the yard's building programme was clearly still struggling to find its feet (equipment shortages were the major contributory factor, but the harsh weather of the New England winter cannot have helped). The second pair of vessels left basin two on 2 February 1942, and the first triple floating out from basin three did not take place until 23 March. The midway point in the contract was reached on 27 July (five days after the entire Richmond contract had been completed) when *Ocean Pilgrim* (Yard No 15) was delivered.

The normal pattern of floating-out was interrupted on Sunday, 16 August when five vessels, *Ocean Wayfarer, Ocean Stranger, Ocean Traveller, Ocean Seaman* and *Ocean Gallant,* took the water from two basins on the same day. This was part of another carefully orchestrated publicity move, it being combined with the launch on the same day of the Liberty ship *Ethan Allen* by the neighbouring South Portland Shipbuilding yard, and the Fletcher class destroyers *Conway* (*DD-507*) and *Cony* (*DD-507*) by Bath Iron Works across the harbour in Portland, to produce the biggest mass launching by one company of the war to date and the headline 'Todd Yards Launch Eight in One Day.' The final three South Portland vessels left their basin on 18 October 1942, and the final delivery, that of *Ocean Glory,* took place exactly a month later, almost four months behind that of Todd-California, but still six weeks ahead of the originally scheduled contract completion date.

The building of the *Ocean Vanguard* took 169 days from keel-laying to delivery, a particularly commendable performance given not only that she was the first of her type, but that her yard was still under construction. To set this in context, the average construction time of an equivalent UK vessel was ten months, or roughly 300 days. Todd-Bath's early performance was some distance behind that of its west coast cousin, with *Ocean Liberty* taking 279 days to complete. Both yards improved their performance dramatically as they reached full efficiency, with Todd-Bath making up for its slow start, the tenth ship to leave her yard taking only three days more to complete than the equivalent Californian ship. By the end of each building run, both yards were steadily completing ships in under three months, although Todd-California maintained a variable advantage throughout.

Opposite page: Launching ceremonies for the Liberty ship *Star of Oregon* by the Oregon Ship Building Corporation at Portland, Oregon, on Liberty Fleet Day, 27 September 1941.
(Old Oregon Photos)

ELLER
OCEAN STRANGER
OCEAN WAYFARER

OCEAN GALLANT

Photographs of the launch of five Oceans at South Portland, Maine, on 16 August 1942.

Top opposite: The triple building basin being flooded in preparation for floating ou t *Ocean Wayfarer*, *Ocean Stranger*, and *Ocean Traveller*.

Bottom opposite: *Ocean Gallant* under tow from her building basin to the fitting out pier with *Ocean Seaman* waiting her turn to the right.

Top: Panorama of the five newly launched ships moored at the fitting out pier (listed clockwise from left foreground): *Ocean Gallant*, *Ocean Wayfarer*, *Ocean Traveller*, *Ocean Stranger*, and *Ocean Seaman*.

Above: *Ocean Stranger* at the fitting-out pier with the bow of *Ocean Seaman* to the left and *Ocean Traveller* tied up across the head of the pier to the right.

(All photos: Office of War Information Photograph Collection/Library of Congress)

Comparative Building Times – Keel-Laying to Delivery

Vessel	Shipyard	Y/N	Laid-Down	Delivered	Days
Ocean Vanguard	Todd-California	1	14.4.1941	27.10.1941	169
Star of Oregon	Oregon	171	19.5.1941	31.12.1941	226
Ocean Liberty	Todd-Bath	1	24.5.1941	27.2.1942	279
Patrick Henry	Bethlehem-Fairfield	2001	30.4.1941	30.12.1941	244
Ocean Vulcan	Todd-California	10	28.9.1941	20.2.1942	145
John Jay	Oregon	181	30.9.1941	28.3.1942	179
Ocean Courage	Todd-Bath	10	9.2.1942	1.7.1942	142
Alexander Macomb	Bethlehem-Fairfield	2023	16.2.1942	2.6.1942	104
Ocean Volga	Todd-California	20	15.2.1942	15.5.1942	89
William Cullen Bryant	Oregon	195	16.2.1942	7.5.1942	80
Ocean Stranger	Todd-Bath	20	15.6.1942	5.9.1942	82
Benjamin Chew	Bethlehem-Fairfield	2045	15.6.1942	21.8.1942	67
Ocean Victory	Todd-California	30	10.5.1942	22.7.1942	73
Matthew P Deady	Oregon	545	11.5.1942	6.7.1942	56
Ocean Glory	Todd-Bath	30	17.8.1942	18.11.1942	93
George Weems	Bethlehem-Fairfield	2068	19.8.1942	7.10.1942	49

A new Ocean, its prefabricated stern post in the foreground, being laid down at the Todd-Bath yard in South Portland, Maine the day after the previous vessel built in the basin had been floated out. *(Office of War Information Photograph Collection/Library of Congress)*

Building times became progressively faster as the building programme developed as evidenced by this shipyard sign recording the launch of *Ocean Angel*, the twenty-sixth vessel built at South Portland, on 27 September 1942. *(Office of War Information Photograph Collection/Library of Congress)*

It is instructive to compare building times of representative Ocean-class vessels with those of Liberty ships built within the same timeframe. For this purpose, four ships built by Henry Kaiser's Oregon Shipbuilding yard at Portland, Oregon, have been matched with vessels from the Todd-California yard laid down at the same time, and four ships built by Bethlehem-Fairfield at Baltimore have been similarly matched with Todd-Bath vessels. Todd-California was significantly more efficient than Oregon Shipbuilding through 1941 and early 1942, but the latter took the lead over the second half of the Richmond production run, enjoying a two-and-a-half-week advantage by the time the last west-coast Ocean was completed. The picture on the east coast was different. While Bethlehem-Fairfield took almost three weeks longer than Oregon Shipbuilding to build its first Liberty, the Baltimore yard was still more than a month faster than the struggling South Portland concern. While building times reduced steadily in both yards, Bethlehem-Fairfield maintained a significant advantage throughout. The overall picture is one of Liberty ship production efficiency outstripping its Ocean equivalent as prefabrication and efficiencies of scale increased, with improvement in the latter being constrained by lower levels of modular construction, a marginally more complex design, and the limited scope for improvement over short production runs.

Considering the difficulties that had been anticipated in accessing a supply of reciprocating steam engines, and the fact that most US marine engineering firms had little recent experience in producing such machinery, the machinery side of the Ocean building programme proved surprisingly straightforward. A single order for all sixty engines was placed with the long-established General Machinery Company of Hamilton, Ohio. Some confusion exists over the identity of this firm, as the name of the engine builder was given as Hooven, Owens, Rentschler & Co. (with the first word often misspelt as Hoover) in the British registry documents of the thirty Richmond-built vessels, and as the General Machinery Co in the case of their Portland-built sisters. The supplier was one and the same. The original Hooven, Owens, Rentschler concern had merged with another company in 1928 to become General Machinery, but apparently continued to use its old brand name in 1941. Although General Machinery did produce the contracted sixty engines, production was run in with large subsequent orders from the US War Shipping Administration for identical power plant for Liberty ships. The result was that the last fourteen sets of the British order were diverted to US hulls, and the final fourteen Portland-built vessels were equipped with identical plant from the production runs of three different Canadian marine engineering firms.

Initial indications had suggested that there might also be a problem with the supply of boilers. The British specification called for coal-fired Scotch boilers of the type still being fitted to most tramp ships being built in UK yards. Beyond homogeneity, such equipment offered the combined attractions of an easy fuel supply and relative design simplicity. Here again, American engineering practice had moved on, in this case to oil-fired water-tube boilers. In the early stages of negotiations, it appeared that existing manufacturers could not produce boilers large enough to meet British requirements, but once again US industry rose to the challenge. Once requirements were clear, it proved relatively easy to procure the required fit of three boilers with superheat per vessel, those for the west coast ships being manufactured by the Western Pipe & Steel Company of Los Angeles and those for their east coast sisters by the American Locomotive Company of Schenectady, New York.

Naming the Oceans

Prior to the arrival of the new American-built vessels, all but a handful of British government wartime acquisitions, be they vessels built to the government account in British yards, second-hand purchases, or ex-enemy prizes, were, as 'a question of principle', given names beginning with the word 'Empire.' The initial assumption among the concerned civil servants in the Ministry of War Transport (MOWT – a new ministry created by the merger of the Ministry of Shipping and the Ministry of Transport on 1 May 1941) was that this practice should continue with the American deliveries. A note to the concerned British representatives in the United States dated 3 July 1941 gives an interesting insight into what might otherwise be assumed to have been the straightforward pursuit of a simple naming convention: 'this prefix rather cramps our style and our ingenuity in finding names is being very heavily taxed so that should you have any ideas as to how we can link up the prefix "Empire" with some names having a local United States or Canadian atmosphere, it would help an overworked christening section of the Ministry.'

Senior British representatives in the United States swiftly disabused their British colleagues of the idea that 'Empire' names would work, making the obvious point that such a system was inappropriate given political sensitivities in the United States. The counter proposal was that names should begin with 'Ocean.' Whitehall made a second attempt with the suggestion that names begin with 'Atlantic', on the grounds that the ships would be committed to the Battle of the Atlantic 'in which the United States are really now our Allies.' This met with an equally simple rebuttal that 'Atlantic' was hardly an appropriate name for vessels launched into the Pacific! In the end, the overseas case won out and the 'Ocean' nomenclature was adopted.

The second part of the naming system for the Pacific vessels was heavily influenced by the American builders, who were very keen to use words beginning with the letter V in line with the slogan 'V-for-Victory.' This was enthusiastically endorsed by British representatives in the United States, and Whitehall agreed, albeit with some moaning that it might not be possible to find thirty appropriate words beginning

— 4 —

THE OCEANS AT WAR

Ocean Wanderer at anchor in UK waters showing the rigging of her Admiralty Net Defence equipment in silhouette. The pillar box mounting on the aft deck house has been replaced with an AA gun, but no armament has yet been mounted on the forecastle, suggesting the photo might have been taken in the second half of 1943. *(©National Maritime Museum, Greenwich, London)*

Vessel Management and Manning

As was normally the case with vessels owned (or for that matter bareboat chartered) by the Ministry of War Transport on behalf of the British government, all the Oceans were manned and managed by commercial shipping companies. It says a great deal for the strength and resilience of British ship-owning that no fewer than forty-four different companies, many of them quite small tramp operators with limited management resources, were allocated at least one of the sixty vessels. Four vessels were managed by Larrinaga of Liverpool and three by Hain of London, while J & C Harrison, Kaye, Bolton, Haldin & Philipps and Mitchell Cotts of London, Raeburn & Verel of Glasgow, Denholm of Greenock, Hogarth of Ardrossan, Cockerline of Hull and Seager of Cardiff managed two each. The example of the last of these illustrates just how large the commitment could be. W H Seager & Co Ltd was a small South Wales company which had entered the war with a fleet of five steam tramps. Four of these had been lost before the summer of 1941, one with all hands and another with only a single survivor. Despite these casualties, Seager managed not only *Ocean Vanguard* and *Ocean Fame*, but also one war-built Empire, one Sam-Liberty, and no fewer than five Canadian-built Forts and Parks. The burden of losses of managed tonnage was unevenly spread, with, for example, Hain losing all three of the Oceans it manned, and Hogarth both of its.

Surviving crew lists make it clear that ships' complements were overwhelmingly British and generally very experienced. By this stage of the war, a fair number of officers and men were likely to have survived at least one sinking. To return to Seager, Captain Wilfred Leslie Brett, who took command of the trail-blazing *Ocean Vanguard*, had already survived having two ships sunk underneath him: *Beatus* by a U-boat during the slaughter of SC 7 in October 1940, and *Salvus* by the Luftwaffe in the North Sea in April 1941. Another three-time survivor was Captain John Cameron of Maclay & McIntyre Ltd. As a first officer, he survived the sinking of *Empire Wave* (the vessel whose plans were Cyril Thompson's

Ocean Valentine photographed at anchor in San Francisco Bay in June 1942 fresh from the builders with only part of her initial weapons fit, the Oerlikons abreast the compass platform, so far mounted.
(Roy Fenton collection)

original blueprint for the Oceans) by a U-boat in October 1941, and then of *Ocean Might* by another German submarine in September 1942. Promoted to master, he had to take to the boats a third time when his company's own *Janeta* was lost to a third U-boat in May 1944.

Manning practices evolved over time. The master and the chief engineer, who had often served together in their previous deployment, were always assigned to new vessels while they were still building. This was the case with *Ocean Vanguard*, to which both Captain Brett and Chief Engineer Ritchie were posted directly from the recently sunk *Salvus*. The normal practice was to time their arrival to coincide with a ship's launch at the Richmond yard, with the lead time being extended up to a month earlier for ships building at South Portland. The remaining crews of the early completions were allocated by the Ministry of War Transport from the pool of officers and men which had been established at Montreal to handle merchant seamen becoming available for new assignments after being signed off in North American ports, returning from hospital, or surviving a sinking. Again, former shipmates often signed on together, the new second and third officers of *Ocean Vanguard*, for example, coming from *Empire Mallard*, sunk in a collision in convoy in the Belle Isle Strait in September 1941.

As 1942 wore on, the need for crews to man the increasing flow of new ships from North American yards, both Oceans from the US and Forts from Canada, outstripped the capacity of the Montreal pool, forcing a change in manning practices. The Master and his immediate subordinates continued to arrive early from the UK to attend the fitting out of their new vessels but would now be followed across the Atlantic by all the remaining crew, sailing as one party in an empty westbound troopship under the charge of their own senior officer. Surviving correspondence between the ministry and William Thomson & Co of Leith, operators of the Ben Line, concerning the manning of *Ocean Valentine*, launched at Richmond on 7 June 1942 and delivered three weeks later, provides an interesting snapshot of the new procedures in action. Thomson's command group of four men, the master J C Harvey, the chief officer G M McGill, the chief engineer J Brow, and the second engineer J Jamieson, were instructed to report at Princes Parade, Liverpool at one o'clock in the afternoon of 14 May prior to embarking on a Cunard–White Star sailing for New York. At the start of June, the company informed Mr A King, the designated second officer, that he would be in charge of a party of forty-two officers and ratings, all of whom had been signed on in Leith to crew *Ocean Valentine*, and report with them at Princes Pier, Greenock no later than ten o'clock in the morning of 3 June to join a trooper sailing from the Clyde for Halifax. His supervisory responsibilities were to extend over the duration of the long ensuing rail journey to the west coast.

The merchant seamen's war was a hard one, and while serious crew trouble was unusual at sea, there could be problems in port. An extreme example occurred on 1 April 1942, when *Ocean Venus* arrived at Portland, Oregon, from New Westminster, British Columbia, to complete loading for her maiden voyage. In the late afternoon, the second officer returned to the ship and reported to the master that he had been assaulted on shore by the ship's firemen. The miscreants in question returned to the ship soon after, threatened all hands, and attacked the third engineer and the carpenter. The officers and engineers locked themselves in the saloon, while the master called the police. The latter duly arrived and marched seven presumably intoxicated firemen to jail ashore, where charges of assault and battery were lodged against them. The ship had to sign on a new black gang before proceeding, and the logbook does not record the fate of the malefactors.

Ocean Venus, the twelfth vessel completed by Todd-California, ready for delivery on 8 March 1942.
(John & Marion Clarkson collection)

A total of 195 men lost their lives in attacks resulting in the sinking or damaging of Ocean-class vessels, all but twelve of them when their vessels were sunk. Of this total, well over three-quarters (153) were attributable to four vessel losses, all to submarine attack. The losses of *Ocean Crusader* and *Ocean Courage* alone accounted for 102 of the fatalities. The overall percentage of crew lost from sunken ships was 16.7 per cent, but if the two ships which together lost almost 95 per cent of the men aboard are separated out, the loss rate for the remaining seventeen was only 8.2 per cent. Partial figures suggest that the average crew death rate from lost Allied merchant ships was in the region of 25 per cent, so even the higher 16.7 per cent Ocean casualty rate appears to have been on the low side. There can be little doubt that the durability of the vessels and their good life-saving equipment provision played a part in saving lives. In addition, some of the distant Ocean losses took place in coastal waters where survivability was high, while the two ships sunk in the Arctic (no crew losses) and the nine sunk in the Mediterranean (eight crew lost in total) were all either in convoy or in port/anchorage, with rescue close at hand.

Armament

The Ocean-class ships were solid in design and construction, fitted with fuel-efficient engines, possessed of a fair turn of speed by contemporary tramp ship standards, and equipped with a good range of life-saving equipment. In one regard, however, they were deficient when put in service. Until US arms manufacture gathered momentum in 1943, there was a serious shortage of weapons to outfit vessels completing in US yards. Early Oceans sailed with nothing more than a single US 3in low-angle deck gun and a motley handful of machine guns. The former was too small to be effective and was unlikely to impress a determined U-boat commander. The latter were similarly unequal to the task of protection against attack by modern aircraft, lacking both range and hitting power. In the event, neither of these weaknesses would have a real impact on losses. Submarine attacks usually took place submerged at night, while those vessels exposed to air attack were in heavily defended convoys or anchorages. Deck armament was upgraded as the war went on, with priority given initially to vessels sailing on Arctic convoys, and then to those deployed to the Mediterranean. Initial progress was slow as there were significant shortfalls in all categories of weaponry, particularly modern automatic anti-aircraft guns, such as the Swiss-designed 20mm

Oerlikon and Swedish-designed 40mm Bofors, until well into 1943.

In common with other war-built ships, a standard arrangement of gun positions was employed when the weapons were available. In the case of the ships built from mid-programme on, the positions themselves were installed while the vessel was still on the building way. The deck gun was installed right aft on the poop, its position still being governed by the anachronistic convention that such a location indicated that the weapon was purely 'defensive.' Five positions for light automatic weapons were commonly located amidships: one on the compass platform, two abreast the bridge wings, and two at the after end of the boat deck. When additional anti-aircraft weaponry was shipped, as was the case for ships deployed in support of the Normandy landings, it was normal practice to install another pair of gun mounts aft of the mainmast. If a second heavier gun was available, practice varied: mid-war arrangements placed it aft in a super-firing position over the existing gun in place of the original pillar box installation, but this arrangement later gave way to a position on the forecastle.

Progress with arming the Oceans for war can be measured by looking at the equipment of vessels lost or damaged during succeeding stages of the war, whose armament was detailed in their casualty reports. No modern weapons were available for vessels fitted out on the west coast in 1941/early 1942. As a result, all that could be shipped was the obsolete 3in gun and an assortment of different US machine gun models.

Ocean Messenger anchored at New York on 19 October 1942 ready for her maiden Atlantic crossing displaying her full array of defensive equipment to good effect with Oerlikons in tubs abreast the compass platform and at the aft end of superstructure, a deck gun and pillar box at the stern, Admiralty Net Defence booms rigged to the fore and mainmasts, and quick-release life rafts at the forward ends of Nos 2 and 5 holds.
(US Coast Guard/Mariners' Museum & Park)

Key: US – American; Br – British, LA – Low Angle; DP – Dual Purpose; 20mm – 20mm Oerlikon; 40mm – 40mm Bofors

Ocean Venture (February 1942) – One US 3in LA, two 0.5in Colt machine guns.

Ocean Venus (May 1942) – One US 3in LA, one twin 0.5in Browning and two single Marlin machine guns.

It is doubtful if any significant upgrades were possible for vessels crossing the Atlantic in the spring and summer of 1942. By the time *Ocean Vagabond* made the first of her two attempts to reach the UK in September, modern automatic anti-aircraft weapons were becoming available, and a few 20mm Oerlikons were being shipped in lieu of some of the machine guns.

Ocean Vagabond (January 1943) – One US 3in DP, two 20mm, two twin machine guns.

Ocean Honour had departed for the Indian Ocean in July 1942 immediately after making good defects and damage from her Atlantic delivery voyage. As a result, the only upgrade to her armament was the addition of a single Oerlikon.

Ocean Honour (September 1942) – One US 3in DP, one 20mm, two twin Lewis and two twin Marlin machine guns.

As had been the case with *Ocean Honour*, *Ocean Vanguard* and *Ocean Justice* made early departures for distant waters without any significant upgrades to weaponry. *Ocean Courage*, which made two Atlantic round trips before her departure south, did receive some new 20mm. Oerlikons. *Ocean Viceroy*, sailing in a homebound convoy from Freetown in the spring of 1943, had received a significant weapons upgrade.

Ocean Vanguard (September 1942) – One US 3in LA, two Hotchkiss, two Colt and two Lewis machine guns.

Ocean Justice (November 1942) – One US 3in DP, two twin Colt and two twin Marlin machine guns.

Ocean Vigil newly arrived at New York from the eastern Mediterranean on 14 September 1943 displaying some typical late war changes in armament, including a pom-pom mounting right forward, and midships Oerlikons re-sited aft to positions with a better field of fire.
(US Coast Guard/John & Marion Clarkson collection)

Ocean Courage (January 1943) – One US 3in DP, three 20mm, two twin Marlin machine guns.
Ocean Viceroy (March 1943) – One Br 12pdr DP, one Br 12pdr HA, six 20mm, two twin Hotchkiss machine guns.

Vessels sailing in the 1942 convoys to Russia, exposed as they were to heavy attack by the Luftwaffe, received priority in the fitting of still rare modern automatic weapons. They were thus significantly better protected than those of their sisters that had made early departures to distant waters.
Ocean Voice (September 1942) – One US 3in DP, four 20mm, one twin Browning, two twin Marlin, two Colt and two Lewis machine guns.
Ocean Freedom (March 1943) – One US 3in DP, one 40mm, six 20mm, two twin Marlin and one twin Colt machine guns.

Vessels deployed to the Mediterranean theatre, originally in support of the North African invasions of November 1942, in the build-up to the invasion of Sicily in July 1943, and then in continuing support operations for the Italian campaign, benefitted from a general improvement in the availability of modern weapons. Most original US 3in guns had been replaced with British weapons or at the very least with dual-purpose LA/HA versions of the original. Similarly, sufficient Oerlikons were available to provide four and in some cases six per vessel. Some machine guns were still in evidence, not least in one vessel which mounted a veritable arsenal of twelve antique Lewis guns.
Ocean Vanquisher (December 1942) – One Br 4in DP, four 20mm, two twin Hotchkiss machine guns.
Ocean Seaman (March 1943) – One Br 12pdr DP, four 20mm, two twin Marlin machine guns.
Ocean Peace (July 1943) – One US 3in DP, six 20mm, one twin Colt and twelve Lewis machine guns.
Ocean Hunter (January 1944) – One Br 4in DP, one Br 12pdr DP, four 20mm, three twin machine guns.

By the time of the massive Normandy invasion operation, shortages of modern anti-aircraft weaponry were definitely a thing of the past. The Oceans committed to the intensive series of convoys supporting the beachhead through June and July 1944 were often as well armed as their close naval escorts. Indeed, modern merchant ships, with their high reserve buoyancy, could accommodate upgrades in firepower far more easily than much smaller naval vessels already struggling with the top weight of radar, gunnery control, anti-submarine weaponry and incremental additions to firepower not allowed for in design. Although the absence of HA (High Angle) direction and range-finding equipment reduced the lethality of non-naval anti-aircraft fire, the sheer quantity of ordnance a mercantile convoy could now project was itself a deterrent to all but the most determined attackers.
Ocean Courier (July 1944) – One Br 4in DP, one 40mm, seven twin 20mm, two twin Colt machine guns.

Other Defensive Equipment

The anti-aircraft armament was supplemented with a rocket-launching installation known as a 'pillar box', the last of a series of such projectors developed by the Royal Navy in the early years of the war when the supply of modern automatic weapons like the 20mm Oerlikon was not sufficient to provide adequate air defence at sea. The 2in 'Rocket Mounting, Mark II, Pillar Box' consisted of a cabinet shaped like a pillar box with a sloping roof. A shaft projected from each side of the cabinet to which were attached angle iron frameworks containing rails and electrical contacts for ten two-inch rockets, which could be elevated through an arc from horizontal to eighty-five degrees using a handwheel located inside the cabinet. The top half of the cabinet was mounted on rollers on top of the fixed lower half and could be rotated through 360 degrees using another handwheel, while the rockets were salvo-fired using pedals. Each rocket weighed 10.25lbs and was made up of four components: fuse, shell, propelling unit and fins, the fuse being activated by a wind vane to detonate the high explosive shell several seconds after arming.

While the pillar box was a great improvement on earlier projectors such as the 'pig trough', it was only capable of use for slow barrage fire. The single operator inside the cabinet had limited ability to track fast-moving targets through the simultaneous use of handwheels, sustained use required an external crew of two loaders and two supply numbers, and the rockets themselves were vulnerable to wind effects, partial correction for which required the overloaded operator to operate a basic wind correction sight while simultaneously adjusting for any changes in his vessel's course. Pillar boxes were a standard part of most Oceans' preliminary weapons fit, the device being placed on a raised position on the stern deckhouse, forward and above the deck gun. No specific mention of its use in action has been found, and while it might have been employed in area anti-aircraft defence of convoys in 1942 and early 1943, it would have been difficult to man it adequately from the small defensively-armed merchant ship (DEMS) gunner detachments then embarked. With the supply of modern guns improving, most, if not all, pillar boxes were removed later in the war.

A more obvious and more effective supplement to defensive equipment was the provision of anti-torpedo protective nets commonly referred to as AND (Admiralty Net Defence). This system involved the provision of anti-torpedo nets capable of use while underway at sea. Wire nets were attached to long booms, one pair of each being rigged to the fore and main masts. For deployment, the booms themselves were swung out at right angles to the centre line of the ship, and the nets then un-rolled and their head drawn along a stay connecting the heads of the booms, the streamed nets thus covering the midships section of the vessel from the forward end of No 2 hold to the after end of No 4 hold. Some convoy commodores appear to have been resistant to the use of nets at sea because of the resulting loss of speed. This loss, however, was calculated to be roughly 17 per cent, a handicap which would not prevent a modern ship with a maximum speed of 11kts from keeping up with a 9kt convoy. Such evidence as there is from reports of net-equipped vessels subject to torpedo attack suggests that AND could be effective, and at least one of the Oceans (*Ocean Pilgrim* in November 1942) was saved from a U-boat torpedo by her nets.

A second, less obvious, innovation was the installation of 'plastic armour' on the exterior of the bridge structure, W/T office and exposed gun positions. This armour was in fact a mixture of bitumen and granite chippings, not unlike road surfacing material, which was formed into sheets or panels. It was effective in absorbing small-calibre bullets, and thus provided valuable protection against low-flying aircraft

A 1947 photo taken aboard the recently salvaged *Ocean Viking* while she was being rebuilt at Palermo for Italian commercial service, showing the wartime plastic armour on the face of the bridge to good effect.
(Archivi C N R Palermo)

which often machine-gunned their target's bridge structure during bomb or torpedo attacks. The armour itself was a British invention but was manufactured and installed in the US under the supervision of specialist 'plastic armour officers' despatched from the UK specifically for that purpose.

There was a progressive improvement in life preservation equipment across the British merchant marine in the second half of the war. The installation of such things as large, durable, and easily launched life rafts was general to the merchant marine, but the Oceans themselves also benefitted from modern lifeboat provision. Four steel lifeboats were carried, two each at the forward and after ends of the midship superstructure. The boats themselves were more durable than the wooden craft fitted to most earlier ships, and were installed on modern gravity davits, from which they could be deployed far more rapidly than was the case with older equipment.

Delivery for War

As already noted, the California Ocean building programme was several months ahead of its Portland, Maine, equivalent, and the first four vessels were delivered before the end of 1941; the fifth, *Ocean Viking*, cleared San Francisco for Canadian loading ports on New Year's Day, 1942. All thirty Richmond-built ships were loaded on the west coast. After a post-builder call at nearby San Francisco, vessels sailed north to load and bunker at ports in British Columbia. Bunkering often took place at Union Bay, a small port on the inward (east) side of Vancouver Island which had been developed exclusively for this purpose in combination with a nearby coal mine. While some government stores were loaded at Vancouver (and in most cases subsequently at Seattle, Washington, or Portland, Oregon), the bulk of the cargo was usually made up of mineral, forest and food products, picked up at smaller Canadian ports such as New Westminster, Comox, Port Alberni and Victoria. After final calls in Washington and Oregon ports, vessels were then routed via Los Angeles and the Panama Canal for the US east coast, where most vessels called at Hampton Roads and New York. They then proceeded to the convoy marshalling port of Halifax, Nova Scotia, for departure across the North Atlantic to Britain.

The use of multiple loading ports in British Columbia, and Washington, Oregon, and California states would normally keep new vessels in western coastal waters for four to five weeks. The experience of *Ocean Vanguard* was typical. Following delivery at Richmond on 27 October 1941, she visited Vancouver, Union Bay, and New Westminster, before calling at Tacoma and Seattle, revisiting San Francisco and finally clearing Los Angeles on 25 November. It then took two to three

Ocean Valour sailing from Halifax on her maiden Atlantic crossing on 3 May 1942 as part of HX 188 with partially disassembled two-engine aircraft across Nos 4 and 5 hatches.
(H B Jefferson Nova Scotia Archives 1992-304/43.1.4.77)

Atlantic Delivery Passages

Vessel	Delivery Date	Atlantic Convoy	Departure	Arrival	Destination
Ocean Vanguard	27.10.1941	HX 168*	2.1.1942		
Ocean Vigil	13.11.1941	HX 170**	13.1.1942		
Ocean Vanguard		HX 171	20.1.1942	1.2.1942	Cardiff
Ocean Vigil		HX 171	20.1.1942	1.2.1942	Glasgow
Ocean Voice	28.11.1941	HX 175	13.2.1942	25.2.1942	Glasgow
Ocean Venture	12.12.1941	**8.2.1942 Torpedoed and sunk off US east coast before arrival at Halifax**			
Ocean Viking	20.12.1941	HX 180	15.3.1942	27.3.1942	Cardiff
Ocean Vestal	6.1.1942	HX 181	21.3.1942	2.4.1942	Liverpool
Ocean Liberty	27.2.1942	HX 181	21.3.1942	2.4.1942	Cardiff
Ocean Vesper	16.1.1942	HX 182	27.3.1942	9.4.1942	Cardiff
Ocean Freedom	18.3.1942	HX 185	14.4.1942	27.4.1942	Manchester
Ocean Valley	28.1.1942	HX 186	20.4.1942	2.5.1942	Manchester
Ocean Vision	6.2.1942	HX 186	20.4.1942	2.5.1942	Bristol
Ocean Vulcan	20.2.1942	HX 187	26.4.1942	8.5.1942	Cardiff
Ocean Peace	3.4.1942	HX 187**	26.4.1942		
Ocean Peace		HX 188	3.5.1942	15.5.1942	Manchester
Ocean Valour	28.2.1942	HX 188	3.5.1942	15.5.1942	Southampton
Ocean Justice	c.10.4.1942	HX 188	3.5.1942	15.5.1942	Cardiff
Ocean Venus	9.3.1942	**3.5.1942 Torpedoed and sunk off US east coast before arrival at Halifax**			
Ocean Honour	c.2.5.1942	HX 191	24.5.1942	6.6.1942	Liverpool
Ocean Faith	9.5.1942	HX 191	24.5.1942	6.6.1942	Manchester
Ocean Vigour	19.3.1942	HX 193	7.6.1942	19.6.1942	Liverpool
Ocean Vanity	30.3.1942	HX 193	7.6.1942	19.6.1942	Glasgow
Ocean Vintage	6.4.1942	HX 193	7.6.1942	19.6.1942	Middlesbrough
Ocean Hope	c.15.5.1942	HX 194	14.6.1942	26.6.1942	Bristol
Ocean Pride	29.5.1942	HX 195	21.6.1942	2.7.1942	Glasgow
Ocean Might	c.7.6.1942	HX 196	29.6.1942	10.7.1942	Liverpool
Ocean Volunteer	14.4.1942	HX 197	6.7.1942	17.7.1942	Manchester
Ocean Veteran	23.4.1942	HX 197	6.7.1942	17.7.1942	Southampton
Ocean Courage	c.12.6.1942	HX 197	6.7.1942	17.7.1942	Liverpool
Ocean Voyager	30.4.1942	HX 198	12.7.1942	23.7.1942	Liverpool
Ocean Fame	22.6.1942	HX 199	19.7.1942	30.7.1942	Manchester
Ocean Vista	8.5.1942	HX 200	27.7.1942	7.8.1942	Manchester
Ocean Strength	8.7.1942	HX 200	27.7.1942	7.8.1942	Manchester
Ocean Trader	15.7.1942	HX 201	2.8.1942	14.8.1942	Liverpool
Ocean Volga	15.5.1942	HX 202	9.8.1942	21.8.1942	London
Ocean Vengeance	21.5.1942	HX 202	9.8.1942	21.8.1942	Manchester
Ocean Vagrant	27.5.1942	HX 203	16.8.1942	28.8.1942	Bristol
Ocean Wanderer	21.7.1942	HX 203	16.8.1942	28.8.1942	Liverpool
Ocean Viscount	31.5.1942	HX 204	23.8.1942	4.9.1942	Newcastle
Ocean Verity	8.6.1942	HX 205	30.8.1942	11.9.1942	Southampton
Ocean Rider	10.8.1942	HX 205	30.8.1942	11.9.1942	Glasgow
Ocean Viceroy	14.6.1942	HX 206	6.9.1942	18.9.1942	Glasgow
Ocean Virtue	24.6.1942	HX 206	6.9.1942	18.9.1942	Manchester
Ocean Valentine	29.6.1942	HX 206	6.9.1942	18.9.1942	Southampton
Ocean Merchant	31.7.1942	HX 206	6.9.1942	18.9.1942	Cardiff
Ocean Athlete	15.8.1942	HX 206	6.9.1942	18.9.1942	Bristol
Ocean Pilgrim	27.7.1942	HX 207	13.9.1942	25.9.1942	Cardiff
Ocean Vanquisher	8.7.1942	HX 208	17.9.1942	2.10.1942	Hull
Ocean Vagabond	12.7.1942	HX 208**	17.9.1942		
Ocean Wayfarer	1.9.1942	HX 208**	17.9.1942		
Ocean Vagabond		HX 209	24.9.1942	29.9.1942 Torpedoed/ returned	
Ocean Wayfarer		HX 209	24.9.1942	9.10.1942	Cardiff
Ocean Victory	22.7.1942	HX 209	24.9.1942	9.10.1942	Liverpool
Ocean Stranger	5.9.1942	SC 103	26.9.1942	14.10.1942	Manchester
Ocean Traveller	12.9.1942	HX 211	8.10.1942	24.10.1942	Liverpool
Ocean Seaman	17.9.1942	HX 211	8.10.1942	24.10.1942	Liverpool
Ocean Gallant	c.22.9.1942	HX 211	8.10.1942	24.10.1942	Manchester
Ocean Courier	28.9.1942	HX 212	18.10.1942	2.11.1942	Liverpool
Ocean Messenger	30.9.1942	HX 213	26.10.1942	10.11.1942	Cardiff
Ocean Angel	13.10.1942	HX 214*	3.11.1942		
Ocean Hunter	20.10.1942	HX 215	11.11.1942	25.11.1942	Cardiff
Ocean Crusader	31.10.1942	HX 216	19.11.1942	**26.11.1942 Torpedoed and sunk**	
Ocean Gypsy	7.11.1942	NG 326	2.12.1942***		
Ocean Glory	18.11.1942	NG 327	6.12.1942***		
Ocean Angel		HX 218	5.12.1942	21.12.1942	Glasgow
Ocean Vagabond		SC 115	3.1.1943	**10.1.1943 Torpedoed and sunk**	

*Returned with collision damage ** Returned with defects *** To Guantanamo and southwards

Ocean Verity arriving at Halifax on 29 August 1942 to sail the following day in HX 205 on the final leg of her delivery voyage to Britain.
(H B Jefferson Nova Scotia Archives 1992-304/43.1.4.207)

weeks to reach and transit the Panama Canal, *Ocean Vanguard* herself clearing Cristobal on 12 December. Finally, the passage through the Caribbean, up the US east coast (with at least one port call), and then north to Halifax, normally took about two weeks, and by the time the Atlantic convoy itself had sailed, the total time elapsed from delivery was between two and two-and-a-half months. To take another example, *Ocean Viking*, whose New Year's Day 1942 departure from San Francisco was noted above, sailed from Halifax in HX 180 on 15 March 1942.

The first vessel to attempt the Atlantic passage, *Ocean Vanguard*, sailed from Halifax with convoy HX 168 on 2 January 1942. In the event, she was slightly damaged in collision with the British motor ship *Tolten* (5,348g/1930) soon after, and returned to Halifax for repairs, later sailing again with HX 171. Here she joined the next vessel to be delivered, *Ocean Vigil*, which had put back from HX 170 with defects. The two ships arrived safely at Avonmouth and the Clyde, respectively, at the beginning of February. Two west coast ships, *Ocean Venture* and *Ocean Venus*, were lost off the east coast of America before reaching the convoy departure point, while a third, *Ocean Vagabond*, was sunk crossing the Atlantic. The remaining twenty-seven arrived safely in UK ports, the last being *Ocean Victory* on 9 October 1942.

The first east coast-built vessel, *Ocean Liberty*, was

Ocean Wayfarer arriving at New York on 14 September 1942 to join HX 208, the first transatlantic convoy to use New York as its departure port.
(US Coast Guard/World Ship Society Ltd)

delivered at the end of February and sailed from Halifax in HX 181 on 21 March in company with the sixth west coast ship, *Ocean Vestal*. The average time between delivery and departure across the Atlantic for Portland-built ships was about four weeks. The upshot of the difference in distance from builder's yard to convoy port was that Portland-built vessels crossed the Atlantic at the same time as Richmond-built vessels completed roughly one-and-a-half months earlier. As an example, *Ocean Vagrant*, delivered on 27 May 1942, sailed in the same convoy (HX 203) as *Ocean Wanderer*, delivered on 21 July 1942. With the beginning of the Portland deliveries, ships from both yards crossed the Atlantic in close succession, occasionally with multiple sailings in the same convoy. The largest group crossing took place in HX 206, which departed on 6 September 1942, and included no fewer than five Ocean-class vessels: *Ocean Viceroy*, *Ocean Virtue*, *Ocean Valentine*, *Ocean Merchant* and *Ocean Athlete*. The next vessel to sail, *Ocean Pilgrim*, crossed in HX 207, the last of the transatlantic HX convoy series to assemble in Halifax, Nova Scotia. The next three ships sailed from the new convoy departure port of New York in HX 208, but only *Ocean Vanquisher* completed the crossing. *Ocean Vagabond* and *Ocean Wayfarer* both returned with defects, re-sailing in HX 209 together with *Ocean Victory*, the final west coast completion. *Ocean Crusader*, the last Maine-built vessel despatched east across the Atlantic, was lost while attempting the crossing. The final two Portland deliveries did not follow the normal deployment pattern and sailed southwards for distant waters, neither arriving in the UK until late 1943. Thus, twenty-seven of the east coast ships reached UK ports safely in 1942, the last, *Ocean Angel*, sailing in HX 218 and arriving on the Clyde four days before Christmas.

Once again, surviving William Thomson & Co documents concerning the firm's management of *Ocean Valentine* provide a helpful illustration of the delivery process in action. The vessel cleared San Francisco on 3 July 1942 and was formally declared ready for delivery under the Liner Requisition Scheme at Union Bay on Vancouver Island on 6 July, loading beginning at New Westminster on the afternoon of 8 July across the Strait of Georgia. After completing loading at Vancouver and San Francisco, she transited the Panama Canal in mid-August, passed safely up the US east coast in convoy to become one of the quintet of Oceans which crossed the Atlantic in September in HX 206. *Ocean Valentine* finished her delivery voyage at Southampton on 23 September, discharging her 8,550-ton cargo between 24 September and 3 October.

Unlike their sisters, the last two Portland deliveries, *Ocean Gypsy* and *Ocean Glory*, took a long time reaching the UK. They sailed south from New York for Guantanamo, Cuba, in successive coastal convoys on 2 and 6 December 1942, after which their paths diverged. *Ocean Gypsy* sailed through the Panama Canal and thence on a long voyage across the Pacific and Indian Oceans to Durban, South Africa, arriving on 26 January 1943. She then made a triangular voyage, north to Abadan, southeast to Bombay and then southwest back to Durban. Her stay at Durban, a port which appeared to suffer

Ocean Gypsy newly arrived at New York on 16 November 1942 to load for a long maiden voyage south to the Panama Canal and then across the Pacific and Indian Oceans to South Africa and the Persian Gulf. *(US Coast Guard/World Ship Society Ltd)*

Distant Ocean Delivery Passages

Vessel	Passage	Convoy	Departure	Arrival
Ocean Gypsy	Maiden passage – New York to Guantanamo	NG 326	2.12.1942	9.12.1942
Ocean Glory	Maiden passage – New York to Guantanamo	NG 327	6.12.1942	13.12.1942
Ocean Gypsy	Ocean passage – Balbao (Panama) to Durban	Independent	16.12.1942	26.1.1943
Ocean Glory	Ocean passage – Trinidad to Table Bay	Independent	4.1.1943	2.2.1943
Ocean Gypsy	Final passage – Freetown to Manchester	SL 137	23.9.1943	4.11.1943
Ocean Glory	Final passage – Gibraltar to Liverpool	MKS 29G	3.11.1943	18.11.1943
Ocean Glory	Coastal passage – Loch Ewe – Methil – Tyne	Various	19.11.1943	22.11.1943

particularly badly from logistical problems and bottlenecks, stretched from 11 June to 9 July, before she finally cleared for Table Bay and thence across the South Atlantic for the River Plate. Having spent most of August in Montevideo and Buenos Aires, *Ocean Gypsy* finally headed homewards, re-crossing the Atlantic to Freetown before sailing for the Mersey in convoy. She arrived at her final destination, Manchester, on 5 November 1943, having effectively completed a circumnavigation of the globe.

Ocean Glory was to take slightly longer getting home. From Guantanamo she went south in another coastal convoy to Trinidad. The waters around Trinidad were something of a happy hunting ground for U-boats in the last third of 1942, and two of her sisters had been lost there between September and November 1942, but she made a safe independent passage to Table Bay, arriving on 2 February 1943. From there, *Ocean Glory* made a triangular Indian Ocean voyage to Abadan, Bombay, and Port Sudan, before heading north through the Red Sea and Suez Canal to Alexandria, where she remained in port from late May to early July. She then sailed in the assault convoy for the Sicily Invasion. After this, she went through a period of active service in the central Mediterranean combat zone, calling at Tripoli (Libya), Syracuse, and Malta, and then successively at Algiers, Bougie and Naples. *Ocean Glory* finally left Malta for Gibraltar on 18 October, spending two weeks there under repair before joining a convoy home to the UK. Even the last stage of her journey was prolonged, as she sailed northwards around Scotland before arriving at the Tyne on 22 November 1943.

North Atlantic Convoy Crossings

Between the first aborted sailing of *Ocean Vanguard* in HX 168 in January 1942 and the second attempted passage of *Ocean Vagabond* in SC 115 a year later, fifty-six Oceans attempted the transatlantic convoy crossing to Britain. Only two failed to arrive, and both these ships were sailing alone when torpedoed, *Ocean Crusader* after turning back, possibly with weather damage, and *Ocean Vagabond* while pressing on alone, having lost touch with her convoy in poor visibility. This high survival rate was less unusual than might be thought. While 1942 would prove the highwater mark for the Ubootwaffe, much of its success came away from the North Atlantic battlefield, first against lightly protected shipping off the US east coast, and then progressively in more distant waters as it searched for other vulnerable targets. In the first half of the year, the west coast Oceans were far more vulnerable as they sailed alone up the eastern seaboard than they were after they joined their convoy at Halifax, and, indeed, neither of the two ships lost, *Ocean Venture* in February and *Ocean Venus* in May, got any further north than Cape Hatteras.

While individual stragglers regularly fell victim to U-boats on passage to distant patrol berths, there were only three successful wolfpack attacks on North Atlantic convoys in the first half of 1942, all of them against slow westbound convoys in the ONS series. The picture changed significantly in the second half of the year as more U-boats were deployed to the theatre and Befehlshaber der Unterseeboote (BdU) married a better early detection rate for eastbound convoys with a doubling in average wolfpack size. Even after this, however, attacks fell disproportionately on the slower convoys, with the result that only two of the HX convoys in which Oceans were sailing suffered successful attacks, HX 209 losing a single US tanker to a solo U-boat attack at the beginning of October, and HX 212 losing six ships to a wolfpack at the end of the same month.

Ocean delivery crossings peaked in September when fourteen of the class were on their first transatlantic voyages. The first UK arrival was that of *Ocean Viscount* in HX 204 on the fourth of the month, and the last US departure was the sailing of *Ocean Stranger* in SC 103 on the twenty-sixth. *Ocean Vagabond* was the only member of this group to become a casualty, being torpedoed by *U 513* on 29 September after turning back from HX 209 with engine problems and limping back to St John's, Newfoundland, for repairs. The largest

U-Boat Wolfpack Attacks on North Atlantic Convoys, January – December 1942

Convoy	Heading	Attack dates	U-Boats	Wolfpacks	ships sunk	tonnage
ONS 67	Westbound	21.2 - 25.2.1942	6		8	54,750
ONS 92	Westbound	11.5 - 13.5.1942	6	Hecht	7	36,284
ONS 100	Westbound	8.6 - 12.6.1942	6	Hecht	5	20,478
ON 115	Westbound	29.7 - 3.8.1942	6 + 7	Wolf + Pirat	3	21,456
SC 94	Eastbound	5.8 - 10.8.1942	17	Steinbrinck	11	53,421
ONS 122	Westbound	22.8 - 26.8.1942	14	Lohs	4	17,235
ON 127	Westbound	9.9 - 14.9.1942	12	Vorwarts	8	51,619
SC 100	Eastbound	18.9 - 25.9.1942	9 + 8	Lohs + Pfeil	5	26,331
SC 104	Eastbound	12.10 - 16.10.1942	10 + 7	Wotan + Leopard	8	43,970
HX 212	Eastbound	26.10 - 29.10.1942	13	Puma	6	51,918
SC 107	Eastbound	30.10 - 5.11.1942	16	Veilchen	15	82,817
ONS 144	Westbound	15.11 - 21.11.1942	13	Kreuzotter	6	26,321
ON 153	Westbound	15.12 - 21.12.1942	13	Raufbold	4	19,551
ONS 154	Westbound	26.12 - 30.12.1942	10 + 9	Spitz + Ungestum	14	69,893

single Ocean crossing took place when *Ocean Viceroy*, *Ocean Virtue*, *Ocean Valentine*, *Ocean Merchant*, and *Ocean Athlete* sailed together in HX 206, the penultimate Halifax convoy departure before the assembly point was moved south to New York. A more detailed study of this convoy provides an opportunity to examine the operational circumstances under which the Oceans went to war.

The forty-six merchant ships of HX 206 departed Halifax on 6 September 1942 under the control of the convoy commodore Admiral Sir E J A Fullerton KCB DSO aboard the British motor ship *Pacific Enterprise*. These vessels were deployed in eleven columns steaming about 1,000 yards apart, composed of three to five vessels following each other at intervals of roughly 500 yards. The columns were numbered from port to starboard so that *Ocean Viceroy* leading the outer port column occupied position 11 (vessel one in column one) and *Ocean Merchant* at the rear of the outer starboard column was in position 115 (vessel five in column eleven). All five Oceans were deployed in the outer columns along with other modern AND-equipped vessels, although it is doubtful if the nets would often have been streamed in North Atlantic sea conditions. Two other aspects of convoy composition are worthy of comment. The presence of no fewer than fifteen war-built ships — five Oceans, two Forts, four Liberties, three Empires, and the Dutch *Pieter de Hoogh*, which had been built (by coincidence in Sunderland by J L Thompson & Sons) as *Empire Halley* — was a fair reflection of the increasing impact of the Allied governments' building programmes on the war at sea. Similarly, the inclusion of fourteen tankers — seven Norwegian, six British and one Belgian — underlines the critical part played by the safe delivery of oil products across the Atlantic to the European war theatre.

Pacific Enterprise (6,736g/1927), photographed arriving at Vancouver on 16 July 1932 on her regular peacetime service between the UK and the North American west coast, served as the commodore ship in HX 206 in September 1942. ***(Walter E Frost/City of Vancouver Archives CVA 447-2540)***

HX 206 Sailing Order

Column 1	Column 2	Column 3	Column 4	Column 5	Column 6	Column 7	Column 8	Column 9	Column 10	Column 11
Ocean Viceroy Br – 7,174/42 gen cargo	*Inventor* Br – 6,210/35 gen cargo	*Empire Chapman* Br – 8,194/42 petrol	*Noreg* Nw – 7,605/31 fuel oil	*Ville de Tamatave* Fr – 6,276/31 gen cargo	*Pacific Enterprise* Br – 6,736/27 gen cargo	*Empire Coral* Br – 8.602/41 gasoil	*Clan Colquhoun* Br – 7,914/18 reefer, general	*Moveria* Br – 4,867/25 gen cargo	*Empire Norseman* Br – 9,811/42 petrol	*Ocean Athlete* Br – 7,178/42 gen cargo
Fort McLeod Br – 7,127/42 wheat, lumber	*Asbjorn* Br – 4,387/35 gen cargo	*D L Harper* Br – 12,223/33 petrol	*Athos* Nw – 8,267/37 fuel oil	*Polartank* Nw – 6,356/30 petrol	*Akaroa* Br – 15,130/14 reefer/passgrs	*Villanger* Nw – 4,884/29 gen cargo	*Edam* Du – 8,871/21 gen cargo	*Skandinavia* Nw – 10,044/40 petrol	*Polarsol* Nw – 10,022/39 petrol, paraffin	*Trentbank* Br – 5,060/29 gen cargo
John P Poe US – 7,191/42 gen cargo	*Nueva Granada* Nw – 9,968/37 oil	*Cardium* Br – 8,236/31 diesel	*Thomas Hooker* US – 7,176/42 steel, general	*Del Norte* US – 4.982/19 gen cargo	*Emile Franqui* Bel – 10,452/37 gasoil	*Bernard Carter* US – 7,191/42 gen cargo	*Manchester Citizen* Br – 5,343/25 gen cargo	*Garonne* diesel Nw – 7,113/21	*Edward F Johnson* Br – 10,452/37 gasoil	*Ocean Valentine* Br – 7,174/42 gen cargo
Ocean Virtue Br – 7,174/42 gen cargo	*Empire Hawk* Br – 5,033/19 phosphate	*Ralph Waldo Emerson* US – 7,176/42 gen cargo			*Tai Shan* Nw – 6,962/29 gen cargo	*Fort Babine* Br – 7,135/42 gen cargo	*Tjimanoek* Du – 5,628/11 gen cargo	*Hegeria* US – 7,588/19 gen cargo	*Jean* US – 4,902/18 gen cargo	*Pieter de Hoogh* Du – 7,168/41 gen cargo
					Penmar US – 5,868/20 gen cargo		*Hercules* Du – 2,317/14 steel, general		*Steel Navigator* US – 5,719/21 gen cargo	*Ocean Merchant* Br – 7,178/42 steel, general

By 1942, the deployment of convoy escorts in the Atlantic had developed into a three-stage procedure in which a Canadian local escort force was responsible for taking convoys to and from the Western Ocean Meeting Point (WESTOMP) at 40 degrees west, with a British local escort force filling the same role between the UK and the Eastern Ocean Meeting Point (EASTOMP) at about 20 degrees west. Ocean escort protection for the main part of the voyage, including through the critical 'air gap' beyond the range of land-based patrol aircraft, was provided by a rotation of permanent escort groups, seven RN groups number B1 to B7 based at Londonderry or Liverpool, and four RCN groups (C1 to C4) and one USN group (A3) based at St John's, Newfoundland. Each group normally took an outgoing convoy from its first ocean meeting point to its second and then picked an inbound convoy to reverse the process, after which it would return to base for rest, refit, and replenishment. At this stage in the war, these groups usually consisted of one or two destroyers and four or five corvettes, only a few of the new River-class frigates having so far entered service. HX 206's Canadian local escort consisted of two old ex-US Town class destroyers and three corvettes, which handed over to the RN group B1 at WESTOMP on 9 September. This in turn remained with the convoy after it reached EASTOMP as it was returning to base to refit, being reinforced along the way by a corvette and three old S-class destroyers from the British local escort force. B1 Escort Group itself comprised the 1940-vintage destroyer *Hurricane*, the old V & W destroyer *Watchman* – which had been converted to a slower but longer-range escort through the replacement of one boiler with added fuel capacity – and four corvettes, *Anchusa*, *Monkshood*, *Snowflake*, and *Wallflower*.

HX 206 would cross the Atlantic unscathed, and indeed without being sighted by the enemy. This was not the product on any lull in U-boat activity or any decrease in their effectiveness. September, in fact, was the worst month of the war for Ocean-class losses, with U-boats sinking *Ocean Might*, *Ocean Vanguard*, and *Ocean Voice*, and a fourth vessel, *Ocean Honour*, succumbing to a Japanese submarine in the Gulf of Aden. Overall, the Ubootwaffe sank ninety-three merchant ships and eight warships in September 1942. Roughly half of these successes (including all the Oceans), however, were achieved in distant waters, most of them off West Africa or off Trinidad and the northeast coast of South America. In the North Atlantic itself, HX 206's safety was partially the product of other convoys' misfortunes. In the first half of the month, two U-boats were running amok in the Gulf of St Lawrence savaging a succession of coastal feeder convoys while a third penetrated the anchorage at Wabana, Newfoundland, to sink a pair of iron ore carriers. In the Atlantic itself, ON 127 was sighted by the newly formed 'Vorwarts' group on 9 September and attacked repeatedly by the twelve-strong wolfpack until 14 September, losing seven merchantmen and the destroyer *Ottawa* of the C4 escort group. A second battle followed almost immediately when a decoded course instruction allowed the interception of SC 100 first by the nine boats of the 'Lohs' group and then by eight more from a second group code-named 'Pfiel.' Although the accompanying A3 escort group had been reinforced by three corvettes on passage to participate in Operation Torch, attacking U-boats managed to sink five merchantmen before the attack was broken off on 25 September. Even after this, some of the boats from the three groups were homed onto a small US–Iceland convoy, sinking three transports and the British destroyer *Veteran*.

Operational Overview, 1942

By 1 July 1942, twenty Ocean-class vessels, thirteen built on the west coast and seven built on the east coast, had

Vessel Deployment, 1942

Vessel	30.6.1942	Route/Convoy	31.12.1942	Route/Convoy
Ocean Vanguard	Port Said	Egypt-Cape-USA	**13.9.1942 Torpedoed and sunk, east of Trinidad**	
Ocean Vigil	Suez	Egypt-Cape-USA	New York	USA-North Africa
Ocean Voice	Murmansk	Repairs bomb damage	**22.9.1942 Torpedoed and sunk, Norwegian Sea**	
Ocean Venture	**8.2.1942 Torpedoed and sunk, US east coast**			
Ocean Viking	Aden	UK-Cape-Egypt	Indian Ocean	India-South Africa-USA
Ocean Vestal	Aden	UK-Cape-Egypt	Southampton	UK-South Africa
Ocean Liberty	Buenos Aires	Plate-Freetown-UK (SL 117)	Barry	UK-North Africa (KMS 7)
Ocean Vesper	Indian Ocean	UK-Cape-Egypt	Guantanamo	USA-Panama Canal-South Africa
Ocean Freedom	Norwegian Sea	UK-North Russia PQ 17	Gibraltar	North Africa-UK (MKS 4Y)
Ocean Valley	East Atlantic	UK-Cape-Egypt OS 30	Pacific Ocean	USA-Panama Canal-South Africa
Ocean Vision	East Atlantic	UK-Cape-Egypt OS 30	New York	USA -Cape-South Africa
Ocean Vulcan	East Atlantic	UK-Cape-Egypt OS 32	Indian Ocean	USA-Panama Canal-South Africa
Ocean Peace	East Atlantic	UK-Cape-Egypt OS 32	Pacific Ocean	USA-Panama Canal-South Africa
Ocean Valour	East Atlantic	UK-Cape-Egypt OS 32	Trinidad	South Africa-USA
Ocean Justice	East Atlantic	UK-Cape-Egypt OS 31	**6.11.1942 Torpedoed and sunk, east of Trinidad**	
Ocean Venus	**3.5.1942 Torpedoed and sunk, US east coast**			
Ocean Honour	Mersey	UK-Cape-Egypt (OS 33)	**16.9.1942 Torpedoed and sunk, Gulf of Aden**	
Ocean Faith	Manchester	UK-North Russia (PQ 18)	Leith	UK-North Russia (JW 52)
Ocean Vigour	Liverpool	UK-Cape-Egypt (OS 35)	West Atlantic	South Africa - USA
Ocean Vanity	Clyde (repairs)	UK-Cape-Egypt (OS 38)	South Atlantic	South Africa - USA
Ocean Vintage	Middlesbrough	UK- USA (ON 111)	**22.10.1942 Torpedoed and sunk, Gulf of Oman**	
Ocean Hope	Barry	UK-Cape-Egypt (OS 36)	New York	USA-Panama Canal-India
Ocean Pride	North Atlantic	Canada-UK HX 195	New York	USA-Cape-Egypt
Ocean Might	North Atlantic	Canada-UK HX 196	**2.9.1942 Torpedoed and sunk off Gold Coast**	
Ocean Volunteer	Halifax, NS	Canada-UK (HX 197)	Table Bay	Egypt-South Africa-USA
Ocean Veteran	US east coast	US- Canada-UK (HX 197)	Clyde	UK-North Africa (KMS 7)
Ocean Courage	Portland, Maine	US- Canada-UK (HX 197)	Freetown	West Africa-Trinidad
Ocean Voyager	US east coast	US- Canada-UK (HX 198)	Mediterranean	Egypt-Tripolitania
Ocean Fame	Portland, Maine	US- Canada-UK (HX 199)	Liverpool	UK-North Africa (KMS 8)
Ocean Vista	Panama Canal	US- Canada-UK (HX 200)	Manchester	UK-North Africa (KMS 7)
Ocean Strength	Fitting out, Portland		Belfast Lough	UK-South Africa -Egypt
Ocean Trader	Fitting out, Portland		Barry	UK-North Africa (KMS 7)
Ocean Volga	US west coast		Swansea	UK-North Africa (KMS 7)
Ocean Vengeance	US west coast		Liverpool	UK-North Africa (KMS 7)
Ocean Vagrant	US west coast		Aden	Egypt-South Africa-USA
Ocean Wanderer	Fitting out, Portland		Liverpool	UK-North Africa (KMS 7)
Ocean Viscount	San Francisco		Liverpool	UK-North Africa (KMS 7)
Ocean Verity	Seattle		Durban	South Africa-USA
Ocean Rider	Building, Portland		Clyde	UK-North Africa (KMS 7)
Ocean Viceroy	Vancouver		Clyde	UK-North Africa (KMS 7)
Ocean Virtue	Canada west coast		Liverpool	UK-North Africa (KMS 7)
Ocean Valentine	San Francisco		Manchester	UK-North Africa (KMS 8)
Ocean Merchant	Fitting out, Portland		Liverpool	UK-North Africa (KMS 8)
Ocean Athlete	Building, Portland		Liverpool	UK-North Africa (KMS 8)
Ocean Pilgrim	Fitting out, Portland		Manchester	UK-North Africa (KMS 8)
Ocean Vanquisher	Fitting out, Richmond		**12.12.1942 Beached at Algiers, limpet mine damage**	
Ocean Vagabond	Fitting out, Richmond		St. John's, Nfld	Repairing torpedo damage
Ocean Wayfarer	Building, Portland		Manchester	UK-North Africa (KMS 8)
Ocean Victory	Fitting out, Richmond		N Atlantic	North Africa-UK MKS 4
Ocean Stranger	Building, Portland		Northeast Atlantic	North Africa-UK MKS 4
Ocean Traveller	Building, Portland		Algiers	North Africa-UK (MKS 5)
Ocean Seaman	Building, Portland		Gibraltar	North Africa-UK (MKS 4Y)
Ocean Gallant	Building, Portland		Algiers	North Africa-UK (MKS 5X)
Ocean Courier			Algiers	North Africa-UK (MKS 5)
Ocean Messenger			Northeast Atlantic	UK-North Africa KMS 6
Ocean Angel			Glasgow	UK-Gibraltar (KMS 8G)
Ocean Hunter			Clyde	UK-Cape-Egypt (ON 158)
Ocean Crusader			**26.11.1942 Torpedoed and sunk North Atlantic**	
Ocean Gypsy			South Pacific	USA-Panama Canal-South Africa
Ocean Glory			Trinidad	USA-Cape-India-Egypt

protective benefits of convoy, were next to defenceless against the U-boats and aircraft ranging freely across their paths to safety. No fewer than twenty-one ships were sunk between 5 and 10 July, including thirteen US, five British and one Dutch merchantmen, a Royal Fleet Auxiliary oiler, and a convoy rescue ship, leaving only fourteen, *Ocean Freedom* among them, to stagger into Archangel.

When the convoy scattered, Captain William Walker of J & J Denholm Ltd had taken *Ocean Freedom* almost due east towards Novaya Zemlya, away from those of her convoy mates which had chosen the more direct southeast course to their destination or were heading north towards the fog banks along the edge of the polar icefield. Along the way, she joined company with the RFA oiler *Aldersdale*, the rescue ship *Zaafaran*, and the minesweeper *Salamander*, one of the small escort vessels which had chosen to ignore the directive to head directly for Archangel. This group made good progress eastwards until the afternoon of 5 July when it was found by a group of four Ju-88s. Although three of the attackers failed to press home their attack through the small convoy's AA barrage, the fourth laid its bombs across *Aldersdale*'s stern, flooding the engine room and leaving the ship completely disabled. *Salamander* went to the oiler's assistance (she would eventually be forced to take off the crew and abandon *Aldersdale* as a drifting derelict to be finished off by *U 457* two days later), leaving the other two ships isolated in the face of further air attacks as they headed east. *Ocean Freedom*'s luck held, but *Zaafaran* was fatally straddled by a stick of bombs and had to be abandoned in turn. While all this was underway, several other vessels had come up and *Ocean Freedom* continued its voyage towards the partial protection of the Matochkin Strait, the narrow waterway between Novaya Zemlya's two main islands, Severny to the north and Yuzhny in the south in the company of a second rescue ship, *Zamalek*, and the minesweeper *Britomart*.

Led by *Britomart*, the small group rounded Cape Stolbovoi on the afternoon of 6 July, where they were soon joined at anchor off the small Russian settlement of Lagerni by other escorts. The small armada in what was promptly named 'Funk Creek' grew over the day to include the anti-aircraft ships *Palomares* and *Pozarica*, the corvettes *Poppy* and *La Malouine*, the minesweepers *Britomart*, *Halcyon* and *Salamander*, and the rescue vessel *Zamalek*, but as the long Arctic twilight began *Ocean Freedom* remained the only merchant ship present, and *La Malouine* was sent back out into the night to look for others. The corvette succeeded in contacti four American merchantmen – the new Liberty ships *Benja min Harrison* and *Samuel Chase*, and the much older *Hoosi* of 1920 and the Panamanian-flagged *El Capitan* of 1917 directing each of them into the anchorage over the followi day, where they were joined by three of the convoy's anti-su marine trawlers, *Lord Austin*, *Lord Middleton*, and *Northe Gem*. Having rejected the idea of sailing through the strait the Kara Sea because of ice conditions, the senior naval offic aboard *Palomares* led the entire group down the west coa of Yuzhny Island at 1900hrs on 7 July. Almost immediate the mini convoy ran into heavy fog, visibility becoming poor that *Benjamin Harrison* returned to the anchorage whi the other ships lost touch with each other and fragment into several smaller groups. Confusion increased when ma of the ships ran into thick offshore ice flows, some taki hours to break free and others sustaining hull damage. *Ocea Freedom* was among the latter, and although she was save by her collision bulkhead when she fractured her stem a flooded her forepeak in a sharp collision, the delay caused h to fall behind her consorts. When the ships did find clear weather, they were strung out over a distance of forty mil and were quickly discovered by a short patrol line of U-boa positioned across what the German command had accurate foreseen would be a likely escape route. The first attacks b Ju-88s of Kampfgeschwader 30 began on the afternoon of July and carried on into the following morning, leaving fir *Hoosier* and then *El Capitan* hopelessly disabled. Both shi had to be abandoned, their crews being rescued by escor several hours before each was finished off by a U-boat. Th enemy bombers returned for the last time in the mornin of 11 July, quickly disabling *Samuel Chase*, although n severely enough to prevent *Halcyon* from towing her int port. *Ocean Freedom* finally arrived in Archangel later th same day, accompanied only by *Britomart* and *Northern Ge* and survived one last attack when in sight of land durin which near misses shattered most of the bridge instrumen and left the master with a serious shrapnel wound to the hi Captain Walker's achievements would be recognised when h was awarded the Distinguished Service Order, one of four P 17 masters to be so honoured in the London Gazette of 2 September, the first occasion on which this military honou had been bestowed on officers of the Merchant Navy.

Only one of the Oceans would survive its deployme to the northern theatre. *Ocean Voice* was lost on her retur trip in QP 14 in September 1942. Following a suspension sailings until the shorter days of the Arctic winter, the two survivors each made a second outward passage, *Ocean Faith* in JW 52 in January 1943, and *Ocean Freedom* in JW 53 a month later (having squeezed in a round trip to North Africa in between). *Ocean Faith* made a safe passage home in March, but *Ocean Freedom* never got a chance to follow her, being bombed and sunk at Murmansk in the same month.

Long-Distance Passages

Elsewhere, vessel deployment at the end of 1942 showed two clear patterns. One group of vessels, largely composed of the earlier arrivals in the UK, had been committed to the long haul around the Cape of Good Hope and up through the Suez Canal to ports in Egypt and Libya in support of the Eighth Army. Six ships were on the return leg of this voyage, which in each case would take them from the Cape northwest across the South Atlantic to Trinidad, and then in a succession of coastal convoys north to New York. Four other vessels, *Ocean Vesper*, *Ocean Valley*, *Ocean Vulcan* and *Ocean Peace*, had already completed this extended trip, and had sailed on their next outward voyage from the US east coast, being joined by the newly delivered *Ocean Gypsy*. In every case, these ships were not being sent across the Atlantic, but rather south to the Panama Canal and then on a long passage across the Pacific and Indian Oceans to South Africa. It is unclear why the longer westward route was chosen. In any event, the first four of these vessels were subsequently sent north from South Africa to Egyptian ports, from where they would be deployed to support the invasion of Sicily.

Operations Against Vichy French Madagascar

The first involvement of the Oceans in support of amphibious operations, a role in which most members of the class would be heavily involved in the last two-and-a-half years of the war, was the redeployment of *Ocean Vesper* and *Ocean Viking* after the completion of voyages from Britain around Africa to Egypt, to the final stages of the capture of Madagascar in September 1942. Allied fears that the Vichy French government might allow the Japanese to use bases on the island for attacks on merchant ships along the supply routes between Britain and the Middle East, India, and Australia, had triggered the successful invasion of the Diego Suarez area in northern Madagascar in May 1942. Vichy authorities in the remainder of the island, however, refused to join the Allied cause voluntarily, with the result that follow-up assaults were mounted in September, first at Majunga on the west coast, and then against Tamatave on the east coast.

Both Oceans participated in Operation Stream against Majunga, arriving in the beachhead area in separate convoys on 10 September – *Ocean Vesper* from Diego Suarez, and *Ocean Viking* from Mombasa. After the successful west coast landings, *Ocean Viking* left Majunga on 13 September as part of Operation Jane against Tamatave where the 18 September landings were completed unopposed, the initial French refusal to surrender being reversed within minutes after a display of air power and the commencement of a naval bombardment. The lack of opposition was fortunate, as some landing craft broached to before reaching the beaches and *Ocean Viking* disgraced herself by running aground twice when she was called forward to her berth to unload her cargo of military vehicles. Having misjudged her approach, she first grounded for two hours in the approaches, and then went aground and became firmly stuck in the outer harbour, where she remained until re-floated the following morning with assistance from the destroyer *Active* and the minesweeper *Cromer*.

Supporting the North African Invasion

The deployment of the remainder of the Ocean fleet went through an even more dramatic change in the last quarter of 1942. The trigger here was Operation Torch (the invasion of French North Africa), the first major Allied amphibious assault in the western theatre, which commenced on 8 November 1942. There were three separate points of attack: around Casablanca on the Atlantic coast of French Morocco, and around Oran and Algiers on the Mediterranean coast of Algeria. The first of these was an entirely American affair, the assault convoys coming direct across the Atlantic from the United States. Ships for the Algerian invasions sailed from the UK, and although British troops were only directly committed to the Algiers attack, the British navy and merchant marine were heavily involved in both assaults. Four Oceans sailed in the assault convoy KMS 1 for the Algiers attack. No fewer than eleven further vessels sailed in the large follow-up convoy KMS 2 three days after the first. Ships carried a mixed cargo of invasion stores, the largest component in most cases being military vehicles, these latter coming aboard with full tanks, pre-loaded with ammunition and other potentially explosive cargoes.

Although Vichy French authorities in North Africa agreed an armistice within a few days, German and Italian forces deployed quickly to Tunisia, and a hard-fought campaign

Ocean Volga, seen here under tow in UK waters, sailed from the Clyde on 22 October 1942 in the North African invasion assault convoy with a cargo of military vehicles for the Operation Torch landings in French North Africa. *(National Maritime Museum)*

began which would last until May 1943. This new front required continuous supply and further Ocean vessels sailed from the UK for Algerian ports in November and December. By the time KMS 5 reached Bone on 27 December, twenty-seven of the fifty Oceans still in service at the end of 1942 had been deployed to Algerian ports (a twenty-eighth, *Ocean Vanquisher*, had been lost at Algiers in December). This intensive deployment would continue into 1943. On New Year's Day 1943, seven Oceans were returning to the UK from the invasion theatre, while sixteen were loading in British ports for North Africa, of which eleven would sail in KMS 7 on 7 January. By the end of January 1943, most of the ships deployed had made their second trip to the theatre.

Deployment in support of the campaign in Tunisia remained heavy through the spring of 1943. The experience of *Ocean Fame* was typical of many ships of her class. She had arrived in the UK on her delivery voyage from North America at the end of July 1942, and after a spell of repairs had sailed for Oran in late October in KMS 2, the first follow-up convoy. She returned to the UK in mid-December and sailed again for North Africa with six sisters in KMS 8 on 21 January 1943. She was back in the Mersey in mid-March, but sailed on her third North African convoy, KMS 13, on 24 April. After this, she finally deployed away from the theatre, sailing from Gibraltar for West Africa and the Gold Coast, and only from there homewards in a convoy from Freetown.

In addition to *Ocean Vanquisher* from KMS 4, which

North Africa Invasion Convoys

KMS 1	Assault Convoy	Sailed, Clyde	22 October 1942
Vessel	**Port of Origin**	**Arrival Point**	**Tanks, vehicles, guns, cased petrol, stores, coal**
Ocean Rider	Glasgow	Algiers B beachhead	123 vehicles, 4 guns, 240t cased petrol, 28t stores
Ocean Viceroy	Glasgow	Algiers A beachhead	130 vehicles, 26t stores
Ocean Volga	Swansea	Algiers B beachhead – Bone	132 vehicles
Ocean Wanderer	Birkenhead	Algiers A beachhead	129 vehicles, 16 guns, 5t cased petrol, 4t stores
KMS 2	**Follow-up Convoy**	**Sailed, Loch Ewe**	**25 October 1942**
Vessel	**Port of Origin**	**Arrival Port**	**Tanks, vehicles, guns, cased petrol, stores, coal**
Ocean Athlete	Penarth	Oran	155 vehicles, 2 guns, 808t stores, 1,250t coal
Ocean Fame	Cardiff	Oran	162 vehicles, 871t stores, 1,257t coal
Ocean Liberty	Glasgow	Oran	136 vehicles, 1 gun, 1,531t stores
Ocean Merchant	Barry	Oran	123 vehicles, 4 guns, 240t cased petrol, 28t stores
Ocean Strength	Barry	Algiers	8 tanks, 145 vehicles, 31t cased petrol, 2,215t stores
Ocean Trader	Barry	Algiers	136 vehicles, 50t cased petrol, 244t stores
Ocean Vengeance	Manchester	Algiers	11 tanks, 96 vehicles, 2 guns, 2,074t stores
Ocean Veteran	Glasgow	Algiers	14 tanks, 124 vehicles, 2 guns, 2,318t stores
Ocean Virtue	Mersey	Algiers	129 vehicles, 110t cased petrol, 2,083t stores
Ocean Viscount	Glasgow	Oran	139 vehicles, 1 gun, 739t stores
Ocean Vista	Manchester	Oran	121 vehicles, 20 guns, 579t.cased petrol, 1,489t stores

Tunisian Campaign Support Convoys

Convoy	Departure	Vessels
KMS 3	8.11.1942	*Ocean Pilgrim, Ocean Valentine, Ocean Victory, Ocean Wayfarer*
KMS 4	26.11.1942	*Ocean Freedom, Ocean Seaman, Ocean Stranger, Ocean Traveller, Ocean Vanquisher*
KMS 5	11.12.1942	*Ocean Courier, Ocean Gallant, Ocean Hunter*
KMS 6	24.12.1942	*Ocean Messenger*
KMS 7	7.1.1943	*Ocean Liberty, Ocean Rider, Ocean Trader, Ocean Vengeance, Ocean Veteran, Ocean Viceroy, Ocean Virtue, Ocean Viscount, Ocean Vista, Ocean Volga, Ocean Wanderer*
KMS 8	21.1.1943	*Ocean Angel, Ocean Fame, Ocean Merchant, Ocean Pilgrim, Ocean Valentine, Ocean Wayfarer*
KMS 9	6.2.1943	*Ocean Athlete, Ocean Seaman, Ocean Stranger*

was crippled at Algiers on 12 December 1942 by Italian frogmen, *Ocean Pilgrim* was saved by her AND nets from damage by a U-boat torpedo in KMS 3 on 20 November, and one other vessel, *Ocean Rider*, was seriously damaged by an air-launched torpedo on 21 January 1943 while on her way to Bone, Algeria, in KMS 7. Two more ships were lost in the remainder of the North African campaign. *Ocean Seaman* was heavily damaged by a U-boat soon after starting a ballast voyage in convoy back to Gibraltar and the UK on 15 March 1943. Although the vessel was towed back to Algiers and beached outside the harbour, she broke in two and was ultimately abandoned as a total loss. On 19 March, a third vessel was lost. Unlike her sisters, *Ocean Voyager* had been operating in the eastern Mediterranean carrying supplies from Egypt for the Eighth Army, which had pushed the Afrika Korps back into Tunisia from the east. She was caught in an air raid on Tripoli, Libya, since January the major supply port in the eastern part of the theatre, with a significant part of her military cargo still unloaded. Set afire by bombs, she subsequently blew up.

The Tonnage Replacement Scheme and Sales to Allied Governments

By the time the Oceans were entering service, the British government had already instituted a scheme for selling vessels to Allied governments. With their own shipyards in enemy hands, the latter had no way of replacing their war losses. They did, however, possess the means for purchasing tonnage, due to payments from UK war risk insurance on war casualties while on British government charter; the expertise to manage new acquisitions through missions already set up under the auspices of their respective governments-in-exile; and the officers and seamen to man replacement tonnage, in the form of survivors from vessels lost. This situation presented Britain with an opportunity to achieve a series of objectives ranging from raising funds to finance further new

Ocean Fame sailing out of Halifax harbour through a summer fog on 19 July 1942 to make her maiden Atlantic voyage as part of HX 199. After repairs to damage suffered in the crossing, she would join fourteen of her sisters in the Operation Torch invasion convoys.
(H B Jefferson Nova Scotia Archives 1992-304/43.1.4.118)

building and spreading the load of manning and managing the merchant fleet, to tying Allied governments more closely into the war effort at sea.

A tonnage replacement scheme was instituted in 1942, which allocated a fixed number and mix of vessels for purchase by each Allied government, calculated as a factor of the number and type of vessels lost in the previous years. While some of the vessels sold under this arrangement were wartime buildings from British shipyards, these were supplemented by the addition of second-hand ex-American vessels acquired in 1940–1. These latter were all over twenty years old, and, while relatively inexpensive, were not otherwise attractive propositions, as they offered no real prospect of profitable operation after the end of hostilities. The Norwegians, both the largest Allied contributors to the merchant shipping war campaign, and the recipients of the highest losses, were forced to take six of the old ships in addition to British new buildings, a fact which appears to have caused some resentment.

A new tonnage replacement scheme was put in place for 1943, with vessel allocations again based on earlier losses. In this case, however, the Ministry of War Transport had already decided to add a portion of the US-built Oceans to the equation. As early as May 1942, with its American building programme still less than half complete, the ministry was considering the inclusion of a quarter of the final sixty-vessel output in the new scheme. Indeed, it was suggested not only that these ships be included, but that their purchase be made a condition of participating in the programme. It was realised that the high price of the US-built ships would be 'a formidable obstacle.' This notwithstanding, there was a clear desire not only to recover full building costs, but also to do so in foreign hard currency. From the outset, the scheme was based on the premises, first that the price to be paid for any of the vessels offered would be 'the cost of such vessels to HM Government,' and secondly that the price of vessels built in the United States would be payable in US dollars. The final proposal added the requirement that financially more attractive British-built vessels could only be acquired if the US-built vessels were purchased as well, this decision echoing the Treasury view that it was 'clearly only right that the allied governments should take their full share of the expensive Todd ships along with the cheaper and better-built United Kingdom replacements.'

The overall allocation of vessels for the second tranche of the replacement scheme included fifteen Ocean-class vessels, in addition to twenty-one British-built steam tramps of broadly similar specifications. Twelve of the Oceans were allocated to Norway (five), the Netherlands (four) and Greece (three), with one each being allocated to Belgium, Poland, and Yugoslavia.

By February 1943, a list of sixteen Oceans had been prepared, from which fifteen would be allocated to the scheme. This list indicated when each vessel would be available for transfer, and the allied governments made a preliminary selection from it on a pre-established rota. There was a preponderance of more recently delivered vessels in the list, of which five were west coast-built and eleven east coast-built, with only three of the nominees having been delivered before May 1942. Two of the older ships, *Ocean Freedom* and *Ocean Faith*, were singled out as being 'fitted for north Russian service', a distinction largely indicative of their being equipped with an enhanced anti-aircraft weapons fit and other defensive equipment. There appears to have been no sentimentality in the choice of vessels for sale, the two with the most iconic names, *Ocean Liberty* and *Ocean Victory*, both being included in the list.

There would be three changes to the final allocation of vessels. In mid-March 1943, *Ocean Seaman*, allocated to the Netherlands, was torpedoed in the Mediterranean, and *Ocean Freedom*, presumably the sixteenth 'spare' vessel, was bombed at Murmansk. Although other vessels on the list would later become available, no effort was made to add a substitute to the Dutch list, and their allocation fell from four vessels to three. Finally, the Poles objected to manning

Replacement Scheme Allocations for 1943

Vessel Type	Norway	Holland	Greece	Belgium	Poland	Yugoslavia	TOTAL
Diesel tankers	3	1					**4**
Steam tankers	1						**1**
Cargo liners		3					**3**
Diesel tramps 5,000t +	2	2					**4**
Steam tramps UK-built 5,000t +	5	5	7	2	1	1	**21**
Steam tramps US-built 5,000t +	5	4	3	1	1	1	**15**
Steam tramps under 5,000t	4	1		1			**6**
Smaller vessels				3			**3**
Gross Tons ('000)	125	110	66	23	13	13	**350**

Vessel Allocations for the Replacement Scheme

Vessel	Builder – Yard Number	Delivery Date	Availability 1943	Allocation
Ocean Viking	Richmond – 5	20.12.1941	End-April	Greece
Ocean Liberty	Portland – 1	27.2.1942	Mid-March	Greece
Ocean Freedom *	Portland – 2	18.3.1942	April	reserve
Ocean Veteran	Richmond – 17	23.4.1942	End-April	Belgium
Ocean Faith **	Portland – 6	8.5.1942	March	Poland
Ocean Vengeance	Richmond – 21	26.5.1942	Early March	Greece
Ocean Vagrant	Richmond – 22	27.5.1942	April	Yugoslavia
Ocean Victory	Richmond – 30	22.7.1942	End-March	Holland
Ocean Merchant	Portland – 16	31.7.1942	Early March	Holland
Ocean Athlete	Portland – 18	15.8.1942	Early March	Holland
Ocean Wayfarer	Portland – 19	1.9.1942	Early March	Norway
Ocean Stranger	Portland – 20	5.9.1942	End-March	Norway
Ocean Traveller	Portland – 21	12.9.1942	End-April	Norway
Ocean Seaman ***	Portland – 22	17.9.1942	End-March	Holland
Ocean Courier	Portland – 24	28.9.1942	End-April	Norway
Ocean Glory	Portland – 30	18.11.1942	May	Norway

* Bombed at Murmansk 13.3.1943 ** Replaced by *Ocean Hope* *** Torpedoed in the Mediterranean 15.3.1943

a vessel for Russian convoy duty, possibly due to ambivalence about supporting the Soviet war effort following the breaking of diplomatic relations between the USSR and the Polish government-in-exile in London in the wake of the Katyn massacre discoveries. Although *Ocean Faith* would not in fact serve in the northern theatre after March 1943, she was removed from the scheme and a substitute, *Ocean Hope*, was provided from outside the original list.

Negotiations appear to have proceeded in a relatively smooth fashion with the representatives of the Netherlands, Belgian and Polish governments. As indicated above, the Dutch replacement scheme went ahead with only three US-built ships. The Dutch took these ships without objection, although the British subsequently discovered that the purchase had gone ahead without approval from the Dutch Ministry of Finance, which had taken 'strong exception' to the price they had been forced to pay. Both Belgium and Poland took the one Ocean offered to them without serious objection, the only issue being the vessel substitution required to facilitate the Polish transaction.

The situation was completely different with Norway and Greece, which had been allocated eight between them. In July 1943, after some of the sales to other nations had been completed, the Norwegian shipping mission informed the Ministry of War Transport verbally that it was 'very anxious' not to be forced to take its quota of five Oceans as a condition of also getting some British-built tonnage, and that it wished to 'sacrifice' the US-built portion of the Norwegian quota. The immediate British response was that the Minister had 'expressed the strongest dissent from any such proposal and had intimated already that he could not consider it', claiming that to do so 'would place him in an impossible position with our own owners and other Allies, apart from the unfairness of saddling the British Treasury with an undue proportion of expensive tonnage.'

Neither side showed any inclination to compromise, each sticking to its guns at a meeting on 24 September. On 20 October, the British issued what can only be described as a final ultimatum in the guise of a formal letter from Lord Leathers, the Minister of War Transport, which gave the Norwegians until the end of the month to accept all the ships offered through the scheme, or to have the complete offer withdrawn. The Norwegians did not respond until 30 October, declining to change their position, and going as far as to state 'the American built standard ships, in our opinion, cannot justly be considered as 'replacement'. They have been constructed in an emergency to meet the requirements of the war and presumably will not be worth very much after the war.' Writing on the same day, the Greeks also declined to participate on financial grounds, stating that 'insurance monies collected by the government as deponent owners could not be invested in those vessels without serious capital loss.' The Yugoslavs also bowed out of the programme, in their case suggesting that their more modest financial means would be better invested in older second-hand tonnage.

The withdrawal of three allies from the replacement scheme, particularly that of the Norwegians, by far the biggest contributors to the shipping war among Britain's European allies, hinted at the very real problem which not only undermined British ship disposal efforts in 1943, but would continue to cause difficulties when the whole war-built fleet was being disposed of in 1946–7. The contract for the Oceans had been

Ocean Victory, photographed here arriving at New York on 20 September 1942 with a full cargo from the west coast including crated aircraft on her aft hatch covers, would be renamed *Jan Steen* following her sale to the Dutch government in August 1943.
(US Coast Guard/Mariners' Museum & Park)

signed in December 1940, when Britain was fighting the war alone, and the very real threat to her survival posed by serious shipping losses seemed to justify the acquisition of new tonnage in the USA without regard to cost. This situation had changed completely by early 1943. Not only was the overall war situation much more positive, but the addition of American productive might, and the introduction of Lend-Lease, had profoundly altered the new tonnage equation. The Norwegian shipping mission, and its Greek and Yugoslav equivalents, were now assessing vessel replacement decisions along the lines of long-term fleet renewal rather than emergency wartime pressure, with a consequent change in strategic, commercial and financial outlook. Putting it simply, buying Oceans with 1940 price tags was already making less and less sense in 1943.

The five sales which did proceed were executed between March and August 1943. In line with their previous practice for wartime acquisitions, the Dutch named their vessels after painters of old (of which the country had an impressive number), and the Belgians used a two-word name beginning *Belgian* (in this case simply replacing *Ocean* and keeping the second word unchanged). The Poles appear to have adopted two separate naming conventions. Two of their 1942–3 acquisitions, *Narwik* and *Tobruk*, took their names from Second World War battles in which Polish troops had distinguished themselves. A third acquisition, *Boryslaw*, took her name from that of a Polish city, as indeed did *Ocean Hope* in her new guise as *Bialystok*. The latter name was, in fact a second choice, it being a replacement for that of another Polish city, *Grodno*, a name declined by the British as there was already an Ellerman's Wilson Line vessel of that name on the UK register.

Sales to Allied Governments, 1943

Vessel sold	Date of sale	New owner	New name
Ocean Merchant	24.3.1943	Netherlands	*Jan Lievens*
Ocean Athlete	10.4.1943	Netherlands	*Govert Flink*
Ocean Veteran	21.6.1943	Belgium	*Belgian Veteran*
Ocean Victory	3.8.1943	Netherlands	*Jan Steen*
Ocean Hope	17.8.1943	Poland	*Bialystok*

Ocean Angel arriving at New York on 4 October 1943 to load for a long voyage to Bombay, the first leg of which would take her from Hampton Roads across the Atlantic and through the Mediterranean to Port Said in UGS 22.
(US Coast Guard/Mariners' Museum & Park)

Vessel Deployment, 1943

Vessel	30.6.1943	Route/Convoy	31.12.1943	Route/Convoy
Ocean Vigil	Newport, Mon	UK-North Africa (KMS 20)	Brindisi	Italy-UK
Ocean Viking	East Atlantic	UK-Sicily KMS 19	**11.10.1943 Mined and abandoned Taranto**	
Ocean Vestal	East Atlantic	West Africa-UK SL 132	Gibraltar	India-Mediterranean-UK
Ocean Liberty	Clyde	UK-North Africa (KMS 20)	Port Said	Egypt-Italy
Ocean Vesper	Alexandria	Egypt-Sicily (MWS.37)	Naples (ex-UK)	North African/Italian ports
Ocean Freedom	**13.3.1943 Bombed and abandoned Murmansk**			
Ocean Valley	Alexandria	Egypt-Sicily (MWS.36)	Gibraltar (ex-US)	USA- Mediterranean-India
Ocean Vision	Alexandria	Egypt-Sicily (MWS.36)	Buenos Aires	River Plate-West Africa-UK
Ocean Vulcan	Alexandria	Egypt-Sicily (MWS.36)	Barry	UK-Italy
Ocean Peace	Alexandria	Egypt-Sicily (MWS.36)	**12.7.1943 Bombed and sunk Avola, Sicily**	
Ocean Valour	East Atlantic	Gibraltar-Freetown OS 50	Murmansk	UK-North Russia JW 55B
Ocean Faith	Halifax	Canada-UK (HX 246)	Naples (ex-UK)	North African/Italian ports
Ocean Vigour	Liverpool	UK-North Africa (KMS 21)	Bombay	India-South Africa-River Plate
Ocean Vanity	Freetown	West Africa-UK	Loch Ewe	UK-North Russia RA 55A
Ocean Hope	Takoradi	West Africa-UK (SL 133)	Sold Poland, renamed *Bialystok*	
Ocean Pride	Alexandria	Egypt-Sicily (MWS.36)	Murmansk	UK-North Russia JW 55B
Ocean Volunteer	East Atlantic	Gibraltar-West Africa OS 50	Indian Ocean	US-Egypt-India
Ocean Veteran	Sold Belgium, renamed *Belgian Veteran*			
Ocean Courage	**15.1.1943 Torpedoed and sunk off West Africa**			
Ocean Voyager	**19.3.1943 Bombed and blew up Tripoli, Libya**			
Ocean Fame	Takoradi	West Africa-UK (SL 134)	Algiers	North African/Italian ports
Ocean Vista	Algiers	North Africa coastal	Gibraltar	Italy-West Africa-Rio de Janeiro
Ocean Strength	Alexandria	Egypt-Sicily (MWS.36)	Loch Ewe	UK-North Russia RA 55A
Ocean Trader	Santos, Brazil	Brazil- West Africa-UK	Port Said	Egypt-Italy
Ocean Volga	Liverpool	UK-North Africa (KMS 20)	Persian Gulf	Basra-Port Sudan-Suez-UK
Ocean Vengeance	East Atlantic	UK-Sicily KMS 19	Gibraltar	Gibraltar-Freetown-Brazil
Ocean Vagrant	Portland, Maine	US-North Africa (UGS 13)	Cochin	US-Suez-India
Ocean Wanderer	Algiers	North Africa-Suez-India	Bombay	India-South Africa-Plate
Ocean Viscount	Swansea	UK-North Africa (KMS 20)	Colombo	India-East Africa- UK-Suez
Ocean Verity	East Atlantic	Gibraltar-West Africa OS 50	Loch Ewe	UK-North Russia RA 55A
Ocean Rider	Liverpool (repairs)	UK-North Africa	Newport, Mon	UK-Italy (KMS 40)
Ocean Viceroy	East Atlantic	UK-West Africa-Plate OS 50	Murmansk	UK-North Russia JW 55B
Ocean Virtue	East Atlantic	UK-Sicily KMS 19	**21.7.1943 Bombed and sunk Augusta, Sicily**	
Ocean Valentine	East Atlantic	West Africa-UK	Augusta	Italy-US
Ocean Merchant	Sold Netherlands, renamed *Jan Lievens*			
Ocean Athlete	Sold Netherlands, renamed *Govert Flinck*			
Ocean Pilgrim	Rio de Janeiro	Brazil-West Africa-UK	Fremantle, WA	Australia-India-Spain-UK
Ocean Vagabond	**10.1.1943 Torpedoed and sunk north Atlantic**			
Ocean Wayfarer	Buenos Aires	Plate-East Africa-Egypt	Red Sea	Egypt-East Africa-Plate
Ocean Victory	East Atlantic	West Africa-UK SL 132	Sold Netherlands, renamed *Jan Steen*	
Ocean Stranger	London	UK-North Africa (KMS 22)	Naples	North African/Italian ports
Ocean Traveller	Oban	UK-North Africa (KMS 20)	Buenos Aires	River Plate-West Africa-UK
Ocean Seaman	**15.3.1943 Torpedoed and abandoned Algiers**			
Ocean Gallant	Bone	North Africa-West Africa	Oban	UK-North Africa (OS 64)
Ocean Courier	Middlesbrough	UK-North Africa (KMS 22)	west Atlantic	North Africa-US GUS 24
Ocean Messenger	South Atlantic	West Africa-River Plate	Murmansk	UK-North Russia JW 55B
Ocean Angel	Glasgow (repairs)	UK-Lisbon (KMS 24)	Indian Ocean	India-South Africa-River Plate
Ocean Hunter	Alexandria	Egypt-Sicily (MWS 36)	East Atlantic	US-North Africa UGS 27
Ocean Gypsy	Durban	South Africa-River Plate	Murmansk	UK-North Russia JW 55B
Ocean Glory	Alexandria	Egypt-Sicily (MWS 36)	Clyde	UK-Italy (KMS 40)

Transferred Vessels

Vessel	30.6.1943	Route/Convoy	31.12.1943	Route/Convoy
Bialystok			Indian Ocean	US-Suez-India
Belgian Veteran	North Atlantic	UK-Canada ON 191	Indian Ocean	India-Australia
Jan Lievens	South Atlantic	UK- West Africa-River Plate	London	UK-Mediterranean
Govert Flinck	Bougie, Algeria	North Africa-UK (MKS 16G)	East Atlantic	UK-Mediterranean KMS 36
Jan Steen			Newcastle, NSW	Australia-New Zealand-Chile

Structural Problems

US war-built war ships suffered a rash of structural failures soon after entering service. Most of these affected Liberty ships, and in the worst cases resulted in the total loss of the ships concerned after breaking in two. The Oceans were not immune to these problems, with a total of nine recorded incidents. None of these resulted in the loss of the ship involved, but in at least two cases, the cracking of deck and hatch comings on *Ocean Angel* and a hull fracture on *Jan Lievens* (ex-*Ocean Merchant*), the damage was serious. The initial assumption in most corners was that the cause of the problem was welded construction. Exhaustive examination did uncover some evidence of poor-quality welding, but it became clear that hull and deck fractures normally did not follow welding joins, running instead through the plates themselves. The issue was complex, but the biggest contributory factor was the relatively brittle nature of some American steel compared to its more ductile British equivalent, which tended to have a higher manganese and carbon content.

Assessment of partial hull and deck failures on the Oceans is complicated by the fact that all nine reported cases involved vessels built on the east coast at South Portland, Maine. This has led to suggestions that cold New England weather might have compromised welding quality. This seems unlikely, as many of the ships concerned were built in the summer (*Ocean Angel*, for example, between July and September) when temperature would not have been an issue. It is possible that the quality of the steel used in hull construction had been compromised by cold weather at the steel yard, but this can only be speculation as data on the sourcing of steel plate is not available. The British maintained a keen interest in the Liberty ship hull failure issue, and although wartime investigation had identified some addressable issues, both structural and operational in nature (the latter including inadequate ballasting on westward Atlantic crossings), a decision to undertake exhaustive comparative tests between riveted and welded vessels had already been made before the war ended.

Operational Overview, 1943

The first half of 1943 saw some dispersal of Oceans back to distant waters, but most ships remained committed to the UK to Mediterranean route. Up until May, the major effort was in support of the campaign in Tunisia itself. Even after the Axis surrender in North Africa in May, a significant part of the fleet was deployed in bringing military stores to the theatre in preparation for the next phase of the campaign, the invasion of Sicily. At the end of June, ten Oceans were either loading in the UK for North African ports or at sea heading for the same destination, while a further five vessels were already in theatre or on their way home from it. Beyond this ongoing commitment, the other major effort was the Sicilian invasion itself in July. Eight Oceans sailed in the invasion convoy from Alexandria, with another four following in support convoys.

The Mediterranean remained the major focus of operations in the second half of the year. A dozen vessels were directly deployed in support of the military campaign in Italy at the end of 1943, most of them operating in shuttle convoys between North African and south Italian ports. Although the Allies enjoyed a greater and greater advantage in numbers, enemy resistance was fierce, even after the Italian capitulation in September 1943. The campaign in the central Mediterranean exposed the Oceans to a consistently higher level of risk than any other employment, save for mid-1942 Russian convoy duty. From the loss of *Ocean Vanquisher* on 12 December 1942 to that of *Ocean Hunter* on 10 January 1944, seven of the sisters fell victim to aircraft, submarines, or mines. Across the wider Mediterranean theatre, however, the changing strategic situation produced an extremely important change in the second half of the year. The successive captures of Tunisia, Sicily and the southern part of the Italian mainland had finally broken the Axis mid-Mediterranean barricade, which had blocked through traffic between Gibraltar in the west and the Suez Canal in the east since the summer of 1940. This eliminated the need for the long and wasteful southwards diversion around Africa. Through convoys could now be run in both directions between the US or UK and the Eastern Mediterranean, with some vessels sailing on to India, where the Oceans were beginning to play their part in reinforcing British forces facing the Japanese on the Bengal-Burma border. The closing months of 1943 also saw a return of the Oceans to the north Russian convoy route, in considerably more favourable conditions than those prevailing during their previous deployment.

The Invasion of Sicily

In contrast to the assault on French North Africa in the previous November, the invasion of Sicily on 10 July 1943 was largely staged from the eastern Mediterranean. The ships of the invasion convoys of Operation Husky and most of the immediate follow-up convoys loaded at Alexandria

Sicily Invasion Convoys

MWS 36 Assault Convoy Sailed, Alexandria 3 July 1943

Vessel	Arrival Beach	Vehicles, cased petrol, stores
Ocean Glory	Bark East	109 vehicles, 22t cased petrol, 150t stores
Ocean Hunter	Acid South	123 vehicles, 114t cased petrol, 110t stores
Ocean Peace	Acid South	103 vehicles, 253t cased petrol, 432t stores
Ocean Pride	Acid South	121 vehicles, 45t cased petrol, 106t stores
Ocean Strength	Acid South	123 vehicles, 44t cased petrol, 108t stores
Ocean Valley	Acid South	98 vehicles, 183t cased petrol, 441t stores
Ocean Vision	Bark East	111 vehicles, 129t cased petrol, 123t stores
Ocean Vulcan	Acid South	124 vehicles, 45t cased petrol, 110t stores

MWS 37 Follow-up Convoy Sailed, Alexandria 6 July 1943

Vessel	Arrival Beach	Vehicles, cased petrol, stores
Ocean Vesper	Acid South	96 vehicles, 680t cased petrol, 1,502t stores

KMS 19 Follow-up Convoy Sailed, Clyde 25 June 1943

Vessel	Port of Origin	Arrival Beach/Port
Ocean Vengeance	Glasgow	Bark South
Ocean Viking	Glasgow	Algiers, Augusta
Ocean Virtue	Swansea	Algiers, Augusta

throughout June and sailed in early July. Merchant ships were not yet being convoyed through the Mediterranean, and the invasion fleet consisted largely of vessels that had remained in theatre after distant ocean passages around South Africa or across the Pacific. The slow portion of the assault convoy, the thirty-seven-ship MWS 36, sailed from Alexandria on 3 July with eight Oceans in its ranks, and a further vessel followed three days later in MWS 37. The first follow-up convoys from the UK, with a longer voyage ahead of them, had sailed in late June, KMS 19 including a further three members of the class, bringing the total commitment to twelve. The composition of the first of these convoys provides a clear indication of the extent to which the Allies were now able to depend on modern tonnage at the sharp edge of the war. Apart from the eight Oceans, MWS 36 included fourteen US Liberties and eleven British war-built Empires, as well as a single Canadian-built Fort, only the remaining three ships dating from earlier than 1940.

The major invasion convoys arrived at the invasion beaches in southeast Sicily almost entirely intact. U-boats managed to sink three ships from KMS 18B off the coast of Algeria, but only one vessel was lost from the main assault convoy in the eastern Mediterranean, again to a submarine torpedo. The beaches were code-named in line with existing practice, but those responsible fell well short of the striking name choices made for the Normandy landings in 1944: the five beaches stretching south and then southwest from Syracuse, revelled in the names Acid North, Acid South, Bark East, Bark South, and Bark West. The beaches themselves, and the roadsteads off the nearby ports of Syracuse and Augusta, became heavily congested. Arriving merchant ships carried some landing craft crosswise over their hatches, but unloading was painfully slow. Although a beachhead was successfully established on the first day, many ships remained unloaded at anchor through the following week. The Allied air forces provided extensive daytime fighter cover over the invasion beaches from bases in North Africa, its effectiveness being only limited by breakdowns in control from afloat. The cover was less extensive at night, and then German and Italian bombers managed to carry out a damaging series of raids. Two Oceans fell victim to these nocturnal attacks: *Ocean Peace* off the Acid South beachhead at Avola on 12 July, and *Ocean Virtue* off Augusta on 21 July. Neither vessel had been unloaded and both caught fire, but their subsequent fates were completely different. *Ocean Peace* blew up despite the efforts of an attendant destroyer to scuttle her with gunfire to extinguish the flames, but *Ocean Virtue* sank of her own accord in shallow water before she could suffer a similar fate, her hulk being re-floated in the autumn to clear the anchorage.

The Russian Convoys, 1943–4

The Admiralty undertook a comprehensive rethink of its Russian convoy strategy after the heavy losses suffered by PQ 16, 17 and 18. Although the last of these had been fought through in September 1942, it had been given close protection by a

Russian Convoy Deployment, 1943–4

Vessel	Convoy	Direction	Departure	Fate of Vessel	
Ocean Vanity	JW 54A	outward	15.11.1943	Arrived safely in convoy	24.11.1943
Ocean Verity	JW 54A	outward	15.11.1943	Arrived safely in convoy	24.11.1943
Ocean Strength	JW.54B	outward	22.11.1943	Arrived safely in convoy	3.12.1943
Ocean Gypsy	JW 55B	outward	20.12.1943	Arrived safely in convoy	30.12.1943
Ocean Messenger	JW 55B	outward	20.12.1943	Arrived safely in convoy	30.12.1943
Ocean Pride	JW 55B	outward	20.12.1943	Arrived safely in convoy	30.12.1943
Ocean Valour	JW 55B	outward	20.12.1943	Arrived safely in convoy	30.12.1943
Ocean Viceroy	JW 55B	outward	20.12.1943	Arrived safely in convoy	30.12.1943
Ocean Strength	RA 55A	homeward	22.12.1943	Arrived safely in convoy	1.1.1944
Ocean Vanity	RA 55A	homeward	22.12.1943	Arrived safely in convoy	1.1.1944
Ocean Verity	RA 55A	homeward	22.12.1943	Arrived safely in convoy	1.1.1944
Ocean Gypsy	RA 56	homeward	3.2.1944	Arrived safely in convoy	11.2.1944
Ocean Messenger	RA 56	homeward	3.2.1944	Arrived safely in convoy	11.2.1944
Ocean Pride	RA 56	homeward	3.2.1944	Arrived safely in convoy	11.2.1944
Ocean Valour	RA 56	homeward	3.2.1944	Arrived safely in convoy	11.2.1944
Ocean Viceroy	RA 56	homeward	3.2.1944	Arrived safely in convoy	11.2.1944
Ocean Strength	JW 57	outward	20.2.1944	Arrived safely in convoy	28.2.1944
Ocean Strength	RA 58	homeward	7.4.1944	Arrived safely in convoy	14.4.1944

naval force of one escort carrier, a light cruiser, two anti-aircraft ships, eighteen destroyers and ten smaller escorts. Even this force had not been able to prevent the loss of ten merchant ships to aircraft and another three to U-boats. Mercantile losses of this level were not bearable on an ongoing basis. Sustainability was also a serious issue for the commitment of escort forces, which faced not only the continued strain of the battle of the Atlantic, but also a major redeployment to support Operation Torch, the November invasion of French North Africa. These considerations led directly to a decision to limit operations to the winter months, a time of near-total darkness in the high northern latitudes through which the convoys sailed. Although this exposed ships to greater danger from weather and ice conditions and put some strain on the always delicate relationship with the Soviet government, it also severely reduced the effectiveness of German interdiction measures. Not only was convoy detection itself much more difficult, but mass air attack became next to impossible and positioning U-boat patrol lines difficult at best.

Only three outward convoys, one split into two sections, were sailed in the first all-winter sequence between December 1942 and March 1943, all of them significantly smaller than those of the preceding summer and autumn. They were immediately successful, U-boats sinking only four ships, all from homeward convoys. A fifth ship was lost to weather. The only Oceans committed to these operations were the two veterans of PQ 17 and 18. Of these, *Ocean Faith* completed one round trip, while *Ocean Freedom* was bombed at Murmansk after arrival, the only vessel to succumb to air attack in the entire cycle.

Eight Oceans were deployed to the northern theatre when

Ocean Messenger underway on the Tyne after returning from Arctic convoy duty to Murmansk on 13 February 1944 in RA 56.
(National Maritime Museum)

the Russian convoys were resumed on a much larger scale in November 1943. Three sailed in JW 54A/JW 54B in November, and five in JW 55B in December, returning, respectively, in RA 55A in December 1943 and RA 56 in February 1944. All but one of these ships were then deployed elsewhere, *Ocean Strength* remaining to complete what would prove to be the class's last Arctic round trip in JW 57 and RA 58 in February–April 1944. The contrast between the last PQ convoys and those of the 1943–4 season was once again striking. Only five merchantmen and one escorting destroyer were lost in the new cycle of convoys, all to U-boats, which themselves lost thirteen of their number between January and May 1944. The other striking development was the extent to which war-built government-designed ships had taken over almost the entire burden of the sailings. In JW 55B, the five Oceans were accompanied by three Canadian-built Forts and nine US Liberty ships, the only pre-war vessels being the escort oiler and another tanker. In the much larger JW 57, in which *Ocean Strength* made the last outward trip of her class, there were no fewer than thirty US Liberty ships, as well as three Forts and three British-built Empires, the only pre-war ships being two escort oilers, three other tankers and a convoy rescue ship.

Vessel Deployment, 1944

Vessel	30.6.1944	Route/Convoy	31.12.1944	Route/Convoy
Ocean Vigil	English Channel	Normandy landings	New York	US-UK (SC 167)
Ocean Vestal	Madras	India-South Africa-UK	Port Elizabeth	UK-South & East Africa
Ocean Liberty	Naples	Mediterranean	Antwerp	Mediterranean-North Europe-UK
Ocean Vesper	Alexandria	Mediterranean	London	UK-Canada (ON 284)
Ocean Valley	Lourenço Marques	East Africa-North Africa-UK	North Atlantic	US-Suez-India (UGS 64)
Ocean Vision	English Channel	UK-Normandy beachhead	Calcutta	India-East Africa-Mediterranean
Ocean Vulcan	Naples	Mediterranean	Barrow	UK-Mediterranean
Ocean Valour	Suez (repairs)	Mediterranean	Haifa	Mediterranean
Ocean Faith	Augusta	Mediterranean	Aden	US-Suez-India
Ocean Vigour	English Channel	UK-Normandy beachhead	Casablanca	Mediterranean-US (GUS 63)
Ocean Vanity	Buenos Aires	River Plate-West Africa-UK	New York	US-Suez-India (UGS 68)
Ocean Pride	Algiers	Mediterranean	Alexandria	Mediterranean-US (GUS 67)
Ocean Volunteer	North Atlantic	UK-US (ON 242)	Buenos Aires	Plate-West Africa-UK
Ocean Fame	West Indies	West Indies-US-UK (HX 300)	Dakar	West Africa-UK
Ocean Vista	English Channel	UK-Normandy beachhead	New York	US-Suez-India (UGS 67)
Ocean Strength	English Channel	UK-Normandy beachhead	North Atlantic	UK-US (ON 275)
Ocean Trader	Bone	Mediterranean	Liverpool	US-UK-Suez-India
Ocean Volga	English Channel	UK-Normandy beachhead	North Atlantic	UK-US (ON 272)
Ocean Vengeance	English Channel	UK-Normandy beachhead	Sunderland	UK-Antwerp
Ocean Vagrant	English Channel	UK-Normandy beachhead	Norfolk, Virginia	US-Mediterranean (UGS 68)
Ocean Wanderer	Methil Roads	Plate-Freetown-UK	Aden	East Africa-Suez-UK
Ocean Viscount	Colombo	India-South Africa-Plate	East Atlantic	UK-Suez-India
Ocean Verity	Red Sea	East Africa-Suez-UK	Suez	East Africa-Suez-US (GUS 67)
Ocean Rider	Algiers	Mediterranean	Piraeus	Mediterranean-UK
Ocean Viceroy	Indian Ocean	South & East Africa-Australia	Indian Ocean	India-Suez-UK
Ocean Valentine	Calcutta	India-Suez-UK	Mauritius	Mauritius-Suez-Mediterranean
Ocean Pilgrim	Port Said	South Africa-Suez-UK	New York	US-Suez-India (UGS 67)
Ocean Wayfarer	Irish Sea	UK-Mediterranean	East Atlantic	Gibraltar-West Africa
Ocean Stranger	Liverpool	UK-Mediterranean	Patras	Mediterranean-US (GUS 70)
Ocean Traveller	Port Said	Mediterranean	Piraeus	Mediterranean-US (GUS 69)
Ocean Gallant	Port Said	Mediterranean	Liverpool	UK-Mediterranean (KMS 77)
Ocean Courier	English Channel	UK-Normandy beachhead	Middlesbrough	Repairing torpedo damage
Ocean Messenger	Alexandria	Mediterranean	Piraeus	Mediterranean-West Africa-UK
Ocean Angel	English Channel	UK-Normandy beachhead	Colachel, India	India-Suez-UK
Ocean Hunter	**10.1.1944 Torpedoed and sunk Mediterranean**			
Ocean Gypsy	Algiers	Mediterranean	Bone	Mediterranean
Ocean Glory	Algiers	Mediterranean	Augusta	Mediterranean
Transferred Vessels				
Bialystok	East Atlantic	Mediterranean-UK (SL 161)	Naples	Mediterranean-US (GUS 66)
Belgian Veteran	East Atlantic	UK-West Africa (OS 81)	Liverpool	UK-Mediterranean (OS 103)
Jan Lievens	Augusta	Mediterranean	Augusta	Mediterranean-US (GUS 67)
Govert Flinck	Mediterranean	UK-Italy (KMS 54)	South Atlantic	Casablanca-Rio de Janeiro
Jan Steen	Liverpool	Liverpool-Barrow (repairs)	Mediterranean	Mediterranean-UK (MKS 78)

Bialystok, the former *Ocean Hope*, arriving at New York in ballast from the Clyde on 9 August 1944 in convoy ON 246 a year after she had been sold to the Polish Government.
(US Coast Guard/Mariners' Museum & Park)

Operational Overview, 1944

Vessel deployment in the first half of 1944 remained heavily oriented towards the Mediterranean. This was not only the product of continued support for the military campaign in Italy, but also of the build-up for Operation Dragoon, the invasion of the south of France. At the mid-point of the year, thirteen Oceans were on long-term assignment in the Mediterranean theatre, while another four were on their way there from the UK. Of the vessels deployed in the Mediterranean, eight would be involved in Operation Dragoon, sailing from assembly ports in the south of Italy. Elsewhere, the other large-scale deployment was to the landings in Normandy. A total of ten Oceans had been assigned to the invasion fleet, an ongoing commitment which required repeated round trips between UK south coast loading ports and the beachheads.

Some vessels were now spending a great deal of time away from European waters. To take one example, the midway point of 1944 found *Ocean Viscount* at Colombo, near the beginning of a voyage from Calcutta for Durban and the River Plate, while by the end of that year the same ship was a week out of Milford Haven on her way back to Calcutta via the Mediterranean and Suez. One of the most unusual voyages undertaken in distant waters was carried out by the Dutch *Jan Steen*. Having already called at several Australian ports, she sailed from Newcastle, NSW, across the South Pacific for Iquique in Chile, making another long return passage to New Zealand ports. This voyage pattern had been common in the last decades of commercial sail, vessels carrying coal out from Newcastle to Chile and loading nitrates in the latter. Cargo data does not survive for the *Jan Steen*'s trans-Pacific odyssey, but as Newcastle remained primarily a coal port, and Iquique's only significant product was nitrates, it seems likely that she was following these old trades.

The first weeks of 1944 had seen the last war loss the class was to suffer, that of *Ocean Seaman* to a German torpedo bomber in the Mediterranean, and there were to be only two cases of non-fatal damage in the remaining months of the war. These last casualties, *Ocean Volga* and *Ocean Courier*, were torpedoed by German S-boats in the same convoy at the end of July, several months into their assignment to supply the Normandy beachheads. Both returned first to the Thames and then proceeded to Middlesbrough for permanent repairs. *Ocean Volga* made the journey under her own power, but

Deployment in D-Day Support Convoys

Vessel	First Convoy	Departed	Arrived	Beachhead	Final Sailing
Ocean Vengeance	ETM 3	8.6.1944	9.6.1944	Gold	7.8.1944
Ocean Vision	ETM 3	8.6.1944	9.6.1944	Gold	30.8.1944
Ocean Volga	ETM 3	8.6.1944	9.6.1944	Gold	30.7.1944*
Ocean Courier	ETM 4	9.6.1944	10.6.1944	Gold	30.7.1944*
Ocean Vista	ETM 4	9.6.1944	10.6.1944	Juno	2.8.1944
Ocean Angel	ETM 6	11.6.1944	12.6.1944	Juno	9.8.1944
Ocean Strength	ETM 6	11.6.1944	12.6.1944	Gold	9.8.1944
Ocean Vagrant	ETM 7	12.6.1944	13.6.1944	Gold	20.9.1944
Ocean Vigour	ETM 7	12.6.1944	13.6.1944	Juno	6.8.1944
Ocean Vigil	ETM 8	13.6.1944	14.6.1944	Gold	4.8.1944

* Torpedoed on return voyage and sent to Middlesbrough for repairs

Ocean Courier was much more heavily damaged, and had to be towed into port. Her repairs would not be completed until March 1945.

By the end of 1944, the overall deployment of the Oceans had become dispersed, a pattern which was reflective of the growing breadth of Allied military operations. While very few ships were being employed on the traditional North America–UK convoy routes, no fewer than twelve were committed to the supply line between the US and the Mediterranean, and an increasing number were sailing direct from the UK or US to the Belgian port of Antwerp, access to which was secured by the clearance of German forces from the banks of the Scheldt estuary late in the year. Finally, more vessels were being deployed on voyages to Indian ports in support of the war effort in Burma. A total of eight vessels were outbound for India directly from the UK or US, while four more were on return voyages; in every case the route followed was through the Mediterranean and the Suez Canal.

Ocean Vigil arriving at New York on 19 September 1944 in ON 251 after coming off Normandy invasion duty.
(US Coast Guard/Mariners' Museum & Park)

Operation Neptune – The D-Day Invasion

A total of ten Oceans – including *Ocean Strength*, which was deployed straight from Russian convoy duties – were committed to Operation Neptune, the naval component of the D-Day landings in Normandy in June 1944. These first sailed in five different support convoys between 8 and 14 June, seven vessels going to Gold Beach, one of the two British landing areas, and three to the Canadian Juno Beach. All ten vessels remained committed to ongoing supply operations throughout June and July, sailing in shuttle convoys between Southend, on the Thames Estuary, and Seine Bay, each ship normally arriving in the latter at roughly two-weekly intervals. The Allies committed huge numbers of escort vessels to protecting the invasion armada and the succeeding supply effort, and increasingly desperate German attempts to interfere produced only limited results at disproportionate cost. There were no Oceans among the handful of merchant ships lost, but, as mentioned above, two were damaged, one of them severely, when a German S-boat flotilla managed to break through Allied defences at the end of July.

Operation Dragoon – The Invasion of the South of France

Unlike the Normandy invasion, the landings ten weeks later in the south of France encountered only limited resistance, particularly at sea. The last U-boat success in the Mediterranean had been the sinking of *Fort Missanabie* by *U 453* south of Taranto on 19 May 1944, and by the time of the landings the Germans could not deploy any significant sea or air assets in the theatre. The fate of *U 230*, the only operational U-boat left in the entire western Mediterranean at the time of the landings, was indicative of how low German fortunes had sunk: her failed attempt to break into the invasion anchorage ended when she ran aground and was blown up by her crew to avoid capture. The landings themselves were centred on St Tropez and extended along a thirty-mile stretch of the Cote d'Azur in four sectors code named (from east to west) Camel, Delta, Alpha and Sitka. American assault troops landed on 15 August, and a follow-up force of two Free French divisions on the following day. The equipment and supplies of the latter arrived simultaneously in a forty-ship convoy of British merchant ships which included eight Oceans. Although two of these vessels were damaged by air attack soon after arrival, the only drama involving an Ocean had taken place at Taranto, where part of *Ocean Rider*'s cargo had to be replaced after a hold fire.

South of France Invasion, Follow-up Convoy TM 1 – Sailed from Taranto, 10 August 1944

Vessel	Beachhead	Personnel, Vehicles & Stores
Ocean Gallant	Alpha	268 personnel, 117 vehicles
Ocean Glory	Delta	289 personnel, 113 vehicles, 29t stores
Ocean Gypsy	Delta	315 personnel, 124 vehicles
Ocean Messenger	Delta	291 personnel, 118 vehicles, 1,189t stores
Ocean Pride	Delta	248 personnel, 110 vehicles
Ocean Rider	Delta	295 personnel, 119 vehicles, 1,287t stores
Ocean Traveller	Delta	304 personnel, 116 vehicles, 1,142t stores
Ocean Vesper	Alpha	300 personnel, 102 vehicles, 103t stores

Operational Overview, 1945

The early months of 1945 witnessed a gradual reduction in sailings to the Mediterranean and a corresponding increase in sailings to the UK and north Europe. Several Oceans spent the war's last winter on the North Atlantic convoy run. *Ocean Vigil*, for example, made her last eastbound crossing in February in SC 167, carrying general cargo from Baltimore, while *Ocean Stranger* and *Ocean Traveller* followed together in March in HX 343, both carrying general cargo from New York for Antwerp. The early spring also saw some vessels making ballast voyages from Britain, South Africa, and the Indian Ocean to the River Plate to help lift the grain harvest, an annual commitment made more pressing by the need to feed the newly liberated people of Western Europe, many of whom had faced starvation in the winter months. Finally, the commitment of tonnage to support the offensive of Slim's Fourteenth Army to liberate Burma from the Japanese continued to grow, the flow of ships into the south Asian theatre increasing further as the British began building up resources in India for an eventual amphibious assault on Malaya.

It was fully reflective of the continued commitment of the Oceans to the wider war effort, that only a handful of their crews would have a chance to celebrate VE Day on 8 May 1945 in home ports. Six members of the class were at sea in North Atlantic convoys, three outbound in ballast to load in Canada and three inbound from the same country fully loaded. *Ocean Stranger* and *Ocean Glory* were making their way west in ON 299 and ON 300, respectively, to load grain at ports along the St Lawrence, while *Ocean Vigour* was following behind in ON 301 to load iron ore at Wabana. Their paths would cross mid-ocean with *Ocean Pride* carrying grain from Quebec City for Manchester in SC 175 and *Ocean Messenger* and *Jan Lievens*, sailing together in HX 354, the former with general cargo from Halifax for Antwerp, and the latter with another St Lawrence grain cargo destined for Glasgow. Just

Vessel Deployment, VE Day (8 May 1945) and VJ Day (15 August 1945)

Vessel	VE Day	Route	VJ Day	Route
Ocean Vigil	Red Sea	Leith-Karachi	Immingham	Hull-Baltimore
Ocean Vestal	Mediterranean	Manchester-Karachi	Bombay	Bombay-Malaya (Op Zipper)
Ocean Liberty	Indian Ocean	Bombay-Durban-R Plate	Liverpool	Liverpool-New York
Ocean Vesper	Central Atlantic	Gibraltar-Buenos Aires	Cardiff	Glasgow-Calcutta
Ocean Valley	South Atlantic	Rio de Janeiro-Gibraltar	Red Sea	Manchester-Colombo
Ocean Vision	Catania, Sicily	South Italy-Middlesbrough	Central Atlantic	Baltimore-Ancona
Ocean Vulcan	Mediterranean	Piraeus-Hampton Roads	North Sea	Middlesbrough-London (repairs)
Ocean Valour	Abadan	Abadan-Bombay	Abadan	Abadan-Bombay
Ocean Faith	Gibraltar	Buenos Aires-Manchester	Freetown	Freetown-London
Ocean Vigour	North Atlantic	Newport, Mon-Wabana	East Atlantic	Barry-New York
Ocean Vanity	Red Sea	Lourenço Marques-Port Said	Port Kembla, NSW	Newcastle NSW-Cairns
Ocean Pride	North Atlantic	Quebec-Manchester	Baltimore	Baltimore-Madras
Ocean Volunteer	Three Rivers, PQ	Three Rivers-Plymouth	Southampton	Southampton-Cherbourg
Ocean Fame	Gibraltar	Algiers-Hampton Roads	Liverpool	Liverpool-Colombo
Ocean Vista	Karachi	Beirut-Karachi	English Channel	London-New York
Ocean Strength	St John, NB	St John-Immingham	North Atlantic	Sorel, PQ-Bremerhaven
Ocean Trader	Mediterranean	Mauritius-Liverpool	Bombay	Bombay-Madras
Ocean Volga	Indian Ocean	Lourenço Marques-R Plate	Glasgow	Glasgow-New York
Ocean Vengeance	London	London-Antwerp	New York	New York-Bombay
Ocean Vagrant	Casablanca	Naples-Hampton Roads	Casablanca	West Africa-West Australia
Ocean Wanderer	Bombay	Bombay-Beira	Suez	Liverpool-Bombay
Ocean Viscount	Dundee	Calcutta-Dundee	Bombay	Bombay-Malaya (Op Zipper)
Ocean Verity	Milford Haven	Glasgow-Bombay	Mediterranean	Mombasa-London
Ocean Rider	Baltimore	Baltimore-Naples	Suez	New York-Calcutta
Ocean Viceroy	Madras	Madras-Durban	East Atlantic	South Africa-Liverpool
Ocean Valentine	Indian Ocean	Swansea-Bombay	Durban	Colombo-R Plate
Ocean Pilgrim	Aden	Lourenço Marques-Aden	Madras	Madras-Malaya (Op Zipper)
Ocean Wayfarer	Norfolk, Virginia	Hampton Roads-Dakar	Hull	Hull-Rangoon
Ocean Stranger	North Atlantic	Tyne-Three Rivers	Sunderland	Sunderland-Rotterdam
Ocean Traveller	Montreal	Montreal-Antwerp	Sunderland	Sunderland-Hamburg
Ocean Gallant	Freetown	Freetown-Tyne	London	London-Clyde-Toulon
Ocean Courier	Portland, Maine	Portland-Bizerta	Manchester	Manchester-Madras
Ocean Messenger	North Atlantic	Halifax, NS-Antwerp	Central Atlantic	Bari-Vitoria, Brazil
Ocean Angel	Galveston	Galveston-Brindisi	Bombay	Bombay-Malaya (Op Zipper)
Ocean Gypsy	Brindisi	Ancona-Bari	Madras	Madras-Malaya (Op Zipper)
Ocean Glory	North Atlantic	Cardiff-Montreal	North Sea	Middlesbrough-Glasgow (repairs)
Transferred Vessels				
Bialystok	Norfolk, Virginia	Hampton Roads-Oran	Mediterranean	Naples-Freetown
Belgian Veteran	Cardiff	Ghent-Cardiff	Antwerp	Montreal-Antwerp
Jan Lievens	North Atlantic	Montreal-Glasgow	Montreal	Montreal-Rotterdam
Govert Flinck	Montreal	Montreal-Cardiff	Karachi	New York-Bombay
Jan Steen	Cardiff	Antwerp-Cardiff	North Atlantic	New York-Rotterdam

two ships' companies spent the day in British ports. *Ocean Vengeance* had been deployed to carry supplies between UK ports and Antwerp since the preceding November and the end of hostilities in Europe found her loading in the London docks for what would prove to be her last departure for the Scheldt on 10 May. Almost four hundred miles to the north, *Ocean Viscount* had only arrived at Dundee on 6 May two-and-a-half months after clearing Calcutta with a cargo of jute, her voyage having been extended by a long stop at Lisbon. Her stay in the UK would be brief – after a passage north around Scotland to load military equipment at Glasgow, she would leave the Clyde on 13 June for a voyage back to India to participate in the August amphibious landings on the Malayan peninsula. The crew of a third Ocean missed any VE Day shore celebrations by the narrowest of margins. *Ocean Verity* had left Glasgow on 3 May carrying military supplies, again for India, and sailed from Milford Haven on VE Day itself after loading a deck cargo of landing craft to deliver along the way in the Middle East.

The months between the German and Japanese surrenders saw most of the Oceans remaining committed either to the North Atlantic supply route, supported by shuttle support voyages between the UK and north European ports, or to the ongoing build-up of men and materiel in south Asia. In the Atlantic theatre, *Ocean Vigour* participated in the last escorted eastbound crossing when she sailed from St John's, Newfoundland, on 27 May with the cargo of iron ore she had loaded up the coast at Wabana to join HX 358 at sea. *Ocean Traveller* had crossed in the previous convoy and landed her grain cargo at Antwerp before beginning a series of shuttle voyages between Southampton and Cherbourg which would see her make four round trips before being repositioned for a voyage to Hamburg. Further south, several vessels remained on duty sailing between the US and the Mediterranean, one such ship, Poland's *Bialystok,* making a convoy crossing to Algeria in May and an unescorted passage to Italy in July. In the Indian Ocean, *Ocean Wanderer* loaded a mixed cargo at Beira, Mozambique and Mombasa, Kenya, for the UK in late May and early June, and after repairs on the Mersey sailed from Liverpool for Bombay on 29 July, while *Ocean Trader*, which had left Liverpool on 22 June, transited the Suez Canal on 5 July and set course for Bombay via Aden.

By VJ Day on 15 August, eighteen Oceans were loading for South Asia, in transit for India or already operating in the theatre. Seven British-flagged vessels were still operating in the North Atlantic, as were three of their foreign sisters, the latter now carrying cereals direct from Canada to ports in their liberated homelands, Antwerp for *Belgian Veteran*, and Rotterdam for *Jan Lievens* and *Jan Steen*. Four British ships were loading in the UK for destinations stretching around from Hamburg to Rotterdam, Cherbourg, and Toulon, but another four were far from home on long voyages in support of the wider war economy. *Ocean Vagrant* was loading phosphates in Morocco for Western Australia and would not arrive at Fremantle until October; *Ocean Viceroy* had passed Gibraltar on 14 August bound for Liverpool with a cargo of tea, copper and general loaded at Durban, Beira and Mombasa; *Ocean Faith* touched at Freetown on VJ Day, itself northbound for London with a cargo of iron ore from the nearby Sierra Leone port of Pepel; finally, *Ocean Messenger* had cleared the Mediterranean on 10 August bound for the port of Vitoria, midway up the coast of Brazil to load another iron ore cargo for the UK.

Jan Steen in port in late 1945 while engaged on a series of voyages carrying North American grain to the Netherlands.
(World Ship Society Ltd)

Ocean Vulcan photographed on the Scheldt during a December 1945 visit to Antwerp, her armament freshly removed during a post-war refit at London. *(World Ship Society Ltd)*

The eastern Indian Ocean would be the scene of the last significant deployment of the Oceans in support of amphibious operations. Allied planning in the spring and summer of 1945 did not anticipate an early Japanese surrender. The United States was embarking on a massive build-up of forces for the invasion of Japan itself, while the British were planning for landings on the west coast of occupied Malaya. The sudden Japanese surrender in August transformed these invasions into occupations, but the British amphibious landing, code-named Operation Zipper, went ahead, as parts of the invasion fleet had to sail in late August from ports on the west coast of India, before the final Japanese surrender documents were signed on board the battleship *Missouri* in Tokyo Bay on 2 September. Two separate landings took place, the first putting 25,000 men ashore at Morib and Sepang on 9 September, and the second 15,000 at Port Dickson on 12 September. The stance of local Japanese forces was not clear when the ships first sailed, but in the event, there was no resistance.

A total of seven Oceans were deployed on these operations, four in assault convoys and three in follow-up convoys. All the vessels involved were veterans of other major operations, and some had served in several theatres. *Ocean Angel* had been part of the D-Day invasion support operation. Both *Ocean Valour* and *Ocean Gypsy* had served on Russian convoys, while the latter, one of the most widely travelled members of her class, had circumnavigated the globe on her prolonged 1942–3 delivery voyage and had also participated in the invasion of the south of France.

The Invasion of Malaya, September 1945

Vessel	Role	Origin	Convoy	Function	Arrived	Destination
Ocean Angel	MT/Store ship	Bombay	JMA 2BS	Assault	12.9.1945	Port Swettenham
Ocean Vestal	MT/Store ship	Bombay	JMA 2BS	Assault	12.9.1945	Beachhead
Ocean Gypsy	MT/Store ship	Madras	JME 2S	Assault	12.9.1945	Port Swettenham
Ocean Pilgrim	MT/Store ship	Madras	JME 2S	Assault	12.9.1945	Beachhead
Ocean Trader	Store ship	Bombay	JMA 3	Follow-up	17.9.1945	Beachhead
Ocean Valour	Cased petrol ship	Bombay	JMA 3	Follow-up	17.9.1945	Beachhead/Singapore
Ocean Viscount	MT/Store ship	Bombay	JMA 3	Follow-up	17.9.1945	Beachhead

— 5 —

WARTIME CASUALTIES

Shown here soon after re-floating in early 1947, *Ocean Viking* had been scuttled to fill a breach in the wartime breakwater at Bari in January 1944, three months after suffering mine damage in the central Mediterranean.
(Archivi C N R Palermo)

Just less than one-third of all the Oceans – nineteen out of sixty – were lost to enemy action between February 1942 and January 1944. At first glance, this might appear to be an abnormally high casualty rate given that the ships arrived after the dark years of 1940–1. Losses, however, were more proportionate than they seemed. 1942 was easily the worst year of the war for British and Allied merchant ship losses. This was overwhelmingly due to the expansion of the German U-boat force and its deployment not just in large wolfpack attacks on Atlantic convoys, but also in distant theatres from the US east coast and the Caribbean, through the South Atlantic, and into the Indian Ocean – areas where most cargo vessels still sailed alone, and available escort forces were grossly inadequate. German U-boats were responsible for ten of the Ocean losses, and another two vessels fell victim to Japanese submarines in the northwestern reaches of the Indian Ocean.

While historians of the U-boat war have tended to concentrate on the large convoy battles in the North Atlantic, 1942–3 losses were particularly heavy in more distant waters. Of the twelve Oceans lost to submarine attack on the high seas, only two – *Ocean Voice* in the Arctic in September 1942, and *Ocean Seaman* in the Mediterranean in March 1943 – were under escort at the time of their loss. Even the two losses from North Atlantic convoys – *Ocean Crusader* in November 1942, and *Ocean Vagabond* in January 1943 – had straggled and were proceeding alone when attacked. Given this fact, it is striking that only four of the losses resulted in heavy casualties. Although most of the attacks happened at night, merchant ship crews were relatively well drilled in escape procedures by 1942–3, and their survival chances were enhanced by the fact that the Oceans were equipped with rapidly deployable gravity davits and four steel lifeboats, as well as the same number of large, quick-release life rafts. The vessels themselves were larger and more resistant to damage than the bulk of pre-war tonnage, and many of those lost only succumbed after multiple torpedo hits. In fact, the four cases of heavy loss of life were all the product of special circumstances: *Ocean Venture*, lost with thirty-one of forty-five crew in bad weather off Cape Hatteras, had two loaded lifeboats destroyed by torpedo explosions; *Ocean Honour*, lost with twenty of fifty-three men aboard in the Indian Ocean, suffered the explosion of a part cargo of munitions; *Ocean Crusader*, lost with all fifty hands off Newfoundland, was alone in heavy weather in the North Atlantic winter; and *Ocean Courage*, lost with fifty-two of the fifty-eight aboard off the Cape Verde Islands, went down at night in less than two minutes because of her cargo of iron ore. In most other cases, casualties were restricted to engineering crew on duty at the time of the attack, and survivors were either rapidly picked up or rowed themselves ashore.

Beyond the overall expansion of the Axis war against British and Allied merchant shipping, the other major reason why the Oceans were exposed to significant danger was their heavy deployment into theatres which might be classified as intensive combat zones. One of these was the Arctic, where convoys to north Russia faced not only U-boats, but a significant Luftwaffe presence, as well as almost impossibly bad weather conditions and the latent threat of intervention by German surface warships. A total of eleven vessels, two of which were lost, sailed in at least one Russian convoy cycle. Far more important, however, was the Mediterranean, where no fewer than seven Oceans were lost in a period of thirteen months between December 1942 and January 1944. Here, the strongest magnets for modern merchant shipping, and the biggest sources of danger, were the successive Allied invasions of North Africa, Sicily, and mainland Italy. The lengthy military campaigns which ensued, first in North Africa up to May 1943, and then in Italy from July 1943 on, required a constant supply of armaments, munitions and general stores. The burden of this ongoing campaign fell most heavily on the more modern half of the Allied merchant marine, the result being that almost all the Oceans made at least one voyage into the Mediterranean war theatre. Here they suffered losses from submarine and air-launched torpedoes, bombs, mines, and underwater explosive devices delivered by frogmen, a fair reflection of the intensity and diversity of the Axis defensive response.

Beyond the losses in the Mediterranean, twelve other Oceans were sunk by the enemy. Two each were lost off the east coast of the United States on their way to the Atlantic convoy assembly point at Halifax, Nova Scotia, and in the North Atlantic convoy system itself. A further two were lost in the Arctic convoys. The remaining six were all sunk in distant waters, two each southeast of Trinidad, off the west coast of Africa, and in the northwest Arabian Sea. All but one of this last group of losses occurred between September and November 1942, and all were at least an indirect product of the closure of the Mediterranean to through traffic. The need to carry almost all supplies from the UK and US around South Africa either to Egypt or India resulted in a very heavy deployment of mercantile tonnage over long unescorted passages. The last distant waters loss, in January 1943, was a product of another resort to lengthy diversions due to operational necessity – in this case the suspension of Freetown–UK convoys due to the diversion of escorts to the North African landings, and the consequent need to route ships homebound from West Africa via a three-sided voyage crossing the Atlantic westwards to the West Indies, sailing north to New York, and then east to the UK in convoy.

To place losses in their appropriate operational contexts, they will be covered by area rather than in strict chronological order, dealing first with the North Atlantic casualties, then those in the Arctic, followed by losses in distant waters, and finally those in the Mediterranean. There were an additional six cases in which vessels survived serious damage: five from torpedoes and one from a bomb. Four of these fit into the operational framework outlined above and will be analysed within it, as will an additional incident in which damage appears to have been prevented by special defensive measures. The final two cases of serious damage happened in the same convoy on its way back from the Normandy beachhead, and will be dealt with separately at the end.

US East Coast

All thirty vessels built in California loaded on the west coast and then sailed through the Panama Canal and up the east coast of North America towards the Atlantic convoy assembly port of Halifax, Nova Scotia. Germany had declared war on the United States before any of the new vessels entered the Atlantic, and although the number of U-boats despatched to US coastal waters was initially small, they had a disproportionately severe impact due to the almost total lack of defensive measures in place. There was no black-out of shore lights or navigational markers, limited deployment of naval anti-submarine vessels or aircraft, and, critically, no system of convoys. Merchant ships proceeding along easily interdicted coastal shipping routes were extremely vulnerable, particularly at night. *Ocean Venture* was sunk in February 1942 off Cape Hatteras and *Ocean Venus* in May 1942 off Florida. The first lost two-thirds of her crew, while the second lost only five, an illustration of how one or two changes in circumstances could spell the difference between death and safety for torpedoed merchant seamen.

Ocean Venture – 8 February 1942

Ocean Venture had loaded 9,115 tons of cargo, largely foodstuffs as well as four aircraft on deck at Vancouver, and cleared Colón at the Caribbean end of the Panama Canal for Norfolk, Virginia, on 1 February 1942. As was common at the time, her defensive armament consisted of only an American 3in deck gun and a pair of 0.5in Colt machine guns. As things transpired, even a heavier armament would have done her no good. On the night of 7/8 February, the vessel reached a buoy about forty miles off the entrance to Chesapeake Bay and proceeded inwards as instructed along a swept channel. Her experienced Larrinaga Steamship Company master, Captain Reginald Craston, was not aware of the abysmal state of naval preparedness and assumed such an important clearing point for shipping would be well protected, afterwards admitting in his survivor's report that 'as I steamed along this buoy channel, I had no qualms whatever about being attacked and thought all my problems were over.' He was disabused of these

Ocean Venture photographed immediately after launch on 27 September 1941 would have a short operational career, succumbing to torpedoes from *U 108* off Cape Hatteras on 8 February 1942, less than two months after delivery. *(Courtesy of San Francisco Maritime National Historical Park)*

sentiments at 0340hrs Eastern War Time when a torpedo struck the starboard side in the way of the engine room.

Ocean Venture was under attack by *U 108,* which had just arrived in American waters under the command of Kapitänleutnant Klaus Scholz. Scholz was an established U-boat ace who had already sunk twelve merchant ships and would go on to account for over 100,000 tons of Allied shipping and survive the war holding the Knight's Cross with Oak Leaves. An orderly evacuation was already underway when Scholz fired another torpedo three to four minutes after the first. Unfortunately, this struck underneath the now manned starboard after lifeboat, the occupants of which were killed in the explosion. Other crew members nearby were blown into the engine room through the broken skylight but were quickly rescued. About ten minutes later, a clearly impatient U-boat commander fired a third torpedo which hit forward at the bulkhead between Nos 1 and 2 holds, almost certainly killing the occupants of the smaller starboard forward lifeboat. The master got away safely as the ship began to sink by the bow on an even keel and joined another fourteen men in the small port forward lifeboat. This crowded boat rode out the remainder of a stormy night with some difficulty and sighted what was thought to be the larger port after lifeboat in the morning, although the sea state was such as to make it impossible to make contact. After several aircraft flew over without spotting them, a low-flying one finally sighted the boat at noon on 9 February, and four hours later the occupants were rescued by the US destroyer *Roe* (*DD-418*), by which time one man had died of exposure and another nine needed hospitalisation for frostbite. Despite an intensive search, the other lifeboat was not found until eleven days later, when it was picked up 180 miles to the northeast in a badly damaged state with only three bodies aboard. Although *Ocean Venture* had been sunk in relatively busy coastal waters, a combination of the incidental destruction of two manned lifeboats, poor weather and the absence of any coherent search and rescue efforts (*Roe* had sailed from Norfolk eight hours after the merchant ship had been attacked but had not been notified of a distress signal which had been received on shore) had sent thirty-one men to their deaths.

Ocean Venus – 3 May 1942

Although she followed almost three months after *Ocean Venture* was lost, *Ocean Venus* was sailing under equally perilous operational conditions after she cleared the Panama Canal and began to make her way up the US east coast at the beginning of May 1942. She was carrying a mixed cargo, largely composed of lead, lumber and canned herrings loaded at New Westminster, British Columbia; Portland, Oregon; and Los Angeles, and was already sailing under her second master, Captain John Park, who had joined at New Westminster after the first appointee had fallen ill. At 0124hrs on 3 May, the ship was heading north in calm seas about twelve miles east-south east of Cape Canaveral, Florida, when her Third Officer (for some reason the author of her survivor's report) was awoken in his cabin by a 'sharp crack.' She too had fallen foul of a U-boat ace – in this case Kapitänleutnant Reinhard Suhren in *U 564*. Suhren was one of the most experienced and respected captains in the U-boat arm, having won the Knight's Cross as first watch officer of *U 48* (the highest scoring U-boat of the

Ocean Venus southbound in North American west coast waters in April 1942 at the beginning of a maiden voyage which would be brought to a premature end off the coast of Florida on 3 May by torpedoes from *U 564*. ***(Vancouver Maritime Museum)***

war) in 1940. He would sink just under 100,000 tons of Allied shipping in *U 564* and survive the war with the Knight's Cross with Oak Leaves and Crossed Swords.

The torpedo had hit *Ocean Venus* abreast the bulkhead between the boiler and engine rooms, flooding both places and killing five engineering staff, including those on watch below and several asleep in their quarters. The force of the explosion was such that the vessel made a complete 180-degree turn before losing way. Despite this, the ship was not sinking rapidly, and the 3in gun crew got off fifteen ineffectual rounds after sighting a conning tower, while the three wireless operators tried in vain to repair the damaged radio equipment. The survivors then successfully got away in the three remaining boats a short while before a second torpedo hit amidships at about 0135hrs (this time on the port side as the vessel had effectively reversed heading). As the boats lay off, the occupants then heard two sharp cracks, either bulkheads giving way or the ship's back breaking, before seeing the funnel collapse at 0230hrs and the ship finally jack-knifing and sinking at 0245hrs. Just over an hour after their ship had gone down, they retained a grandstand view when another merchant ship hove in sight and was then sunk by two separate torpedoes. The second vessel was the Dutch-flagged *Laertes,* operated by the Amsterdam-based subsidiary of Britain's Blue Funnel Line. It was reflective of the combat conditions still prevailing off the American eastern seaboard, that a second U-boat, *U 109*, under the command of yet another ace, in this case Kapitänleutnant Heinrich Bleichrodt (who by coincidence had won his Knight's Cross on *U 48* at the same time as Suhren) should strike in the same place, thousands of miles from base, within a few hours of its comrade.

While there were many similarities in the losses of *Ocean Venture* and *Ocean Venus*, not least the impunity with which their attackers operated in what should have been protected coastal waters, there were two critical differences. In the first instance, the *coup de grâce* was not administered to *Ocean Venus* until after the survivors had got safely away, and there were thus no secondary casualties. In the second, the sea state was calm and the weather mild. The motor lifeboat made it safely to shore under her own power. The remaining two boats, together with two from *Laertes*, were taken in tow by a motor fishing boat under the command of a US Navy ensign and landed at Canaveral Lighthouse at 1100hrs. While no further men had been killed after the initial explosion, W W Bewick, the author of the survivor's report, was no more impressed with defensive measures than the captain of *Ocean Venture* had been three months before. Disturbed both by the appearance of coloured lights on shore and the proximity in time and place of other losses, he complained: 'in view of the fact that six ships have been sunk in this vicinity in seven days, and that routeing officers had not altered the routes of ships leaving after such losses, I consider that operations off the Florida coast are rather sinister.'

North Atlantic Convoys

A total of fifty-six Oceans attempted to complete their delivery voyages to the UK in North Atlantic convoys, the only exceptions being the two vessels lost early off the US eastern seaboard and the last two vessels delivered, *Ocean Gypsy* and *Ocean Glory*, which sailed south for the Caribbean and thence to distant waters. Of these, fifty-four arrived safely and only two were lost. One ship, *Ocean Vagabond*, tried twice, turning back safely with torpedo damage on the first occasion, but being sunk on the second. On neither occasion was the vessel under escort when sunk. *Ocean Crusader* had lost contact with her convoy before she was sunk and may have turned back with engine or weather damage. *Ocean Vagabond* had also lost touch in bad weather but was attempting to complete her passage alone. Both ships went down in the North Atlantic winter, but there the similarity ends. All but one of the crew of *Ocean Vagabond* were rescued, while their compatriots on *Ocean Crusader* were all lost without trace.

The fact that fifty-four out of fifty-six vessels made safe passages across the North Atlantic in the worst year for Allied merchant ships is worthy of comment. As is clear from the overall profile of Ocean losses, there was heavy attrition in distant waters where vessels usually sailed alone. Most losses in the North Atlantic theatre itself were either stragglers or members of the relatively small number of convoys whose escorts were stretched beyond breaking point by a large wolfpack. The Atlantic was a big place in which to find a convoy, British convoy controllers had become accomplished at diverting their charges around U-boat concentrations, and U-boats had only a limited ability to redeploy on those occasions when their controllers at Lorient developed timely and accurate target information. Between the safe arrival of *Ocean Vanguard* and *Ocean Vigil* in HX 171 at the beginning of February 1942, and that of *Ocean Angel* in HX 218 in mid-December, U-boats sank only eight vessels while they were sailing in company and under escort in HX convoys. The only HX convoy to be savaged by U-boats during this period was HX 212, which lost six vessels, some of them stragglers, in late October. *Ocean Courier* was sailing in this convoy but escaped damage. The slower SC convoys were a completely different story, losing no fewer than forty-one vessels, but thirty-three of these went down in just three convoy battles, and most slow convoys also crossed unscathed. In any event, only two Oceans tried to complete their maiden voyages in SC convoys – *Ocean Stranger* in SC 103 in September/October 1942, and *Ocean Vagabond* in SC 115 in January 1943 – and, while the latter was lost, the attack took place after she had lost touch with her convoy.

Ocean Vagabond – 29 September 1942 & 10 January 1943

Ocean Vagabond, the penultimate California delivery, was unique in being torpedoed on each of two separate attempts to cross the Atlantic. After an abortive attempt to sail in HX 208, the vessel finally departed in HX 209 on 26 September 1942 with 9,470 tons of wheat and lumber under the command of Captain John Smith of the W G Runciman Shipping Company. Two days later, *Ocean Vagabond* developed serious engine trouble and on the following morning was ordered back to St John's, Newfoundland, with four other vessels. At 1730hrs a torpedo was sighted passing across the bows, and immediately afterwards a second struck the starboard side under the bridge at the after end of No 2 hold. Her assailant was *U 513*, on her maiden patrol under Korvettenkapitän Rolf Rüggeberg, during which she had already sunk two iron ore carriers in a daring attack on the anchorage at Wabana, Newfoundland.

The explosion destroyed all the fittings on the bridge and blew a 28ft by 15ft hole in the side of No 2 hold. The vessel listed some 35 degrees to starboard, submerging the deck rail, and although the master thought the lumber would keep the vessel afloat, the crew panicked, and he was forced to join them in the boats. The whole complement was safely picked up by a corvette which was now in attendance. After some four to five hours, the vessel righted herself and the master, together with the three deck officers, the four engineers, the carpenter and the bosun (the only volunteers), re-boarded. Although two tugs arrived at 0300hrs on 30 September and towed *Ocean Vagabond* into St John's, Captain Smith was convinced the vessel could have made the passage under her own steam.

Having unloaded some cargo, completed repairs, and then topped up her cargo with wood pulp from Botwood, *Ocean Vagabond* sailed from St. John's on 3 January 1943 and joined SC 115 at sea a day later. The weather was extremely stormy with heavy snow, and the visibility deteriorated to almost zero. By 0300hrs on the fifth, no other ships in the convoy could be seen. Concerned about the dangers of collision, Captain Smith reduced speed slightly for half an hour to drop behind the convoy. By daylight, the visibility had not improved and there were still no other ships in sight. With the compasses in error, the ship's exact position was unclear. The master held a conference with his officers and, having agreed that turning back would be just as dangerous as sailing on, decided to proceed eastwards via the pre-established stragglers' route.

Ocean Vagabond proceeded safely until the evening of 10 January, when at 2300hrs the ship was hit by a torpedo on the

Ocean Vagabond arriving at New York from the west coast on 12 September 1942 prior to the first of two failed attempts to reach Britain in convoy, one which would see her towed into St John's, Newfoundland, with torpedo damage inflicted by *U 513*.
(US Coast Guard/Roy Fenton collection)

starboard side in the way of No 2 hold, only slightly forward of the position of her previous hit in September. A large hole was blown in the hold, all the hatch covers blown off, and the bridge wrecked. The vessel took an immediate 15-degree list, and the master ordered the engine's stopped and the vessel abandoned. Both forward boats were wrecked, but the larger after boats were safely launched, the starboard one in water-logged condition. All the crew got away safely apart from Captain Smith, and James Wilson, the senior wireless officer, who remained behind to repair his equipment and to send a distress message.

About half an hour after the first strike, *Ocean Vagabond* was hit a second time, on this occasion on the port side amidships in No 3 hold. The explosion blew the master overboard and almost certainly killed the wireless officer. Captain Smith was picked up by the starboard boat, from which he observed the submarine surface and fire a third torpedo into his command. This again struck amidships on the port side, setting the vessel afire and causing her to sink soon after. James Wilson, however, had managed to send a distress signal before he was killed, and his sacrifice had not been in vain. About noon on 11 January the occupants of both boats were rescued by the British destroyer *Wayfarer*, which had picked up the cry for help while still several hundred miles away from the sinking and had found the survivors because of Wilson's distress broadcast.

Ocean Vagabond's assailant on this occasion had been Kapitänleutnant Siegfried Hesemann in *U 186*, another new boat on her first patrol. Like *U 513* (which would be sunk by aircraft off Brazil in July 1943), *U 186* would not enjoy a long career, and would be depth-charged to destruction with her entire crew northwest of the Azores on her next patrol.

Ocean Crusader – 26 November 1942

There is no survivor's report for *Ocean Crusader* as she, alone among her class, was sunk with all hands. The last Ocean delivered to attempt a maiden voyage across the Atlantic, she sailed from New York in HX 216 on 19 November 1942 for Avonmouth with almost 9,000 tons of general cargo. Poor conditions slowed the passage, and on the night of 25 November the ship parted company with the convoy, apparently due to stress of heavy weather. The only evidence of what happened to her comes from German sources. In the afternoon of 26 November, she was found by *U 262* in heavy fog about 330 miles northeast of St John's, Newfoundland, on a course which would suggest she was heading back to port. At 1657hrs two of a spread of three torpedoes hit the port side of *Ocean Crusader*, one forward and one amidships. The Germans reported that the ship stopped, fired two flares, and began to settle slowly by the bow. Heavy seas prevented Oberleutnant-zur-See Rudolf Heinz Franke from continuing the attack with gunfire. He had expended most of his other torpedoes in earlier attacks on ONS 144 (during which he had sunk the Norwegian corvette *Montbretia*), and he missed when he fired the last one aboard to hasten his victim's demise. Nonetheless, when *U 262* left the scene half an hour later, her victim's bow was well down and the rudder and screw out of the water. Although a distress signal was sent and picked up, no trace was ever found of Captain Ellis Parry of Dodd, Thomson & Co Ltd and his crew of forty-nine.

Ocean Crusader newly arrived at New York on 15 November 1942, less than two weeks before she was torpedoed and sunk with all hands by *U 262* after losing touch with her convoy in heavy North Atlantic weather. *(US Coast Guard/John & Marion Clarkson collection)*

Ocean Voice at anchor on the Clyde in May 1942, after her anti-aircraft armament had been upgraded for Russian convoy duties but before she had loaded her cargo of military equipment and stores.
(Roy Fenton collection)

The Arctic Convoys

Three vessels were committed to the north Russia convoy programme immediately after their arrival in the UK, availability in each case being delayed by repairs, the installation of an upgraded anti-aircraft weapons suite, and the assembly of complex cargoes of weapons, vehicles, and military stores. *Ocean Voice*, which had arrived at Glasgow from HX 175 on 26 February, would sail from Reykjavik on 21 May as commodore ship of PQ 16. *Ocean Freedom*, which had arrived in the Mersey in HX 185 on 27 April before proceeding up the Manchester Ship Canal to unload, would leave Iceland in PQ 17 on 27 June. *Ocean Faith* followed the same initial path as her Portland sister, moving up to Manchester to unload after reaching the Mersey in HX 191 on 6 June, but made a round trip to Reykjavik in July before returning to sail with PQ 18 on 2 September. These were to be the three most hotly contested convoys of the campaign. Despite a heavy escort, PQ 16 lost seven merchantmen, while PQ 18, with an even more formidable warship presence, lost eleven. In between, the unfortunate PQ 17 lost twenty-four – twenty-one of them after an ill-considered decision to scatter left individual vessels at the mercy of marauding bombers and submarines. The three Oceans survived this carnage, although *Ocean Voice* was damaged by air attack. Both she and *Ocean Freedom*, however, were lost subsequently – the first on her homeward passage in QP 14, and the second in port in Russia after completing her first round trip, also in QP 14, and making a second outwards voyage in JW 53.

Ocean Voice – 27 May 1942 & 22 September 1942

Ocean Voice sailed from the Clyde for Loch Ewe and Reykjavik on 5 May. There she became the commodore ship for PQ 16, easily the largest convoy yet despatched to north Russia with thirty-six merchant ships. The convoy sailed on 21 May, losing one ship to a U-boat on 26 May. On the following day, PQ 16 came under the most sustained air assault yet encountered on the route, with over 100 aircraft attacks being logged, mostly by Ju-88 bombers of Kampfgeschwader 30. Six merchant ships were sunk and four damaged. One of the latter was *Ocean Voice*, which suffered a bomb hit forward in an early evening attack by six Ju 88s. The best available record of what ensued comes from Commander Richard Onslow, the senior officer of the escort in the Tribal class destroyer *Ashanti*: 'When the smoke cleared away, I observed that her side plating abreast No 1 hold was ripped away to within 2ft of the water line leaving a gaping hole about 20ft by 10ft. Her foretopmast was over the side and her bridge severely damaged, and she was on fire. I had little hopes of her survival, but this gallant ship maintained her station, fought her fire and with God's help arrived at her destination. Had any sea arisen No 1 hold would have filled and there would have been little hope of saving the bulkhead to No 2 hold.' Commodore N H Gale, RNR was awarded the DSO, the master the DSC, two embarked naval personnel the DSM, the second officer the MBE, and two crewmen the BEM.

Having repaired the bomb damage suffered in PQ 16, *Ocean Voice,* under the command of Captain Harold Kay (like the master of *Ocean Venture*, a Larrinaga man), sailed from Archangel on 13 September 1942 as commodore ship for Convoy QP 14. Cargoes were scarce for homebound vessels, and she was only partially loaded with 1,121 tons of sulphite pulp and 858 standards of timber. In addition to her own crew of forty-eight and ten gunners, she also carried Commodore Dowding and his staff of five, nine survivors from vessels sunk in PQ 17, and no less than twenty Russian passengers, 'including men, women and children', making a total of ninety-eight.

to be responsible for a series of atrocities, but the instruction to kill survivors had not yet been issued, and *I-29* did not approach, much less molest the two lifeboats. The boats, however, were some distance from shore, and the occupants suffered an ordeal by heat and thirst before they were rescued. The men in the master's boat were picked up on the night of 19 September by the British steamer *City of Ripon* and landed at Aden. The other boat did eventually reach shore, but the occupants were not picked up from an isolated beach until 28 September, by which time they were in a very weak condition.

Ocean Vintage – 22 October 1942

Just over a month after the loss of *Ocean Honour*, the Japanese submarine arm claimed one of her west coast-built sisters, again in the northwest reaches of the Arabian Sea. *I-27* was on her fourth war patrol, having left Penang for the Gulf of Oman on 4 October. On the eighteenth of the month, she had hit *Empire Bowman* with two torpedoes amidships, but both had been duds. Her prey escaped, but four days later, on 22 October, *Ocean Vintage* was not so lucky. Unfortunately, there is no extant survivor's report, so we know only the basic details of the sinking.

Having arrived at Middlesbrough on 26 June at the end of her delivery passage in HX 193, *Ocean Vintage* had successfully re-crossed the Atlantic in ON 111 in July, before sailing from New York on a long voyage for Abadan and Bandar Shapur via Key West, Trinidad and Durban with 9,300 tons of general cargo. She was approaching her destination when I-27 hit her with one torpedo near Masirah Island in the Gulf of Oman. All forty-four crew and six gunners got away safely in the boats before their ship went under, and in this case, rescue was swift, a Royal Air Force launch towing the lifeboats to Ras al Hadd harbour in Oman.

Ocean Vintage anchored at New York on 29 May 1942 with a full deck cargo of aircraft in crates prior to sailing for Halifax to join the UK-bound convoy HX 193. *(US Coast Guard/World Ship Society Ltd)*

Trinidad Waters

Port of Spain in Trinidad was a clearing and bunkering port for vessels crossing the South Atlantic on voyages between South Africa or the Gold Coast and North America, and also a loading terminal for locally mined bauxite. The waters around the island were thus a vulnerable 'choke-point' which began to attract long-range U-boats in the second half of 1942. At this time, local escort forces and patrol aircraft were still in short supply and the introduction of a comprehensive coastal feeder convoy system remained a slow process. As we have seen, many of the Oceans passed through the area while returning from the Middle East and South Africa for American east coast ports. Two of these vessels would be lost in just under two months east of Trinidad. Thankfully, there were two strong positives which impacted on the survival of crews in these waters. The first was that the weather and sea conditions were generally benign. The second was that coastal waters, while not yet properly patrolled, were nonetheless relatively busy and rescue was likely to be near at hand.

Ocean Vanguard – 12 September 1942

The first of her class to enter service, *Ocean Vanguard* had an active, but brief, war under the command of Captain Wilfred Brett of W H Seager & Co. Having survived a collision with the British motor ship *Tolten* in HX 168 and crossed the Atlantic

The first vessel of her class to complete a transatlantic roundtrip, *Ocean Vanguard* arrives in ballast at New York on 8 March 1942 to load a military cargo for the Middle East.
(US Coast Guard/John & Marion Clarkson collection)

at her second attempt in HX 171, she unloaded at Cardiff in February 1942. She subsequently re-crossed the North Atlantic in ON 69, leaving Liverpool on 20 February and arriving at New York on 8 March. *Ocean Vanguard* then sailed south at the end of the month on a long passage to South Africa. After spending all but the last day of May at Table Bay and Durban, she proceeded north to Port Sudan and Aden before arriving at Suez. From there she passed through the Suez Canal to Port Said, where she would have unloaded supplies for the war in the Western Desert. By 8 July, she was back at Suez, and after calls at Aden and Lourenço Marques, she cleared Cape Town on 19 August on an independent voyage for Trinidad and New York in ballast. The trip was uneventful until the evening of 12 September when the ship was torpedoed about 45 miles east of Galera Point, Trinidad.

The torpedo struck *Ocean Vanguard* on the starboard side between the boiler and engine rooms. The engine room rapidly filled to the cylinder heads, and the fourth engineer and a fireman were either killed in the explosion or trapped and drowned. Three boats got away safely with most of the crew, except the officers, who were still aboard when a second torpedo struck the ship, this time in the way of No 4 hold. Most of the officers now got away safely in the remaining boat, but *Ocean Vanguard* was sinking rapidly, and the master and senior wireless operator were forced to jump when she settled. She ultimately sank stern-first on an even keel within ten minutes of the first explosion. Unfortunately, the second torpedo hit capsized one lifeboat, drowning those aboard. The rest of the crew, who were in the other boats or were picked up by them from rafts, survived the night, the weather being mild, and had begun to sail for Trinidad with every prospect of a short, safe passage when they were all discovered and picked up by the Norwegian motor ship *Braga* which landed them at Port of Spain the same afternoon. A total of forty men had survived the sinking, but eleven had been lost, including the fourth engineer and the bosun. It was the third time that Captain Brett had survived the sinking of his ship, having, as noted already, previously lost *Beatus* in 1940 and *Savus* in 1941.

Ocean Vanguard had succumbed to yet another Kriegsmarine U-boat ace, on this occasion Kapitänleutnant Werner Henke of *U 515*. Henke was in the process of launching his career in command in spectacular fashion, *Ocean Vanguard* being the third of nine ships he would sink between 12 and 23 September. He would continue in this fashion for the next year and a half, winning the Knight's Cross at the end of 1942 and adding the Oak Leaves in July 1943. By the end of that year, he had sunk twenty-five ships totalling over 150,000 tons, making him the undoubted star of the last successful stage of the German submarine war.

Ocean Justice – 6 November 1942

Ocean Justice enjoyed an even briefer career than her sister, lasting only seven months after completion. Commanded by Captain William Venables of the Hain Steamship Co, she crossed the Atlantic to Cardiff in May 1942 in HX 188 and then departed Liverpool with a cargo of government stores on 11 June in OS 31 for Freetown, West Africa. From there she sailed south as an independent to Table Bay and Durban, before making a triangular Indian Ocean voyage to Karachi, Bombay and back to Durban. On 6 October, she left Durban to make a solo passage to Trinidad and then on to New York, carrying 600 tons of manganese ore, presumably with additional water ballast. A week later, off Cape Agulhas, she picked up two British gunners from a raft, survivors of the sinking of the Belgian steamer *Belgian Fighter* by *U 68* on 9 October. The crossing of the South Atlantic was uneventful, although the receipt of no fewer than four diversion signals from the Admiralty gave an indication that the ship might be sailing into danger. This was indeed the case, and in the early evening of 6 November, when *Ocean Justice* was zigzagging into Trinidad waters in calm weather conditions, she was struck simultaneously by two torpedoes on the starboard side.

The first torpedo hit *Ocean Justice*'s forepeak, bursting the cofferdam and No 1 bulkhead, and blowing the hatches off No 1 hold. The second hit under the bridge in the way of No 2 hold, blowing its hatches onto the bridge. Within seconds, the entire forward part of the ship was submerged, and the propeller was out of the water. The two forward boats went under before they could be launched, but the larger boats mounted further aft were safely lowered by what was clearly a disciplined and well-trained crew. Although the ship sank completely within fifteen minutes, all forty-five crew, nine gunners and two passengers got away at the cost of only two minor injuries. The submarine surfaced and cruised around the scene for some time, alarming the master, who had more reason than most for not wishing to be taken prisoner. Venables had been chief officer of Hain's *Trevanion* when she was sunk by the German pocket battleship *Admiral Graf Spee* in October 1939 and had been a prisoner aboard the pocket battleship until released at Montevideo after the Battle of the River Plate. He was spared any sort of repeat when the submarine disappeared into the night. Although *Ocean Justice* had not been able to send a distress signal, the survivors were all safely on land within twenty-four hours of her sinking. The master's lifeboat was motorised and completed the 75-mile trip to Trinidad by the morning of 7 November. The chief officer's boat was sighted by an aircraft on the same morning, and its occupants safely rescued by a motor launch.

In contrast to Henke and *U 515*, neither Oberleutnant-zur-See Peter Zschech nor *U 505* were to have successful careers after sinking *Ocean Justice*. Zschech would only sink the one ship and lost his life in tragic circumstances when he apparently suffered a nervous breakdown during a heavy depth-charge attack in October 1943 and committed suicide with his service pistol in the control room of the boat. Although *U 505* had sunk seven ships under another commander before Zschech, his successor achieved nothing. *U 505* herself was captured after an engagement with a US hunter-killer group off French West Africa on 4 June 1944. Taken back to the United States, she was eventually gifted to the Chicago Museum of Science & Industry, where she is preserved to this day.

West African Waters

Vessels sailing from the UK for West Africa or South Africa and the Middle East were escorted in OS convoys to the latitude of the Canaries. There the convoys were dispersed, ships making either short, escorted passages to West African ports or much longer independent ones to Table Bay. Most Oceans made the latter journey in 1942 and, given the almost constant presence of U-boats in the waters immediately to the south of the dispersal point, it is perhaps not surprising that there was one fatal encounter.

West Africa itself was the source of a large volume of raw material, most notably metal ores, and vegetable oils. Vessels bound homewards for the UK would normally sail in SL convoys from Freetown. Ships bound for the United States, in contrast, would make independent passages across the central Atlantic to Trinidad to pick up coastal convoys for east coast American ports. The ocean passage was usually relatively safe, although there was still a chance of encountering the enemy at either end of the route. One ship would be lost to a submarine in September 1942 and another in 1943, a third vessel later surviving torpedo damage while in convoy.

Ocean Might – 2 September 1942

There is no survivor's report covering the loss of *Ocean Might*, but other sources provide a fair amount of information. The vessel had sailed from the Mersey for South Africa and the Middle East on 9 August with a cargo of guns, ammunition, and other military stores under the command of Captain William Park of Maclay & McIntyre Ltd. After dispersing from OS 37 she was southwest of Takoradi on the Gold Coast when sighted by *U 109* on the evening of 1 September. The submarine worked into a favourable position to attack, but a three-torpedo spread missed due to the target zigzagging away, as did a fourth torpedo shortly afterwards. *U 109* then surfaced and had worked into a favourable position for another attack just before midnight. A fifth torpedo missed, but a sixth did not. The crew of *Ocean Might* would have been safely away in the lifeboats before a seventh torpedo finished the vessel off. Four men were lost, but the remaining fifty members of the crew made their way safely ashore by sail and oar, landing at Ningo, 35 miles east of Accra. It was the second sinking for both Captain Park and Chief Officer John Cameron, and the latter would survive his third sinking after his promotion to master, when his new command, Maclay & McIntyre's *Janeta,* was sunk in the middle of the South Atlantic on 1 May 1944 by *U 181*. Cameron again reached shore in a ship's boat, on this occasion reaching Brazil after an epic seventeen-day journey.

U 109 was under the command of Kapitänleutnant Heinrich Bleichrodt. A veteran of the U-boat campaign, who had won the Knight's Cross in 1940 as commander of *U 48* in company with First Watch Officer Reinhard Suhren, who had sunk *Ocean Venus* in May 1942. Bleichrodt was approaching breaking point, burnt out by the strain of two years of command, but would sink two further ships in the weeks following his sinking of *Ocean Might* to bring his score to twenty-five vessels of 150,000 tons. Awarded the Oak Leaves to his Knight's Cross on his return from patrol, he would make one more sortie before being posted to training duties, where he would survive the war.

Ocean Courage – 15 January 1943

While weather, distance from land and proximity of rescue vessels were frequently the difference between life and death for the crews of torpedoed vessels, so too were the cargoes they carried. At one end of the safety spectrum, cargoes of lumber and wood products could keep a vessel afloat for some time (and on occasions allow salvage despite multiple hits). At the other, cargoes of metal concentrates and ores, as well as of steel and scrap iron, could be as dangerous as explosives. A ship torpedoed while carrying a cargo like iron ore had little reserve buoyancy once her hull was breached and could sink before the crew had any chance to get up from below, let alone lower the lifeboats. *Ocean Courage*, the last of her class to succumb to submarine attack in distant waters, suffered the highest number of casualties, precisely because of the cargo she was carrying.

Ocean Courage sailed from Freetown on 12 January 1943 under the command of Captain Thomas Kemp of the Hain Steamship Co, carrying a cargo of 8,956 tons of iron concentrates on an independent cross-ocean passage to Trinidad. Such a cargo would not normally have been taken on such a crossing, but the normal northbound SL convoys had been suspended in the run-up to the invasion of French North Africa, and UK-bound cargoes were still being diverted to a long, three-legged route, westwards to Trinidad, north to Halifax and then east to their destination. At 0215hrs on the night of 15 January, about 200 miles south of the Cape Verde Islands, *Ocean Courage* became an indirect victim of Operation Torch when she was hit by a torpedo on the port side under the bridge in the way of the after bulkhead of No 2 hold. The second officer, Robert Smith, had the watch and was knocked off his feet by the force of the explosion.

Ocean Courage silhouetted against a late afternoon sky at New York on 16 August 1942 after crossing the Atlantic in ballast from Liverpool in ON 117 five months before her loss with heavy casualties south of the Cape Verde Islands to a *U 182* torpedo.
(US Coast Guard/John & Marion Clarkson collection)

Recovering, he attempted to launch a lifeboat with the aid of a deckhand, failed, and then rushed to the starboard after life raft. By this time, the ship's forepart was already under water, and before he could knock the slip from the raft, *Ocean Courage* plunged under, at his estimation, only one-and-a-half minutes after being torpedoed.

Luckily, the raft broke free, and having been under water for what seemed an age, Smith surfaced and spotted it. He managed to climb aboard and found five fellow survivors aboard. There appeared to be other men in the water with red survival lights showing, but none were close enough to rescue in the dark. At daybreak, another raft was sighted two miles away, and what looked to be a hatch cover somewhat closer, each carrying two men. Neither, however, could be reached as they were each to windward, and both had disappeared by the end of the day. An empty raft was successfully paddled to and the two were roped together, each providing a home for three men with enough canvas sleeping bags for all. While the upcoming days were temperate, the nights were very cold, and the sleeping bags helped keep the men warm.

Although Smith's party was well equipped considering the manner of their ship's loss, all other circumstances were against them. There had been no time to send a distress signal, they were far from land, outside any major shipping lane, and confined to an unweatherly craft that could make little headway to the safety of West Africa. Luckily, they had one large smoke float, and when a vessel did come into sight on 21 January, they were able to attract its attention. Their rescuer was the British motor ship *Silverwalnut* on its way to Norfolk, Virginia. Smith, the third officer, one apprentice, two gunners and the mess room boy would remain aboard her for her passage home and arrived back in the UK on 23 February, Smith later being awarded a richly deserved MBE. They were the only survivors. No sign was ever found of the rest of the crew, a total of fifty-two men having lost their lives.

Ocean Courage's assailant had been *U 182*, a new submarine on her way to operate off South Africa under the command of Kapitänleutnant Nicolai Clausen. Yet again, an Ocean had fallen foul of a Knight's Cross-winning U-boat ace. Clausen, however, was on his last patrol. Having sunk another four vessels, *U 182* was lost on her return voyage. She was almost certainly the submarine depth charged by a USAAF. B-24 Liberator North West of Madeira on 15 May 1943, and if not sunk in this attack was finished off by the US destroyer *MacKenzie (DD-614)* a day later.

Ocean Viceroy – 29 March 1943

Given the rapid sinking of the iron ore-laden *Ocean Courage* and the heavy casualties it caused, it is interesting that a second vessel with the same cargo survived a torpedo hit two-and-a-half months later. Like some of her sisters, *Ocean Viceroy* had been re-directed from Gibraltar to Pepel in West Africa after completing a supply run to the North African combat zone. Having loaded 8,650 tons of iron ore, she sailed from Freetown for Loch Ewe on 12 March 1943 under the command of Captain N MacFadyen of Patrick Henderson & Co. Her convoy, SL 126, was the first to depart Freetown for the UK after the winter suspension to take account of Operation Torch. The convoy ran into extremely bad weather on 16 March, which did not begin to moderate for almost a week. As a result, by the evening of 29 March the ships were still only about 425 miles northwest of Cape Finisterre, and high-level enemy reconnaissance aircraft had been sighted on each of the last three days. By this stage of the war, U-boat attacks were relatively rare this close to home waters, but the convoy was now attacked in succession by two enemy submarines.

Ocean Viceroy, steaming at the head of the port column in position 11, was the first ship to be hit. A torpedo which had been fired from off the port bow struck the ship at an angle just abaft No 5 bulkhead. The explosion was extraordinarily violent, lifting the after end of the vessel completely out of the water and causing the bows to submerge and fill up. The stern then slammed back down, causing widespread flooding aft. Plunged into darkness and up to their waists in water, the crew aft began to panic and rush the after lifeboats on the boat deck. Before an officer could intervene, one had been lowered, while a second had capsized after the falls had been cut prematurely. A total of twenty-three men abandoned the ship, of whom eighteen were quickly picked up by an escorting corvette, the remaining five being lost. A third lifeboat appears to have been destroyed or lost in the confusion, but the master had time to intervene and prevent the lowering of the last remaining boat. In the meantime, *Ocean Viceroy*'s assailant, *U 662*, had also torpedoed the two vessels immediately to starboard, while *U 404*, operating on the starboard side of the convoy, would shortly torpedo two more. All four of the other ships torpedoed, *Empire Whale*, *Empire Bowman*, *Nagara*, and *Umaria*, were lost, and although there were only four casualties in the last three vessels combined, *Empire Whale*, loaded with iron ore, sank very quickly leaving only ten survivors from her crew of fifty-seven men.

Ocean Viceroy, seen here alongside in a British port late in the war, survived serious torpedo damage from *U 662* on 29 March 1943 while homebound in convoy from West Africa, her master performing a consummate display of seamanship to bring her safely into port.
(National Maritime Museum)

Captain MacFadyen did not think that his ship was sinking, but, given the threat of a second torpedo, and the chance that her cargo of iron ore could send her quickly to the bottom without warning, he and his officers displayed tremendous courage and cool headedness in striving to save their ship. The main steam pipe had broken, and the engine room was full of steam, but the engineers went below wrapped in coats and blankets, managed to shut off the steam, and reported back that the engine room itself was dry and undamaged. Investigation by the deck officers revealed that No 5 bulkhead was buckled and pushed forward but was not leaking. They also went down the tunnel escape to discover that half the stern gland had been blown away and the tunnel itself was flooding rapidly, but the Master later reported that he 'was not unduly concerned about this as the watertight door was shut and there was no danger of the engine room flooding.' The steering gear, however, was 'crumpled up like a concertina' and the steering engine had fallen onto the quadrant. The chief and second officers managed to clear this with the help of the poop winch, and then to rig relieving tackles for steering the ship. At daylight, the chief officer also climbed over the quarter on a ladder to inspect the external damage, discovering that three blades of the propeller were damaged, and the rudder and sole plate twisted to port. Again, in Captain MacFadyen's own words, 'I thought the matter over and finally decided I could reach the United Kingdom if I was lucky.'

Ocean Viceroy began her tortuous voyage home to safety at 0815hrs on 30 March. The weather had once again deteriorated, and, facing heavy seas and swells, it proved difficult to bring the ship round on course. Even when this was achieved, the ship could make only 4.5–5kts with her head swinging about six points each way. After three days, she reached the south coast of Ireland, but was forced to sail up the west side of the country as she could not be brought round to steer for the relative safety of the Irish Sea. Finally, at 0400hrs on 3 April, when the ship was forty miles off Eagle Island, the master felt he could break radio silence to ask for a tug. One arrived in the late afternoon, and *Ocean Viceroy* was brought safely into Belfast. Captain MacFadyen's laconic comment on the voyage home was simply that 'from the time I was torpedoed until the time I contacted the tug off Belfast I did not see one ship or aircraft. I should have felt a lot happier if I had only sighted one British patrol plane or some surface craft.' Not surprisingly, he was fulsome in his praise of the ship itself: 'this ship was one of the new American welded ships and considering what she went through it speaks very highly for the new type of welded construction. She stood up to the explosion very well and ploughed her way through very heavy seas, although badly damaged with a large cargo of iron ore. If this ship had not been welded, I think she would have leaked aft and flooded No.5 hold when I should not have been able to bring her home.' The real star was MacFadyen himself, who was deservedly awarded an OBE and the Lloyd's War Medal.

The Mediterranean (1) – The North African Campaign

The Mediterranean theatre saw the heaviest concentration of Oceans of the war. As we have seen, thirteen were deployed in the initial North African invasion convoys in November 1942, and many more vessels also sailed in subsequent supply convoys, supporting the war against Axis forces in Tunisia from the UK, and in Libya from Alexandria. There was then a significant build-up of ships, men, and material in the eastern Mediterranean to support the invasion of Sicily in July 1943 when twelve Oceans were involved in the original invasion convoys. In the first campaign, Vichy French resistance ended after the first few days, but Axis forces deployed rapidly to Tunisia where fierce fighting continued through the winter months. Even after the Axis surrender in North Africa in May 1943, the invasion first of Sicily and then of the Italian mainland also encountered stubborn defence. Although the Allies built up an ever-increasing material superiority, the central Mediterranean remained a dangerous place until 1944. No fewer than seven Oceans were lost in the Mediterranean campaign and two others damaged. By this time of the war, North American shipbuilding was getting into full swing and Allied tonnage shortages were gradually becoming a thing of the past. In addition, ship repair facilities in the theatre were limited, and most captured ports were heavily damaged and clogged with sunken wrecks. Although at least three of the lost vessels might have been salvaged, none were – at least during the war.

Ocean Pilgrim – 20 November 1942

Although *Ocean Pilgrim* was attacked in the Atlantic, west of Gibraltar, she was sailing in KMS 3, the first large support convoy to sail for the Algerian beachheads. Under the command of Captain A Phillips of the Dene Shipping Co, the vessel had been ordered to stream her AND nets on 18 November. On the morning of 20 November, he was instructed to move across from his steaming position in the middle of the convoy to take up a new post in the starboard wing column, in line with a general order for net-equipped vessels to move to the flanks. *Ocean Pilgrim* had moved ahead of the convoy and was steaming across its head to take up her new position when *U 263* attacked. Two ships, the British steamship *Grangepark* and the Norwegian motor vessel *Prins Harald*, were hit immediately (both would sink later), but Captain Phillips had time to alter course to port before another torpedo detonated in his starboard protective nets abreast the engine room.

The explosion itself was described as 'terrific', but because of the net it took place a considerable distance from the ship. There was no serious internal structural damage, while externally there were only some minor indentations in the shell plating. *Ocean Pilgrim* remained with the convoy and arrived at Algiers without further hindrance. She was even able to re-rig the remnants of her starboard nets while underway to cover the boiler and engine rooms. Not surprisingly, Captain Phillips was numbered among the supporters of welded construction, stating 'I consider we must thank the Americans for the idea of welding, because I am sure if she had been a riveted ship, the rivets would not have held.'

Ocean Pilgrim at anchor in UK waters with the booms for the AND nets, which would save her from probable loss by a torpedo from *U 263* on 20 November 1942 while she was on her way to the beachhead at Algiers in the first major British support convoy for Operation Torch, showing clearly in silhouette. *(John & Marion Clarkson collection)*

Ocean Vanquisher at New York on 8 September 1942 with a full deck cargo of crated aircraft at the beginning of a war career that would be brought to an early end by an Italian frogman attack at Algiers three months later.
(US Coast Guard/Mariners' Museum & Park)

Ocean Vanquisher – 12 December 1942

Although two crewmen from *Ocean Vista* had been killed in an air raid on Bougie, Algeria, on 21 November, the first Ocean lost in the Mediterranean was a victim of one of the theatre's more unusual weapons systems. *Ocean Vanquisher*, commanded by Captain William Fitzgerald of Hogarth & Sons, had arrived in Algiers Bay from the Clyde in KMS 4 with a cargo of military stores and coal on the afternoon of 10 December 1942. No attention was received from the harbour authorities until the following morning, when the vessel was instructed to move closer inshore to an established anchorage. The master was also instructed to have steam raised at 1400hrs on 12 December for an entry into the harbour itself. At 0555hrs on that morning, however, the vessel was rocked by an explosion amidships which threw up a large column of water on the starboard side. The stokehold and engine room flooded, the latter to the height of the cylinder tops within five minutes. No 3 top and 'tween deck hatches were blown off, and the lower hold also began flooding. The second engineer and a fireman were killed by the explosion while on duty below, and two other crew members would subsequently be taken to the hospital with burns. The crew were ordered into the lifeboats, all four of which remained alongside. When it was seen that the ship was not sinking rapidly, the Master ordered the crew back aboard, but the presence of explosives and ammunition in No 2 hold meant that only one gunner and one seaman were prepared to accompany the officers back aboard.

In the mid-morning tugs came out from Algiers, and by noon *Ocean Vanquisher* had been towed into the harbour. Harbour tugs then attempted to move the vessel alongside, but due to her increased draft she grounded some thirty feet from the quay. Inspection of damage revealed a 28ft-by-23ft-wide hole in the port side in the way of the cross bunker stretching from the bilge keel to the centre line keel and extending from bulkhead to bulkhead. There were extensive hull and deck bulges and fractures around the site of the explosion, the bunker 'tween decks being buckled and fractured from starboard to port. The vessel was taken over by the naval authorities, who discharged the cargo to re-float the ship. *Ocean Vanquisher*, however, was too heavily damaged amidships to permit local repair and the vessel was eventually left beached. She was written off as a loss, and her register closed in February 1943.

Captain Fitzgerald's report assumed that *Ocean Vanquisher* had fallen victim to a torpedo, but this was not the case. While Italy's Regia Marina has not generally been favourably treated by historians of the Second World War, there is no doubt that its special attack units, particularly those which operated underwater, were brave, skilful, and effective. On the night of 11/12 December, frogmen from the submarine *Ambra* succeeded in attaching hollow charges to five merchant vessels in the Bay of Algiers. Four of these ships, including *Ocean Vanquisher*, were badly damaged by the subsequent explosions, the smallest victim, the Norwegian steamer *Berto*, sinking, and the British steamers *Empire Centaur* and *Harmattan* being beached but subsequently returned to service after major repairs.

Ocean Rider – 21 January 1943

Ocean Rider, under the command of Captain W S Keay of the Larrinaga Steamship Co, sailed from the Clyde on 6 January with a cargo of 4,000 tons of military stores in the invasion follow-up convoy KMS 7. In the early morning of 21 January, the convoy was some four-and-a-half miles west of Cape Caxine, Algeria, when it came under sustained attack by German and Italian torpedo bombers. *Ocean*

mainland as supply centres for the military campaigns in the theatre. One of the key aspects of this process was port clearance. Every harbour of any significance was at least partially blocked by wrecked shipping, some dating back to the early years of the Mediterranean campaign, but most from the period after November 1942, when Allied airpower systematically destroyed Axis port facilities and the vessels making use of them.

Seven Oceans had been lost in the Mediterranean. Of these, three were not candidates for salvage. *Ocean Hunter* had been torpedoed and sunk in deep water at sea, while *Ocean Voyager* and *Ocean Peace* had been destroyed by explosions which had left little behind but scrap. The preliminary salvage assessment of *Ocean Voyager* stated that she had been reduced to 'tangled metal' and that salvage was necessary only in as much as required for port clearance. While *Ocean Peace* had not been so comprehensively destroyed, her wreck was submerged in open water off Avola, four miles east of Syracuse, and there was no salvage imperative.

The remaining four were all potential candidates for salvage. *Ocean Vanquisher* was in Algiers harbour, where she had been beached after an Italian limpet mine had broken her back in December 1942. *Ocean Seaman* had been beached near the entrance to the same port after being torpedoed by a U-boat. *Ocean Viking* had been scuttled as a blockship to reinforce a breakwater at Bari, there being little short-term imperative to repair her mine damage. Finally, *Ocean Virtue* had been sunk in shallow water off Augusta, Sicily, to prevent her from blowing up after catching fire due to bomb damage.

One partial piece of salvage had been accomplished before a systematic programme of theatre-wide work was begun in 1944. *Ocean Virtue* had been raised at the end of September 1943 and patched up sufficiently to be towed to Catania the following April. Her amidships accommodation was burnt out, her decks buckled, and her shell plating badly holed in the way of No 1 hold, while there were many minor holes elsewhere in the forward part of the hull. With no immediate prospect of repair, she had been placed in service as a coal hulk and remained afloat in unrepaired condition after the war ended.

While *Ocean Virtue* had received early partial salvage, *Ocean Seaman* was rapidly eliminated as a candidate for similar treatment. Having been beached in an exposed location outside Algiers harbour, she had been stripped of all her deck gear, and had subsequently broken in two around the torpedo-wrecked engine room. The initial salvor's assessment was that the two halves could be re-floated, but it would be necessary to allow for the replacement of 60ft of the hull around the engine room and the installation of completely new machinery and equipment. There was no port clearance imperative and, with the hull continuing to deteriorate, it was ultimately decided to sell her for scrap where she lay. Little account was taken of requests to remove the wreck from the French port authorities, and negotiations to sell the wreck to a Gibraltar breaker did not begin until 1946.

The other salvage candidates each presented a different challenge. *Ocean Virtue* was in many ways the most straightforward as she had already been re-floated and moved to port. *Ocean Viking* was resting on the bottom with her hull partially above water as part of a harbour breakwater, and although access to her was complicated by the proximity of other blockships, re-floating itself was only a matter of sealing mine damage to one hold and pumping. Finally, *Ocean Vanquisher* was in port, but her hull was fractured over the top from bilge keel to bilge keel in the way of the forward end of the stokehold, and she had not been re-floated.

Starting to bring the first two vessels back to life awaited only the end of hostilities and the repair and re-opening of Italian shipyards. With temporary repairs completed at Catania, *Ocean Virtue* was taken north to Genoa for permanent repairs in March 1946. Progress with *Ocean Viking* was dependent on Italian salvage work on other blockships in the Bari breakwater. She was finally sold to an Italian salvage firm in September, to be raised and towed to Palermo for repair in the following spring. The reclamation of *Ocean Vanquisher*, a ship considered by J R Smith, director of merchant ship repairs for the western Mediterranean, to be 'one of the best salvage prospects in the area', proved a more attenuated process.

The hulk of *Ocean Vanquisher* had been requisitioned by the Recovery Department of the Ministry of War Transport for use as a store for recovered equipment and salvage material. The ship was upright on the bottom, adjacent to a quay and forming an extension thereto. The lower holds and compartments were flooded but the 'tween deck spaces and deck accommodation had been converted by the Recovery Department to meet their requirements. Following damage, she had been temporarily stiffened, and then sunk in the harbour by flooding all holds, a process which broke away the stiffening. The engine room was intact but flooded, and accommodation and most of the portable gear had been removed. Recovery would require first a renewal of the temporary stiffening, followed by re-floating and a tow to a repair port. There it would first be necessary to renew 35ft of hull structure, together with the amidships superstructure, and then to undertake a complete overhaul of machinery and re-equipment of vessel throughout. Pumping began in mid-May 1945, but at the end of the year, the re-floated vessel was still at Algiers awaiting a tow to an Italian shipyard. She finally arrived at Palermo on 6 February 1946, where it was estimated that repairs would cost £100,000 and take six months. It was decided to go ahead with the work, not least because what were termed 'political considerations' made it expedient to provide local employment.

No thought appears to have been given to bringing the repaired vessels back to the UK for sale to British owners. There was, in any event, an extremely strong market for modern tonnage in Italy. The Italian merchant marine had been all but wiped out during the war; the pre-war fleet of 3,322,000 tons had shrunk by just over 90 per cent to only 321,000 tons. Long-established shipping firms were desperate for tonnage with which to rebuild their businesses. In addition, there were strong policy reasons for helping with the restoration of the Italian economy, of which shipping was a significant part. Following the overthrow of the Fascist regime in September 1943, Italy had re-entered the war on the Allied side. Although her armed forces were dismembered, she was otherwise treated as a friendly power in need of assistance with reconstruction, help with economic recovery being judged particularly vital because of fears that unrest might push the country into the arms of communism. The sale of the three born-again Oceans was one small part of this process.

Two ships were sold to the same owner, both *Ocean Vanquisher* and *Ocean Viking* going to Societa Ligure di Armamento of Genoa to be renamed *Nereo* and *Alceo*, respectively, after rebuilding by Cantieri Navali Riuniti at Palermo. Both ships appear to have been sound investments, each giving their owner a decade and a half of service before sale in 1963–4. Finally, *Ocean Virtue* was sold to Ditta Giacomo Costa fu Andrea, also of Genoa, and renamed *Andrea C.* Before the war, the Costa family had owned a fleet of small cargo vessels employed mainly in the edible oils trade in the

Ocean Viking in dry dock at Palermo in 1947 after salvage, undergoing repair and reconditioning for Italian commercial service as *Alceo*. *(Archivi C N R Palermo)*

Alceo ready to leave Vancouver with a full deck load of lumber on 19 June 1954 midway through her career under the Italian flag after post-war salvage. *(Walter E Frost/City of Vancouver Archives CVA 447-3038.1)*

western Mediterranean. After hostilities ceased, however, Costa embarked on an entirely new, and much grander, shipping venture; one which would see their born-again purchase go through a profound transformation.

Europe experienced a wave of mass emigration in the years following the end of the Second World War. The war itself had produced a veritable army of displaced persons, estimated to have totalled some fourteen million, refugees from both the bitter fighting which had ravaged central Europe in 1944–5, and from the political upheavals, notably the spread of state communism, which had followed. In addition, the European economy had been severely damaged, the damage being so severe that recovery would take more than a decade. Parts of Italy had suffered heavily in the slow Allied push first through Sicily and then up the mainland peninsula from 1943, and out-migration was further fuelled by severe economic dislocation, the fear of the country falling victim to the communist 'domino-effect' from the East, and the desire of those associated with some two decades of Fascist rule to escape discrimination or revenge. A high proportion of Italian emigration was to South America, particularly Brazil, Uruguay, and Argentina, all of which had been common destinations for earlier generations of Italian migrants.

Most of the Italian passenger fleet had been sunk during the war, and the need for established operators to rebuild capacity, often from scratch, combined with the demands of mass emigration, left considerable scope for new operators to enter the field. These latter found tonnage where they could, in some cases, converting war-built Liberty ships to emigrant carriers by erecting a basic one-deck superstructure over some of the holds, and converting the 'tween decks into dormitories. Costa would enter the South American trade with three ancient vessels bought from the American Luckenbach Line. These would carry only a limited number of passengers and would be transferred to a North American service after a year, to be replaced by two newly acquired ships. The first of these was the ex-British *Southern Prince*, a sister of the *Western Prince*, sunk under Cyril Thompson on his way back to Britain in December 1940. Renamed *Anna C*, she had her existing passenger accommodation increased. The second was *Ocean Virtue*/*Andrea C*, which would go through a much more dramatic transformation, arguably one of the most profound undertaken on a wartime-built standard ship.

Taken in hand at Genoa by Cantieri del Tirreno, the vessel had her coal-fired boilers and steam-driven reciprocating engines stripped out, to be replaced by a war-built eight-cylinder FIAT diesel. A long, low superstructure was erected over the after two-thirds of the hull, which was surmounted by a low motor ship funnel. This produced first-class cabin passenger accommodation for seventy-nine, for whom the designers managed to squeeze in a swimming pool. Less obvious externally, save for an increase in lifeboat provision and the appearance of scuttles, was the creation of berths for 384 third-class passengers in dormitories in the 'tween decks. In this guise, *Andrea C* sailed from Genoa on her maiden voyage to South America on 27 June 1948 to make calls at Santos, Brazil; Montevideo, Uruguay; and Buenos Aires, Argentina.

Above: The salvaged *Ocean Virtue* after her initial reconstruction as the passenger liner *Andrea C*, photographed being towed to the berth at Montevideo, Uruguay, her decks crowded with Italian immigrants.
(R Maya/Wm Schell collection)

Below: *Andrea C* at Malta in 1974 while in service as a cruise ship, her third and most comprehensive rebuilding rendering her unrecognizable as a war-built cargo vessel.
(Wm Schell collection)

Andrea C completed sixty-two round voyages between 1948 and 1959, these being supplemented in the late 1950s by a variety of cruises as the emigrant traffic began to thin. By 1959, the Costa passenger fleet had grown considerably with the arrival of a series of larger liners and the spread of the route network across Central and South America. Rather than pensioning off the ageing *Andrea C*, however, her owners decided to undertake a comprehensive upgrade. The ship acquired her third engine, a new and more powerful FIAT Grandi Motori diesel. In addition, her accommodation block was extended, her hull was graced by a longer and more raked bow, and a larger funnel was installed. Internally, some of the remaining cargo space was replaced with passenger accommodation, the dormitories were removed, and total capacity increased to 122 first-class and 354 third-class passengers, all in cabins.

In this third manifestation, the ship completed another decade of service, much of it as a cruise ship. During the 1960s, most of her remaining sisters had gone to the breakers, including her two Italian-flagged counterparts. When *Andrea C* was withdrawn from service in 1970, however, it was not the prelude to a short trip to the scrapyards at La Spezia or Vado Ligure. Rather, she was taken in hand for another comprehensive modernisation. Most of the changes were internal, including remodelled public rooms, and the installation of full air-conditioning and private facilities in every cabin. As modified, passenger capacity was now 464 in a single class. The vessel was then employed almost full time in the cruise market, not just in her traditional haunts, but in Mediterranean waters as well. She lasted yet another decade in this guise, only being taken out of service at the end of the 1981 season. She was finally broken up at La Spezia in 1982, forty years and half a world away from her birth. By this time, she had been the only former Ocean in service in the West for a clear decade. Indeed, her only compatriots which might have still been afloat were the Chinese *Zhan Dou 26*, built as *Ocean Merchant* and sold to the Netherlands during the war to become *Jan Lievens*, and her fleet-mate *Zhan Dou 75*, formerly *Ocean Athlete* and *Govert Flinck*, the date and circumstances of whose final disposal are unknown.

The Post-War Vessel Disposal Programme

Unlike all but two of the Forts, all the Parks, and all the British-operated *Sam*-Liberties, the Oceans were British government property and, like the Empires built in British shipyards, candidates for peacetime sale. The Ministry of War Transport had turned its mind to selling its war-built tonnage to commercial operators as early as the summer of 1944, but progress had been limited. Only a handful of owners were prepared to contract for purchase of war-built vessels for eventual peacetime delivery while the war was still going on. This was only partially due to uncertainty as to when the war would end. In complete contrast to the unbridled optimism about peacetime market prospects prevailing at the end of the First World War, there was widespread caution about the outlook after the end of the Second. There was also an issue with the price owners were being asked to pay for government-owned war construction. The formula employed in 1944–5 was based on the building cost of the vessels concerned, with a depreciation allowance for accelerated wartime wear and tear. As wartime building costs were generally accepted to have been inflated, and as the vessels themselves might be considered as of standardised but inferior quality to peacetime equivalents built to owners' individual specifications, potential buyers would have been looking for a significant discount to new-building cost. There is little evidence that the Oceans were even considered for disposal at this stage. This was simply a matter of the price that had been paid for them, which, as we have already seen, was as much as three times higher than the equivalent figure for British-built Empires.

With the war over, the ministry began to think through its targets and plans for the disposal of government-owned shipping on a more systematic basis. At this stage, there were some 400 war-built ships yet to be disposed of, including seventy coal-burning tramps (seventeen of them still under construction), thirteen partially refrigerated tramps, and nineteen diesel tramps (four still under construction). It also counted thirty-seven coal-burning Ocean-class tramps, of which thirty-six were in service and one, *Ocean Viking*, was still resting on the sea floor at Bari, her British registry remaining open until her October 1946 sale to Italian salvors. The ministry divided this tonnage into three categories:

(i) Cargo liners, intermediate tramps, motor tramps, and ocean-going tankers likely to be attractive to commercial owners because of the general shortage of British tonnage of the types in question.

(ii) War-built dry bulk cargo steamers, together with similar ships built in the last war, and old tramps from the British share of the enemy tonnage – vessels considered to be useful primarily for filling the immediate gaps in the deep-sea tramp fleet, but most of which were thought to have 'little long-term usefulness.'

(iii) Small and specialised tonnage which would be difficult to accommodate within a structured overall disposal scheme, for which the best approach might simply be to 'knock it down to the highest bidder.'

In mid-November 1945, the ministry began to develop a comprehensive plan for selling off its wartime fleet. The basic thinking behind the scheme was laid down in three sentences in a memorandum dated the fifteenth of the month. 'Management and operation by private operators of government owned tonnage under peacetime conditions on government account in competition with privately owned ships would be a very unsatisfactory device, especially if it was adopted after failure to come to reasonable disposal terms to dispose of the government owned ships to private operators. Our main effort, therefore, must be to propound a scheme which would enable all the serviceable ships to be taken from the government on acceptable terms by private operators. It is proposed … that the scheme should include sale by the ministry in suitable cases and long-term bareboat charters to private operators in other cases.'

The memorandum went on to lay out three 'principles' for governing disposal policy:

(i) 'If we are to cover our requirements while our merchant marine is re-built, it will be necessary to keep the bulk of this Government owned tonnage in service for some years.'

(ii) 'On the other hand it is essential that the disposal of this tonnage should not hinder or restrict the prospects of orders in our shipbuilding yards on a substantial scale, and should also not absorb the resources of the shipping industry in investment in these war-built or second-hand ships to the detriment of their plans for building new and up-to-date tonnage of competitive types in order to win back a predominating position for the British merchant marine.'

(iii) 'While these reasons of policy should be taken into full account in our decisions, any scheme must be fair to the taxpayer. In other words, we cannot dispose of tonnage to the British shipping industry on terms involving the Treasury in a cash loss except on well-defined and generally acceptable grounds which can be justified to public opinion.'

Having gone this far, the same document then effectively tore up the third principle, stating that various considerations would justify leaving the exchequer to bear a substantial proportion of the cost of building or obtaining the ships intended for disposal. It reiterated the existing mantra that these ships had been built for wartime purposes at high prices created by war conditions, and that they were of a 'standard type not very suitable for commercial operation.' In line with general policy in the disposal of weapons and materials of war, it argued that it was clear that some part of their cost must be borne by the nation as part of the total loss imposed by the war. Moving into territory which impacted directly on the disposal of the Oceans, it stated that the other governments which had contributed shipbuilding to the war effort were already committed to accepting heavy losses in disposing of their output. Critically, it pointed out that both the Canadian and US governments had written off more than a million dollars, equivalent to nearly two-thirds of the initial price, on the cost of each standard dry cargo ship they planned to put up for sale. This meant that the market was already being governed by pricing decisions taken in North America, and that Britain's own disposal programme would need to be based on force majeure.

Moving on to consider the specific problems of pricing and selling war-built steam tramps, the ministry maintained the basic negative view that such ships were of limited peacetime utility. It was asserted that the ministry did not wish 'to make heavy inroads into the limited capital of the shipping industry available for building, merely in order to take the wartime ships off our hands.' The conclusion was thus drawn that, while the possibility should be left open for owners to buy if they wished, they should also be offered the alternative of long-term bareboat charter on terms which would reasonably cover the taxpayers' interest.

The ministry then embarked on a preliminary exercise in pricing mathematics, suggesting two outline schemes. Both would start by establishing an average cost of building, after which the first would make a flat deduction of 10 per cent before allowing wartime depreciation at the rate of 10 per cent per annum, and the second would deduct an average depreciation of 30 per cent and add or subtract 6 per cent for each year by which ship was younger or older than average. The first method would give a price range for the standard Empire tramps of between £107,000 and £160,000, and the second a range of £114,000 to £148,000. The document went on to suggest that charter rates should be established at a flat percentage annual rate on the mean floor price, offering 8 per cent as the rate for a ten-year charter, 9 per cent for a five-year charter, and 10 per cent for a shorter agreement. The strongly preferred ten-year chartering option was unrealistic, being unlikely to attract a tramp operator, even in more certain market conditions than those prevailing in 1945–6. The preliminary calculations of sales price were, however, moving in the right direction. So too was the suggested approach to selling the US-built vessels, the ministry taking the pragmatic view that these vessels 'would be put into the scheme on the same basis as the Empire ships; that is to say the extra cost of building in the USA would be ignored and the ships would be at the same price as British-built standard tramps of the same size.'

On 18 December 1945, the Minister of War Transport made a statement in the House of Commons, announcing that the government had decided that dry cargo ships, other than those employed in trooping or other direct military or naval service, would be released from requisition on the termination of voyages after 2 March 1946, when present charters expired. This cleared the way for the sale or charter of government-owned tonnage, arrangements for which gathered momentum with the ministry hoping that disposals could take place 'more or less' concurrently with derequisitioning. Policy makers grasped the nettle on both sales prices and charter rates. In the first case, a simplified formula was employed, whereby the average cost of each class of ship was reduced by about 25 per cent to discount some of the excess wartime cost, to produce a new nominal first cost. To arrive at the individual floor price for each ship, further depreciation would be applied at 6 per cent per annum from the date of delivery by the builders to 3 March 1946. In the case of chartering, the ministry took heed of representations from external industry advisers that its vision of ten- or even seven-year charter parties was unrealistic, as 'chartering for so long a period was extremely speculative for an owner.'

The final scheme priced vessels for sale in an approximate range from £105,000 to £130,000 depending on age. The alternative chartering scheme offered three- and five-year options, at rates of £1,025 per month in the first case and £825 per month in the second. The sales proposal achieved Treasury sanction following acceptance of the MOWT assurance that it could reasonably expect 'real competition among ship owners to buy the ships', a point to which it claimed to attach 'considerable importance.' There was real concern that the sale of vessels would attract speculative buyers who might re-sell their acquisitions at a profit if market conditions produced a rise in second-hand prices – a very real prospect, considering first the likelihood that trade would become more robust as wartime dislocation relaxed, and second, that shipyards could not possibly produce enough ships to meet the demand for replacement tonnage for some years to come. This desire to avoid a situation where the ministry might be accused of allowing speculators to profit at the expense of both the taxpayer and the bulk of the shipping industry, resulted in an important condition of sale being included in the tender document. The restriction on the subsequent sale of purchased vessels stated baldly that 'except with the sanction of the Minister and on such conditions as he may determine, the vessel shall not for a period of three years from the date of delivery hereunder (a) be transferred to any person, or (b) cease to be registered in the United Kingdom, the Channel Islands or the Isle of Man.'

Government Sales and Charters

The early uptake on the offer to purchase government-owned tonnage was muted. The end of the war was still less than a year in the past, economic dislocation was unwinding in a slow and uncertain fashion, and the geo-political outlook remained clouded. Many shipowners, particularly those in the tramp sector who were not driven by the imperative of protecting liner conference shipping quotas, were content to wait until they could get a firmer indication of future market conditions, and thus second-hand vessel pricing. The result was that a large majority of the war-built steam tramps offered in tender documents, the first of which was published on 25 January 1946, were taken up on charter rather than purchased outright.

A total of sixty-three steam tramps were chartered. Of these, twenty-one were placed on three-year charters at a total of £25,200 per month (or an average per ship of £1,200 per month). The remaining forty-four ships were placed on five-year charters at a total of £41,900 per month, or an average per ship of £900 per month. The demand for chartered tonnage was evidently robust, as the Ministry of Transport, which had succeeded the Ministry of War Transport in March 1946, was able to achieve charter rates significantly above the floor rates established when setting up the scheme (£1,200 compared to £1,025 for three-year charters, and £900 compared to £825 for five-year charters). Overall, charters accounted for just under two-thirds of the standard tramp vessels potentially qualified for inclusion in the disposal scheme, some of which had not yet been released due to ongoing government commitments. Three Oceans fell into the latter category: *Ocean Trader*, which would go straight to sale in April 1947, and *Ocean Vulcan* and *Ocean Vigour*, which would not follow until 1948.

Sales of Oceans for purchase got off to a slow start, with only six vessels being sold in 1946, four of them to their wartime managers. The first to go, and coincidentally the oldest of the class left afloat, was *Ocean Vigil*, sold to the Bolton Steam Shipping Co Ltd of London and, in line with their long-established convention of using the names of painters beginning with the letter R, renamed *Ramsay*. The other London-registered ship, *Ocean Volga*, also kept her existing registry port, being sold in the summer to Henry M Thomson, once again her wartime manager, and renamed *Sithonia*. Thomson was one of the rare private shipowners left in the business, owning his vessels in person rather than through a limited company. He had been a partner in William Thomson & Co, the company which managed the long-established, Leith-based Ben Line, but had resigned in 1921 following a family rift. He had then gone into business on his own, and in the words of the Ben Line historian, ran his tramp shipping business 'practically single-handed from his home in Edinburgh' until he retired in 1961. By coincidence, two of the other ships sold went to the Ben Line, run by the remainder of the Thomson family. *Ocean Valentine* was renamed *Benlomond*, while *Ocean Gallant* became *Bennevis*. The last two sales of the year involved *Ocean Vestal*, which went to Thompson Steamshipping of London, and was renamed *Farningham*, and *Ocean Rider*, which joined the small London fleet of N G Kyriakides as *Nicholas K*. While Kyriakides was a recent arrival on the UK shipping scene, the Thompson company dated back to the nineteenth century, but was facing a fleet replacement challenge common to many British operators of its type. Having lost all four of its steamers by the spring of 1942, it had to start again from scratch in 1945–6. War risk insurance payments had allowed it to build up financial reserves of £370,000 which it used to purchase three war-built steamers, two Empires and *Ocean Vestal*, and to convert all three to oil-firing. With little scope for further

Benlomond was a 1946 purchase by the Ben Line, who had managed her during the war as *Ocean Valentine*. *(World Ship Society Ltd)*

Early British Commercial Acquisitions, 1946

Original Name	Acquired	Buyer	Port of Registry	New Name
Ocean Vigil	1.4.1946	Bolton Steam Shipping	London	*Ramsay*
Ocean Valentine	6.6.1946	Ben Line of Steamers	Leith	*Benlomond*
Ocean Volga	30.7.1946	Henry M Thomson	London	*Sithonia*
Ocean Gallant	21.8.1946	Ben Line of Steamers	Leith	*Bennevis*
Ocean Vestal	18.11.1946	Thompson Steamshipping	London	*Farningham*
Ocean Rider	22.11.1946	N G Kyriakides Shipping	London	*Nicholas K*

Ocean Viceroy, photographed at Cape Town in the livery of her charterer, the Clan Line, would be renamed *Clan Kenneth* after Clan bought all seven of the Oceans it had chartered.
(Ships in Focus)

capital expenditure, it completed its renewal programme by taking two further US-built vessels, *Ocean Vesper* and *Ocean Wayfarer* on five-year bareboat charter.

The remaining ships available for commercial service in 1946 were taken up on charter by British owners, seventeen on five-year and ten on three-year agreements. Two companies took up well over a third of the available vessels between them. The first to move was the long-established Teesside tramp operator, Sir Robert Ropner & Co Ltd (the company had recently relocated its offices to Darlington, but it retained its original base of West Hartlepool as its port of registry). Ropner took up six vessels, three for each of its two ship-owning firms. The Pool Shipping Co Ltd took *Ocean Pilgrim*, *Ocean Valour* and *Ocean Vanity* on five-year bareboat charter, while the Ropner Shipping Co Ltd took *Ocean Fame*, *Ocean*

Ocean Vengeance alongside at Cape Town under charter to Robert Ropner & Sons, who would rename her *Ingleby* after exercising their option to purchase her and five of her sisters in 1947.
(V H Young and L A Sawyer)

Ocean Faith at Cape Town in the early part of her charter to Neill & Pandelis before the wartime life rafts and gun positions were removed. *(John & Marion Clarkson collection)*

Pride and *Ocean Vengeance* on the same basis. Later in the year, an equally venerable liner company, Cayzer, Irvine & Co Ltd's Glasgow-registered Clan Line of Steamers Co Ltd took up seven more on a mixture of three- and five-year charters: *Ocean Courier*, *Ocean Glory*, *Ocean Gypsy*, *Ocean Messenger*, *Ocean Verity*, *Ocean Viceroy*, and *Ocean Viscount*.

The other fourteen vessels were taken up by nine different tramp operators, of which only three, Lyle and Denholm of Glasgow, and Baltic Shipping from Newcastle upon Tyne, were not London-based. These charterers represented a fair cross section of the sector. Four – Lyle, Saint, Thompson, and Denholm – were independent British operators which had been in business since the nineteenth century, while a fifth survivor of the Victorian age, Alexander Shipping, now operated as a subsidiary of the Furness-Houlder Group. Two

British Commercial Charters, 1946–7

Name	Delivered	Charterer	Port of Delivery	Length of Charter
Ocean Traveller	21.3.1946	Lyle Shipping	Cardiff	5 years
Ocean Glory	10.4.1946	Clan Line	Middlesbrough	5 years
Ocean Vengeance	22.4.1946	Ropner Shipping	Boston, Mass	5 years
Ocean Courier	11.5.1946	Clan Line	London	5 years
Ocean Vista	15.5.1946	Saint Line	Tyne	3 years
Ocean Vesper	29.5.1946	Thompson Steamshipping	Singapore	5 years
Ocean Faith	1.6.1946	Neill & Pandelis	Liverpool	5 years
Ocean Viceroy	21.6.1946	Clan Line	Swansea	3 years
Ocean Strength	22.6.1946	Denholm Line	London	3 years
Ocean Valour	26.6.1946	Pool Shipping (Ropner)	Sydney, NSW	5 years
Ocean Valley	27.6.1946	Alexander Shipping	Middlesbrough	3 years
Ocean Liberty	30.6.1946	Neill & Pandelis	Durban	5 years
Ocean Pride	13.7.1946	Ropner Shipping	Melbourne	5 years
Ocean Vision	15.7.1946	Aviation & Shipping	Aden	3 years
Ocean Wayfarer	15.7.1946	Thompson Steamshipping	London	5 years
Ocean Vagrant	16.7.1946	Baltic Shipping	Liverpool	3 years
Ocean Gypsy	28.7.1946	Clan Line	Leith	5 years
Ocean Volunteer	31.7.1946	Alcyone Shipping Finance	Liverpool	3 years
Ocean Pilgrim	5.8.1946	Pool Shipping (Ropner)	Newcastle, NSW	5 years
Ocean Fame	7.8.1946	Ropner Shipping	Avonmouth	5 years
Ocean Messenger	21.8.1946	Clan Line	Sydney, NSW	5 years
Ocean Angel	28.8.1946	Alcyone Shipping Finance	Vancouver, BC	3 years
Ocean Wanderer	29.8.1946	Bolton Shipping	N/A	3 years
Ocean Stranger	14.9.1946	Alcyone Shipping Finance	N/A	3 years
Ocean Verity	23.9.1946	Clan Line	Liverpool	3 years
Ocean Vanity	18.10.1946	Pool Shipping (Ropner)	N/A	5 years
Ocean Viscount	9.1.1947	Clan Line	Swansea	5 years

Ropner's *Heronspool*, which the company had first chartered as *Ocean Valour*, photographed with a tug alongside at Adelaide.
(V H Young and L A Sawyer)

of the others, Baltic Shipping, and Noel Purvis's Aviation & Shipping Co, were post-war arrivals, the former a small, short-lived venture, the latter an ambitious experiment in integrated transport operations which soon concentrated solely on tramp shipping. The final pair of charterers were both representatives of the transnational Greek shipping community. Neil & Pandelis had moved management of its small fleet from Piraeus to London in the 1930s, while Alcyone Shipping Finance was a new venture of Adelphi Vergottis, itself part of a family shipping group which had entered the business from the Ionian island of Cephalonia in the late nineteenth century.

Of the charterers, it was Ropner which would make the earliest move to ownership. Ropner had signed a five-year charter party at a rate of just under £900 a month per vessel, equal to £5,300 a month for the six ships taken together. On 3 January 1947, less than three months after it had taken delivery of its last charter, it wrote to the Ministry of Transport, seeking to explore the possibility of outright purchase of all six. The letter expressed the wish 'to purchase and pay for the vessels as soon as practicable and allow the transfer to take place at the next favourable opportunity.' It went on, however, to point out that the concerned clause in the charter party agreement was not clear as to whether the company had 'the liberty to purchase and take delivery of these steamers now.' It concluded by claiming that 'it would appear that it would be in the interests of all concerned to terminate the bareboat charter agreement by purchase without further delay.'

The Ropner request produced outright confusion at the Ministry of Transport. While the draft legislation and related documentation put together in early 1946 had included a clear option-to-purchase scheme with an associated pricing system, for some reason this had been excluded from the material put before the cabinet for approval, and, as Ropner had pointed out, had been left unclear in final form of the charter party. There followed an undignified scramble as Whitehall tried to sort out the mess. The Treasury Solicitor was consulted and informed the ministry that, as far as the relevant documentation was concerned, the option to purchase could only be exercised at the end of the charter, but that the ministry was at liberty to relax this provision. A bout of hand wringing ensued. The price of second-hand tonnage had been firming up as market prospects became clearer, with the effect that allowing the exercise of the option would mean that purchasers would get the benefit of the basic

Sir R Ropner & Co Ltd Acquisitions, 1947

Original Name	Acquired	Purchasing Company	New Name	Disposal
Ocean Pilgrim	6.2.1947	Pool Shipping Co Ltd	Pikepool	1959
Ocean Fame	7.2.1947	Ropner Shipping Co Ltd	Firby	1955
Ocean Pride	13.2.1947	Ropner Shipping Co Ltd	Oakby	1959
Ocean Vanity	18.2.1947	Pool Shipping Co Ltd	Teespool	1960
Ocean Vengeance	23.2.1947	Ropner Shipping Co Ltd	Ingleby	1960
Ocean Valour	26.2.1947	Pool Shipping Co Ltd	Heronspool	1955

Cayzer, Irvine & Co Ltd Acquisitions, 1947–52

Original Name	Purchase	Price (£)	New Name	Disposal (Loss)
Ocean Courier	31.12.1947	106,466	*Clan Macbean*	1960
Ocean Glory	31.12.1947	107,343	*Clan Macbeth*	1959
Ocean Gypsy	31.12.1947	108,185	*Clan Macbride*	1958
Ocean Messenger	31.12.1947	108,087	*Clan Macbrayne*	1961
Ocean Verity	31.12.1947	106.270	*Clan Keith*	(1961)
Ocean Viceroy	31.12.1947	104,809	*Clan Kenneth*	1958
Ocean Viscount	31.12.1947	107,949	*Clan Kennedy*	1959
Ocean Wayfarer	2.2.1951	189,500	*Clan Macquarrie**	(1953)
Ocean Vesper	20.4.1951	184,500	*Clan Macqueen**	1958
Ocean Vestal	25.3.1952	360,000	*Hellenes***	1958

* Acquired by Thompson in 1950 without change of name and then resold to Clan; *Clan Macqueen* transferred to Houston 1953 and renamed *Herminius*
** Acquired by Thompson in 1946 and renamed *Farningham*; transferred to the British & South American Steam Navigation Co Ltd (Houston Line (London) Ltd, managers) and renamed *Hellenes*

price originally fixed, when there was no doubt that the ministry could get much higher prices if it offered the ships for purchase to third parties. It recognised, however, that it had originally let the ships concerned on bareboat charter because there were no offers to purchase them. At that stage, preference had been given to offers to purchase, and it had been open to any owner at that time to bid for them.

The inevitable conclusion was finally reached that 'in accordance with the general principles of our scheme', owners must be given the option to make their own decision regarding purchase based on their judgement as to the value of the ships to their business. In what seems no more than a salve

Clan Kennedy, formerly *Ocean Viscount*, at her home port of Glasgow. *(John Solomon/R A Priest/Nautical Association of Australia Collection)*

to conscience, the view was taken that most of owners who had ships on bareboat charter would not decide to exercise the option to purchase then, or in the future, especially if it was made clear 'that there can be no profit taking by re-sale.'

The ministry finally wrote back to Ropner on 31 January, informing the company that it could exercise its option to purchase at the end of the current month of the hiring period. Things then moved quickly, and all the purchases were completed before the end of February. The ships stayed with the subsidiary companies which had been operating them, and adopted the separate nomenclature conventions of each, those going to the Ropner Shipping Co Ltd being given names ending in *-by*, and those going to the Pool Shipping Co Ltd, being given names ending in *-pool*. One ship from each company would be sold for further trading as early as 1955, while the remainder would sail on until 1959–60, when they too went to other operators.

The other large charterer, the Clan Line, also purchased all the vessels it was operating, in this case at the end of 1947. As already stated, Clan had chartered seven ships. Of these, two were taken on three-year charters and five on five-year charters, at monthly rates of £1,100 and £875 respectively. Cayzer & Irvine would subsequently add another three vessels. Two were transferred from the newly acquired Thompson Steamshipping Co Ltd in 1950–1, while the third would also come from Thompson but would be assigned to a subsidiary company, the Houston Line, in 1952. Clan adopted a quirky variation on its *Clan* naming convention for its first seven acquisitions, giving the three California-built ships names beginning *Clan K-* and the four Maine-built ships names beginning *Clan Macb-*. The two Clan ex-Thompson vessels introduced a third convention, getting names beginning *Clan Macqu-*, while the Houston ship stayed within the long-established naming convention of that company, being given a classical Greco-Roman-style personal name beginning with the letter H. The three late additions would bring Clan Line's ex-Ocean fleet to ten, easily the largest group of the sisters operated by any operator, and almost a third of those surviving under the red ensign.

Other charterers began to purchase their vessels as 1947 unfolded, with another five ships being sold to five different buyers, one of which, Bolton, had already purchased a ship in the previous year. A further seven vessels were sold in 1948, leaving only five in government hands, of which three were

Photographed at Auckland, New Zealand, *Cape Nelson* had been purchased as *Ocean Vulcan* by Lyle Shipping in February 1948 after she had completed trials for the Admiralty's Welding Sub-Committee. *(Malcolm Cranfield collection)*

Other British Commercial Acquisitions, 1947–51

Original Name	Acquired	Purchasing Company	Port of Registry	New Name
Ocean Traveller	21.2.1947	Lyle Shipping	Glasgow	*Cape Corso*
Ocean Strength	22.2.1947	Denholm Line	Greenock	*Broompark*
Ocean Trader	1.5.1947	Drake Shipping	London	*Merchant Royal*
Ocean Vision	14.5.1947	Aviation & Shipping	London	*Avismere*
Ocean Wanderer	28.11.1947	Bolton Steam Shipping	London	*Ruysdael*
Ocean Vulcan	5.2.1948	Lyle Shipping	Glasgow	*Cape Nelson*
Ocean Vista	15.2.1948	Saint Line	London	*Saint Edmund*
Ocean Liberty	1.3.1948	Aviation & Shipping	London	*Avismoat*
Ocean Faith	1.3.1948	Aviation & Shipping	London	*Avisvale*
Ocean Stranger	14.5.1948	Alcyone Shipping Finance	London	*Alcyone Fortune**
Ocean Vagrant	16.8.1948	Baltic Shipping	London	*Atlantic Vagrant*
Ocean Vigour	13.12.1948	British Steamship (Cory)	Cardiff	*Ramillies*
Ocean Valley	26.3.1949	Alexander Shipping	London	*Malmesbury*
Ocean Angel	27.4.1949	Alcyone Shipping Finance	Glasgow	*Alcyone Angel*
Ocean Volunteer	26.7.1949	Alcyone Shipping Finance	London	*Alcyone Union*
Ocean Vesper	29.1.1951	Thompson Steamshipping	Glasgow	*Clan Macqueen***
Ocean Wayfarer	29.1.1951	Thompson Steamshipping	Glasgow	*Clan Macquarrie***

* Transferred to Panamanian flag in 1951 as *Calygera*; returned to British flag in 1954 as *Alcyone Faith* ** Ships only renamed after re-sale to the Clan Line

sold in 1949 and two in early 1951. The three ships left out of the chartering scheme due to extended government commitments were all sold during this period, *Ocean Trader* in May 1947 to Drake Shipping, the London-based arm of another international Greek concern, Lykiardopulo & Co, *Ocean Vulcan* in February 1948 to join *Ocean Traveller* in the Lyle Shipping fleet after release from the Admiralty hull testing programme, and *Ocean Vigour* at the end of the same year to John Cory & Sons following her involvement in the Exodus affair. Only one of the chartering companies did not exercise its option to purchase, Neil & Pandelis arranging to terminate its charters of *Ocean Liberty* and *Ocean Faith* to allow both vessels to be purchased by a subsidiary of Purvis Shipping's Aviation & Shipping concern. Purvis also purchased *Ocean Vision* off its own charter, renaming the three vessels *Avismoat*, *Avisvale*, and *Avismere* in line with its established nomenclature. This triple acquisition was later matched by Alcyone Shipping, which purchased *Ocean Stranger*, *Ocean*

N V Reederij Amsterdam's *Amstelveen*, which had seen wartime service for the British as *Ocean Victory* and the Dutch government-in-exile as *Jan Steen*, is seen here leaving Vancouver on 4 July 1956. *(Walter E Frost/City of Vancouver Archives CVA 447-3125.2)*

Foreign Government Disposals, 1946–51

Name	Flag	Sold	Purchasing Company	New Name
Jan Steen	Netherlands	1946	N V Reederij 'Amsterdam', Amsterdam	*Amstelveen*
Jan Lievens	Netherlands	1946	N V Reederij 'Amsterdam', Amsterdam	*Amstelstad*
Govert Flinck	Netherlands	1946	Koninklijke Rotterdamsche Lloyd, Rotterdam	*Ternate*
Belgian Veteran	Belgium	1948	Cie Maritime Belge (Lloyd Royal) SA, Antwerp	*Capitaine Lauwerins*
Bialystok	Poland	1951	Polskie Linie Oceaniczne, Gdansk	*Bialystok*

Angel, and *Ocean Volunteer* in 1948–9 towards the end of their three-year charters, giving them two-word names beginning *Alcyone*. Three other operators made later purchases to bring their complements of Oceans up to three. Ben Line, the only liner company apart from Clan to enter the field, purchased its third vessel from an interim buyer in 1950, as did Bolton, one of the longer-established participants in tramp shipping. The final buyer was Thompson Steamshipping, whose late purchase of its second and third acquisitions from long-term charter was a consequence of its takeover by the Clan Line.

In addition to the thirty-six ships disposed of by the British government, there were another five vessels which had been sold to Allied governments during the war, each of which was a candidate for resale following the return to peace. Four of these vessels were indeed sold into private hands, two of the Dutch ships going to a tramp operator and the third to the cargo liner fleet of Rotterdam Lloyd, and *Belgian Veteran* going to Belgium's only large liner company. Ownership of the Polish ship, however, had been assumed by the new communist state, and while title to the vessel was eventually transferred from the government to a corporate entity in 1951, the latter was state-controlled, and the switch did not even involve a change of name.

Peacetime Operations under the Red Ensign

There was a widespread expectation in official circles that war-built tramp ships would prove of limited commercial utility after hostilities ceased and would thus only fill a short-term bridging role until new purpose-built vessels could replace war losses. This expectation proved mistaken, most of the ships involved serving British owners well into the 1950s, and then going on to compete with these operators until the mid-1960s under flags of convenience (FOCs). There were

Ramsay, seen here at Adelaide, had become the first Ocean to enter British commercial service when purchased in April 1946 by Bolton Steam Shipping who had managed her during the war as *Ocean Vigil*, but she was sold out of the fleet in 1951 along with two sisters when her owners balked at the cost of remedial hull strengthening.
(Jim Freeman/R A Priest – Nautical Association of Australia collection)

three broad reasons why the ships built to government order in Britain, Canada and the US proved more useful and more durable than expected. The first was that the ships themselves were not as sub-standard as many civil servants seem to have believed. Basic design and construction were in line with the more modern portion of the British deep-sea tramp fleet and represented a significant advance over surviving ships built in the 1920s. The second reason was that British shipyards were simply not capable of providing enough new ships to rebuild fleets ravaged by war losses and were soon quoting lead times of three to five years to book berth space. Finally, government policy in the immediate post-war period exacerbated the shortage of domestic shipbuilding capacity by placing restrictions on accessing other sources of supply. Any owner wishing to build new or purchase second-hand tonnage abroad had to obtain official permission. Permission to build abroad was almost invariably refused, as was permission to buy second-hand in dollar-currency countries. These restrictions were not lifted until 1951.

Faced with waiting well into the 1950s for new tonnage, many owners were willing to pay moderate prices to acquire war-built vessels and to make an additional investment in modernisation to allow a decade or more of commercial service. Many vessels were converted from coal- to oil- burning, some relatively quickly, but others well into the 1950s. While there is little mention of it in available records, most owners must also have invested in the significant stiffening of midship hull structures required by Lloyd's when problems began to emerge in the late 1940s. The problems themselves largely concerned the buckling of hull plates and even some girders amidships, the most common area being under the cross-bunker. Lloyd's required that in all cases where transversely framed welded cargo ships suffered from 'significant deflection' of bottom plating, additional longitudinal stiffening should be fitted, extending 'over half the length amidships.' The buckling problem and the remedial instructions applied not only to the Oceans, but also to their similarly welded half-sisters, the Liberties. It is also worth noting that there also appears to have been hull buckling problems with a significant number of riveted Canadian-built Forts. This suggests that at least part of the problem must have been related to the limitations of wartime building practice.

Most buyers appear to have accepted the need for remedial strengthening as a reasonable addition to the cost of fitting their purchases for peacetime service. At least one, the Lyle Shipping Co Ltd, simply arranged to have the structural work carried out at the same time the vessel was in dockyard hands for conversion to oil-firing. Only one British owner was sufficiently concerned about the hull buckling problem to dispose of recently acquired war-built tonnage. Bolton Steam Shipping of London had managed *Ocean Vigil* and *Ocean Viking* during the war. The scuttled *Ocean Viking* had been sold off to Italian salvors for rebuilding, but Bolton purchased *Ocean Vigil* in April 1946 as soon as she became available, renaming her *Ramsay*. Initial experience operating this ship must have been positive, as two of her sisters were acquired. *Ocean Wanderer* had been chartered at the same time as *Ocean Vigil* had been purchased, and in November 1947 she too was acquired, to be renamed *Ruysdael*. Both vessels were converted to oil-firing at an approximate cost of £60,000 per vessel. As a side note, the firm also undertook significant modernisation of crew quarters and amenities. The view of one of the partners that it was 'disgraceful asking men to live and work in such conditions' might be taken as fair judgement on the bath-deleting austerities imposed by Whitehall warriors at the time the vessels were built. Two years later in December 1949, Bolton bought a third sister, the former *Ocean Vagrant*, which had been trading for another owner as *Atlantic Vagrant*, maintaining the tradition of giving their ships famous painters' names beginning with the letter R by renaming her *Raphael*.

Unlike every other British operator, Bolton reacted to the hull-buckling issue by selling off the vessels concerned. The company historian states baldly that this was done 'to avoid the incurrence of heavy costs (particularly in bottom stiffening).' The change in policy was sudden, the most recent acquisition, *Raphael*, being sold in December 1950, only a year after acquisition, and the modernised *Ramsay* and *Ruysdael* following in February and September 1951 respectively. This fire-sale was not restricted to the company's ex-Oceans, as its only other war-built ship, the former Liberty *Reynolds* (ex-*Samcebu*) was disposed of at the same time. The company historian also claims that these disposals were undertaken 'in order to make way for the next generation of custom-built ships', but as these three were only to arrive from builders in Middlesbrough and Sunderland at yearly intervals between 1952 and 1954, there might be an element of post-facto justification in this claim.

Apart from the three Bolton vessels, there were two other departures from the red ensign in 1950–1. In neither of these cases, however, was the change the result of a real sale. *Merchant Royal* (ex-*Ocean Trader*) of Drake Shipping and *Alcyone*

Fortune (ex-*Ocean Stranger*) of Alcyone Shipping were each owned by the London arm of long-established Greek family shipping companies, Lykiardopulo in the first case and Vergottis in the second. Both vessels left the UK register in 1950, but each 'transaction' was no more than a transfer to a FOC, in both instances that of Panama. Flagging-out of this sort was to be an ever-strengthening trend in the tramp shipping industry as the new decade wore on, although here, *Alcyone Fortune*, having spent three years as the Panamanian *Calygera*, then made a second appearance under the red ensign, returning to Alcyone Shipping colours as *Alcyone Faith*.

There would be no more disposals for further trading from the British flag until 1955, but well before this time one vessel had made a premature trip to the breakers. *Clan Macquarrie*, one of the three Oceans added to the Clan Line fleet via the acquisition of Thompson Steamshipping, was making a winter ballast voyage around Scotland from Dundee to Glasgow when she encountered a fierce gale off the Western Isles on the last day of January 1953. With winds gusting to 112mph., the vessel became unmanageable, and although Captain de Vall put out two anchors, the vessel was driven onto the foreshore at the village of Borve on the northwest coast of the island of Lewis. Local villagers rescued the entire crew of sixty-six while the storm was still

Clan Macquarrie (ex-*Ocean Wayfarer*) high and dry on the foreshore at the village of Borve on the northwest coast of the island of Lewis after being blown ashore in a gale on 31 January 1953 – although successfully re-floated, she would be broken up after proving uneconomical to repair. *(Comunn Eachdraidh Nis/Ness Historical Society)*

The ill-fated *Clan Keith* (ex-*Ocean Verity*), photographed in happier days on the Mersey, was the last Ocean in Clan Line service when she was wrecked in the Mediterranean with terrible loss of life on 5 November 1961. *(World Ship Society Ltd)*

raging, but the ship was left on the rocks completely out of the water at low tide. *Clan Macquarrie* was re-floated with some difficulty and taken to Stornoway, but it was decided that this did not constitute a 'place of safety' as specified by the Lloyd's Open Form salvage agreement, and she was subsequently towed to the Clyde. She was dry-docked at Elderslie, where she was valued at £242,500. A request for tenders to carry out repairs garnered five responses, but these ranged from £329,500 to £341,600, and management decided to abandon her as a constructive total loss. *Clan Macquarrie* had cost £189,500 when purchased from the government as *Ocean Wayfarer* near the end of her five-year charter in 1951, after which she had been converted to oil-firing, which will have contributed to the escalation of her insured value to £409,000. The Salvage Association sold the unfortunate vessel to the Liberian company Sea Tankers Inc, but the latter appear only to have sold her on to the shipbreakers, and she was scrapped at Troon. The other casualty of the incident was Captain de Vall, who was deemed to have been responsible for the loss of the ship due to 'serious errors of judgement' and asked to resign.

The other complete loss under the red ensign took place eight years later and involved another member of the Clan Line fleet. The similarities with the 1953 casualty ended there; indeed, the appalling circumstances of the second incident were completely out of step with the operations of an established British liner company in the second half of the twentieth century and were more reminiscent of the dangers of navigation in the Victorian era. By 5 November 1961, *Clan Keith* was the only former Ocean still sailing under Clan Line colours. She was near Cape Bon, Tunisia, in transit through the Mediterranean on a voyage from Middlesbrough for Colombo with general cargo, when Captain L G W Pitts discovered that he was south of his intended position. A gale was blowing, and visibility was poor, but the master made the fatal decision to pass south rather than north of Galita Island, taking his ship into dangerous waters, and ultimately onto the rocks at Eceuils des Sorelles. The vessel broke in two, the stern section sinking immediately and the rest on the following day. There were suggestions that the vessel's hull was in poor condition, but the loss of sixty-two of the sixty-eight men aboard (including all but one of the fifty-four Asian seamen) appears to have been more due to the master's failure to send out prompt distress signals, and a damning shortfall in boat-drill and general emergency training. A Ministry of Transport inquiry found Pitts solely to blame for the tragedy and suspended his certificate for eighteen months, and Clan Line dismissed him from its service.

There were no further departures from the UK register for four years after the triple Bolton sale and the two cases of flagging-out in 1950–1. There were, however, nine changes of ownership between British counterparties. Three of these involved acquisitions by Scottish buyers. The Ben Line, the early purchaser of *Ocean Valentine* and *Ocean Gallant* (renamed *Benlomond* and *Bennevis,* respectively), acquired *Alcyone Union* (ex-*Ocean Volunteer*) from her London-Greek owners in late 1950, renaming her *Benrinnes*.

Charles Dickens arriving at Eastham in 1962, the same year in which she would be sold to Greek buyers and renamed *Cleo*. She had been built as *Ocean Gallant* and had served the Ben Line as *Bennevis* between 1946 and 1959. *(Des Harris/Malcolm Cranfield collection)*

The Glasgow tramp owner Andrew Crawford & Co Ltd, a relatively small concern which had only operated chartered tonnage in the early post-war years, purchased *Broompark* (ex-*Ocean Strength*) from J & J Denholm in 1951, renaming her *Garryvale*. Four years later, Crawford bought a sister, Cory's *Ramillies* (ex-*Ocean Vigour*) which entered the fleet as *Galavale*.

The remaining six transactions all involved London buyers, two of these being the Bolton and Houston/Clan acquisitions already covered. Three of the others involved members of the London-Greek shipping community. Nicholas G Kyriakides, whose fleet already included *Nicholas K* (ex-*Ocean Rider*), purchased *Firby* (ex-*Ocean Fame*) from Ropner, renaming her *Irene K*. Two other ships were acquired by Alexander Tsavliris, a post-war entrant to the business, who purchased *Malmesbury* (ex-*Ocean Valley*) from Alexander Shipping, and *Avismoat* (ex-*Ocean Liberty*) from the Aviation & Shipping Co, employing a different corporate entity for each, the Trafalgar Steamship Co Ltd in the first instance and the Romney Steamship Co Ltd in the second. Like Kyriakides, Tsavliris named his ships after family members, the new acquisitions becoming *Granny Suzanne* and *Claire T*, respectively. The first of the two honoured the memory of the formidable grandparent in question for the fourth time in a decade. Finally, the Rodney Steamship Co Ltd, one of five subsidiaries of the Anglo-Danubian Transport Co, bought the Ben Line's *Bennevis* (ex- *Ocean Gallant*) at the end of the decade, renaming her *Charles Dickens*.

The Evolution of the Post-War Shipping Market

British tramp shipping entered the peacetime era in a relatively strong competitive position. Even though shipowners had to replace heavy losses, war risk insurance compensation had left them with the means to make an immediate start, while the British, Canadian, and US governments all prioritised enabling industry recovery over recouping national defence expenditure, and began to offer their Empire, Ocean, Fort/Park and Liberty/Victory fleets up for sale at commercially attractive prices. Additionally, British owners enjoyed a substantial head start over most of their traditional competitors. The fleets of European wartime allies had all suffered heavily, none more so than that of Greece, which had offered the stiffest competition in traditional tramp markets before 1939. Shipowners from the three defeated Axis powers, all traditional peacetime rivals, were in an even worse position. The entire German mercantile marine had either been sunk or surrendered as reparations, with a vengeful Soviet Union sweeping up everything her Western allies did not want. Italy was only marginally better off – Mussolini's precipitate plunge into war in June 1940 had left part of his fleet isolated and exposed to seizure in distant ports, while most of the remainder had been destroyed during the long Mediterranean campaign. Finally, US submarines and aircraft had hunted Japanese merchant ships to near extinction, leaving the Pacific tramp trades particularly open to British owners.

The global economy had to go through a long and painful period of adjustment before a new maritime trade network could emerge. Widespread destruction of industrial and transport infrastructures, devastation of most major cities, and displacement of whole populations in both Europe and Asia presented British tramp operators with a series of opportunities. Although Britain's own dependence on imported foodstuffs, particularly cereals from North and South America, was falling due to wartime agricultural improvements, large parts of continental Europe faced severe shortages and, in some places, even starvation. This crisis produced a stream of profitable charters to lift cargoes from Australia, the Plate and the Canadian and US east and west coasts from both governments and large commercial grain merchants. Demand for other traditional bulk cargoes was equally strong, the destruction of synthetic fertiliser production facilities across Europe led to an immediate need for imported nitrates and phosphates, while the forced replacement of lost light and heavy machinery underpinned charters from steel plants for iron ore from Spain, Algeria and West Africa and scrap metal from North America.

Economic dislocation, however, also presented British owners with some sharp challenges. In the first years of peace, for example, they still had to obtain official permits for voyages which were often denied by the Board of Trade and replaced by less profitable directed freights. Exceptional circumstances also produced sharp fluctuations in key freight markets. In 1946, a prolonged strike by American coal miners triggered a wholesale switch by US shipowners from coal to grain exports, depriving British tramps of a staple inbound cargo. In the following year, industrial recovery at home absorbed almost all domestic coal production, denying tramp operators their staple outward cargo, and forcing them to accept long ballast voyages to find return cargoes. Volatile freight markets were a normal feature of the tramp shipping market, but post-war conditions made it particularly difficult to position ships to take advantage of regional upswings.

These difficulties notwithstanding, the first decade of peace offered satisfactory profits for British tramp operators,

Ropner's *Teespool* (ex-*Ocean Vanity*) alongside at Vancouver on 5 November 1950. *(Walter E Frost/City of Vancouver Archives CVA 447-8507)*

Most of the Oceans serving British tramp owners spent much of their time trading around the Pacific basin, from the Canadian west coast in the north to Australia and New Zealand in the south.

Above: *Galavale* (ex-*Ramillies*, ex-*Ocean Vigour*) a 1955 addition to the fleet of Andrew Crawford & Co, arriving at Wellington, New Zealand. *(V H Young and L A Sawyer)*

with the outbreak of the Korean War in 1950 adding boom conditions to the mix. Some companies had already moved their fleets wholesale to the trans-Pacific trades, and strong market conditions would see former Oceans such as the Ropner sextet, Lyle's *Cape Corso* and *Cape Nelson* duo, and Crawford's later acquisitions, *Garryvale* and *Galavale,* spending the bulk of their careers under the red ensign there. By the mid-1950s, however, problems were looming – problems which would result in many of the Oceans being sold off the register by the end of the decade.

Some traditional competitors had returned to the market in the late 1940s, and the Greek and Italian tramp fleets were revived by block transfers of Liberty ships, while US operators, some of them expatriate Greeks, tapped the same pool of tonnage to enter the business. Elsewhere, rebuilt modern shipyards in countries like Japan and Italy began supplying their own flag carriers with efficient bulk-carrying tonnage capable of operating profitably at rates which Britain's war-built fleet could not match. In South Asia, independence for India and Pakistan exposed UK tramps to increasing competition from low-cost native tonnage, most of it purchased second-hand from British companies, while elsewhere in the world growing economic nationalism stimulated increased investment in domestically owned shipping. Finally, the use of FOCs to allow operation in less demanding regulatory and fiscal environments grew rapidly, rising from marginally above 1 per cent of the world fleet in 1946 to just over 4 per cent in 1948 and to almost 16 per cent a decade after that with most of the growth occurring on the new Liberian register. Greek shipowners, particularly new arrivals like Onassis, Niarchos and Livanos, and US corporations specialising in the bulk trades accounted for most of the growth, but older international businesses such as the London-Greek shipping community and long-established Italian operators also joined in.

From the Red Ensign to Worldwide Ownership

Only five Oceans had left the red ensign in the early 1950s, all to FOC companies controlled by prominent Greek shipowners. Three of the departures were the result of Bolton Shipping's early disposal of its war-built tonnage, *Raphael* and *Ramsay* hoisting the Panamanian flag as *Siram* and *Stork* for Embiricos and Goulandris respectively, and *Ruysdael*

Okeanis at Hull while operating under the Greek flag for the Lykiardopulo family, having previously served the same owners under the British and Panamanian flags as *Merchant Royal* and *Oceana* respectively after wartime government service as *Ocean Trader*.
(C Hill/George Robinson collection)

becoming the Costa Rican flagged *Santa Irene* for a Panama-domiciled company controlled by the Pateras family. The other two departures were transfers rather than sales: the London-Greek owners of *Alcyone Fortune* (Vergottis) and *Merchant Royal* (Lykiardopulo) moved their ships to Panamanian-flagged subsidiaries, the first being renamed *Calygera*, the second *Oceana*. The subsequent careers of this pair provide a neat case study in international tramp ownership in the new FOC environment. Vergottis moved *Calygera* back to its British-flagged Alcyone Shipping Co in 1954, renaming her *Alcyone Faith*, and then sold her two years later to Salvatores of Genoa, Italy, who registered her with a Liberian-flagged subsidiary as *African Baron*. Lykiardopulo also made a second change of flags, moving *Oceana* to the Greek register as *Okeanis* in 1960 before selling her to another Italian FOC operator, Consulich of Trieste, with whom she returned to Panamanian colours as *Fides*.

Sales off the UK register commenced again in the mid-1950s. By this time, some vessels were undoubtedly beginning to face substantial maintenance costs to keep them in class. Above this, however, the twin pressures of the progressive globalisation of ship ownership and increasing competition from FOC operators were squeezing British companies' profit margins harder and harder. Three ships left the home flag in 1955. Of these, two, *Avisvale* and *Avismere*, were sold by the Aviation & Shipping Co, which was replacing its steamships with second-hand motor ships of similar vintage. The identities of the new owners of these vessels provide an insight into the changing face of the global tramp shipping industry. The first ship went to Sebastiano Tuillier, an Italian expatriate domiciled in Lugano, Switzerland and raised the Costa Rican flag as *Uje*, while the second went to the Tidewater Corporation, a Baltimore-based management company set up by Alberto Ravano fu Pietro of Genoa and was registered in Liberia as *Deep River*. The other seller was Ropner, which sold *Heronspool* to yet another Italian operator, Achille Lauro of Naples, who extracted another twelve years of service from her as *Liana* after conversion to diesel propulsion.

Three more vessels left the red ensign in 1956, all for the Liberian flag. Adelphi Vergottis sold Alcyone Shipping's last two Oceans to two different Italian-controlled offshore companies, *Alcyone Angel* joining the recently acquired *Deep River* in Ravano's Tidewater fleet as *Continental*, and *Alcyone*

Above: *Uje*, photographed at Port Said on 25 May 1960 flying the Panamanian flag and wearing the colours of the Lugano-based Italian expatriate Sebastiano Tuillier, had previously sailed under the red ensign as *Ocean Faith* and *Avisvale*. *(Dr George Wilson)*

Below: *Liana* (ex-*Heronspool*, ex-*Ocean Valour*) her profile changed by the low raked funnel fitted when her new Italian owner Achille Lauro converted her to a motor ship, arriving at Venice in May 1965. *(Malcolm Cranfield collection)*

Faith becoming *African Baron* for Salvatores' West African Navigation Ltd, as described above. The third, Ben Line's *Benlomond*, marked the first Ocean disposal by a British liner company apart from Clan Line's forced sale of *Clan Macquarrie* to the breakers in 1953, the vessel joining the tramp trade as the Greek-owned, Liberian-flagged *Yangos*.

An Italian ship in Liberian colours, *African Lady* (ex-*Garryvale*, ex-*Broompark*, ex-*Ocean Strength*) was one of a pair of Oceans acquired from British owners in 1956–7 by Salvatores & C of Genoa. *(World Ship Society Ltd)*

The tramp shipping market collapsed in 1957 and remained in a depressed condition until the end of the decade, prompting a general clear-out of older tonnage among British owners. The Glasgow-registered *Galavale* and *Garryvale* were both sold in 1957. In this case, the Crawford family, tramp ship owners for half a century, sold all their shares in the Buchanan Shipping Co Ltd to a London finance house which then disposed of the three-vessel fleet and converted their corporate acquisition into an investment company. The two ex-Oceans both went to Italian owners, *Galavale* hoisting the Italian flag as *Confidenza* for Corrado of Genoa, and *Garryvale* becoming *African Lady* for Salvatores, the same FOC operator who had acquired *Alcyone Faith* the year before. In the following year, Alexander Tsavliris transferred both *Granny Suzanne* and *Claire T* to Panama-based subsidiaries, the vessels themselves joining the Liberian registry as *Free Enterprise* and *Free Trader*, names which might have been a sly acknowledgement of the benefits of going offshore.

The two largest British tramp owners of ex-Ocean tonnage, Lyle Shipping of Glasgow, and Ropner of West Hartlepool, both sold off their remaining war-built ships in 1959–60. As recently as January 1957, Lyle had sold the ex-Liberty *Cape Verde* for £515,000 to FOC buyers. By April 1959, depressed market conditions had convinced the company that its two ex-Oceans, *Cape Corso* and *Cape Nelson*, were 'unable to make money on today's rates of freight.' *Cape Corso*, which was facing a potentially expensive survey at the end of the year, became the first of her class to be scrapped after the unlucky *Clan Macquarrie*, realising only £57,500 on sale to Hong Kong breakers. *Cape Nelson* went to owners in the same port several months later as *Happy Sunshine* and, although sold for further trading, still fetched only £72,500. Ropner, for its part, had been forced to lay up seven of its fleet of fifteen vessels by the spring of 1958. With a series of new motor ships arriving from the builders, it too began to sell off its 1940s-vintage steamers. Two ships were sold in the summer of 1959, *Pikepool* joining the Livanos fleet under the Greek flag as *Marigo*, and *Oakby* hoisting Lebanese colours for Pateras, another Greek owner, as *Erinio*. The final pair left in the first half of 1960, *Teespool* going to the Clipper Steamship Co Ltd of Hong Kong where she was managed by Wallem & Co on behalf of the underlying owner Y K Pao, as *Wynn* without change of registry, and *Ingleby* being transferred to the Bahaman flag as *Maratha Enterprise* after sale to the shipping arm of Chowgule & Co Ltd, a diversified Indian industrial group with its headquarters in Goa.

These sales were mirrored by a clear-out of ex-Oceans by the liner operators. The Ben Line sold *Benrinnes* to a Bahaman-flagged, Hong Kong-based operator in January 1959 and, as highlighted above *Bennevis* to a London tramp owner a month later. The Clan Line group sold *Clan Macbride* and

was purchased in 1955, she served first as the British *Granny Suzanne*, then successively as the Liberian *Free Enterprise* and the Greek *Alexandros Tsavliris*, then as the provisionally registered British *Newdene*, a name she retained during her brief stay on the Haitian register, and finally as the Cypriot *Free Navigator* before going to the breakers in 1969.

Overseas Sales and Other Disposals by British Owners

Final British Name	Sale	New Name	Flag (Domicile)	Owner	Nationality
Raphael	12.1950	*Siram*	Panama	Embiricos	Greece
Ramsay	2.1951	*Stork*	Panama	Goulandris	Greece
*Alcyone Fortune**	6.1951	*Calygera*#	Panama	Vergottis	UK/Greece
Ruysdael	9.1951	*Santa Irene*	Costa Rica (Panama)	Pateras	Greece
*Merchant Royal**	10.1951	*Oceana*	Panama	Lykiardopulo	UK/Greece
Heronspool	2.1955	*Liana*	Italy	Lauro	Italy
Avisvale	2.1955	*Uje*	Costa Rica (Panama)	Tuillier	Switzerland/Italy
Avismere	3.1955	*Deep River*	Liberia	Tidewater/Ravano	USA/Italy
Benlomond	3.1956	*Yangos*	Liberia (Panama)	Mazarakis	Greece
Alcyone Faith	7.1956	*African Baron*	Liberia	Salvatores	Italy
Alcyone Angel	1956	*Continental*	Liberia (Panama)	Tidewater/Ravano	USA/Italy
Galavale	1957	*Confidenza*	Italy	Corrado	Italy
Garryvale	1957	*African Lady*	Liberia	Salvatores	Italy
*Claire T**	1.1958	*Free Trader*	Liberia (Panama)	Tsavliris	UK/Greece
*Granny Suzanne**	1.1958	*Free Enterprise*	Liberia (Panama)	Tsavliris	UK/Greece
Herminius	3.1958	*Ekberg*	Panama	Wallem/P S Li	Hong Kong
Clan Macbride	5.1958	*Alice*	Panama	Wheelock Marden/C S Koo	Hong Kong
Hellenes	6.1958	*Janmada*	India	Malabar	India
Clan Kenneth	10.1958	*Omonia II*	Greece (Panama)	Xenios	Greece
Benrinnes	1.1959	*Twinbear*	Bahamas	Great Southern/F Tsao	Hong Kong
Clan Macbeth	4.1959	*Madonna*	Panama	Wheelock Marden/E Tsu	Taiwan
Cape Corso	6.1959			Shipbreakers	Hong Kong
Pikepool	6.1959	*Marigo*	Greece (Panama)	Livanos	Greece
Oakby	7.1959	*Erinio*	Lebanon (Panama)	Pateras	UK/Greece
Clan Kennedy	8.1959			Shipbreakers	Japan
Cape Nelson	12.1959	*Happy Sunshine*	Hong Kong	World-Wide/Y K Pao	Hong Kong
Teespool	1.1960	*Wynn*	UK/Hong Kong##	Clipper/Y K Pao	Hong Kong
Ingelby	6.1960	*Maratha Enterprise*	Bahamas	Chowgule	Goa, India
Clan Macbean	8.1960		-	Shipbreakers	Japan
Clan Macbrayne	3.1961		-	Shipbreakers	Japan
Sithonia	12.1961		-	Shipbreakers	UK
Saint Edmund	5.1962	*Lucrino*	Italy	Lauro	Italy
Charles Dickens	11.1962	*Cleo*	Panama	Ioannou	UK/Greece
Winchester Queen	11.1966		-	Shipbreakers	Spain
Winchester King	12.1966	*Pacific Trader*	Panama	Intercontinental	Hong Kong

* Re-flagged without change of ownership # Returned to the British register 6.1954 as *Alcyone Faith* ## Remained on the West Hartlepool register

Sales and Disposals by Overseas Owners

Initial Name	Flag	Previous name	Sold	New Name	New Flag (Owner)
Amstelveen	Netherlands	*Jan Steen (Ocean Victory)*	1959	*Polly*	Taiwan
Amstelstad	Netherlands	*Jan Lievens (Ocean Merchant)*	1959	*Dunn*	Hong Kong
Ternate	Netherlands	*Govert Flinck (Ocean Athlete)*	1959	*Kasert*	Hong Kong (PRC)
Capitaine Lauwerins	Belgium	*Belgian Veteran (Ocean Veteran)*	1961	*Sanrocco*	Panama (Switzerland/Italy)
Alceo	Italy	*Ocean Viking**	1963	*Allegra*	Panama (Italy)
Nereo	Italy	*Ocean Vanquisher**	1963	Japanese shipbreakers	
Bialystok	Poland	*Ocean Hope*	1971	Spanish shipbreakers	
Andrea C	Italy	*Ocean Virtue**	1982	Italian shipbreakers	

* Post-war salvage

Marine Discoverer (ex-*Happy Sunshine*, ex-*Cape Nelson*, ex-*Ocean Vulcan*), photographed steaming up the Derwent River to Risdon on 25 June 1961, became the last Ocean marine casualty when she was beached near Chittagong in 1966 due to a serious cargo fire and then sold as a constructive total loss to the breakers in Japan.
(David Kirby/R A Priest/Nautical Association of Australia collection)

The End of the Line

Apart from the two Clan Line losses, six other vessels would become marine casualties, all after leaving British ownership. Only the first of these, the Greek-flagged *Santa Irene*, became a total loss in the incident itself. Of the other five, two were recovered after stranding, and three survived serious fires (with the last four incidents taking place within a month and a half of each other in the spring of 1966), but as all the ships were over twenty years old, it is not particularly surprising that each was declared a constructive total loss and sold to the shipbreakers. The ships concerned

Post-War Losses from Marine Causes

Name	Flag	Last UK Name	Date	Particulars	Fate
Clan Macquarrie	UK	*Clan Macquarrie*	31.1.1953	Stranded, Hebrides	Scrapped
Clan Keith	UK	*Clan Keith*	5.11.1961	Wrecked, Cape Bon	Sank
Santa Irene	Greece	*Ruysdael*	2.11.1962	Wrecked, Tarifa	Broke up
Roumeli	Lebanon	*Ramsay*	3.2.1963	Stranded, Gijon	Scrapped
Omonia II	Greece	*Clan Kenneth*	13.4.1966	Fire, Amsterdam	Scrapped
Newgrove	Cyprus	*Newgrove*	14.5.1966	Stranded, Cuba	Abandoned
Susana K L	Liberia	*Oakby*	16.5.1966	Fire, West Pacific	Scrapped
Marine Discoverer	Hong Kong	*Cape Nelson*	23.5.1966	Fire, Chittagong	Scrapped

were tramping all over the world until the end, with the last four losses occurring in a north European port, in the West Indies, and in the Pacific and Indian Oceans. Registration, too, was a worldwide phenomenon, with the casualties flying five different flags.

The first ex-Ocean to go to the breakers after the unfortunate *Clan Macquarrie* in 1953 was another Glasgow-registered vessel, Lyle Shipping's *Cape Corso*, which made its final voyage to a Far East scrapyard in September 1959. In total, five of the first six ships broken up had only served one British owner (although *Clan Kennedy* did sail for Japan as *Kelly*, having been sold to a Taiwanese concern for the delivery voyage only). One of these, Henry M Thomson's *Sithonia*, was destined to be the only other vessel apart from *Clan Macquarrie* to be broken up in the UK. Disposals from the worldwide fleet progressed steadily through the 1960s, with the peak occurring in 1966–7, when eleven ships were broken up. Further scrapping of eight vessels in 1968–9 left just five afloat at the start of the 1970s. Two of these, Achille Lauro's *Lucrino* and Poland's *Bialystok*, were gone by the end of 1971, leaving the much-converted *Andrea C* to soldier on alone in western waters into the early 1980s. While information on their final fate is lacking, the last survivors were almost certainly the Communist Chinese sisters *Zhan Dou 26* and *Zhan Dou 75*, which probably went to the breakers in the mid-1980s.

Lucrino, seen here sailing from Durban in 1968 with a deck cargo of motor vehicles, had served the Saint Line for sixteen years first as *Ocean Vista* and then as *Saint Edmund* before sale to Achille Lauro, who would operate her until 1970, when she made her last voyage to the breaker's yard at La Spezia. *(Trevor Jones)*

The Last Voyage

Name	Owner	Flag (Domicile)	Last UK Name	Date	Breakers
*Clan Macquarrie**	UK	UK	*Clan Macquarrie*	1.1953	Troon, UK
Cape Corso	UK	UK	*Cape Corso*	9.1959	Hong Kong
*Kelly***	Taiwan/ UK	Taiwan	*Clan Kennedy*	3.1960	Japan
Continental	USA/Italy	Liberia (Panama)	*Alcyone Angel*	7.1960	Taiwan
Clan Macbean	UK	UK	*Clan Macbean*	8.1960	Hong Kong
Clan Macbrayne	UK	UK	*Clan Macbrayne*	3.1961	Japan
Clan Keith	UK	UK	*Clan Keith*	11.1961	wrecked
Sithonia	UK	UK	*Sithonia*	12.1961	Preston, UK
Janmada	India	India	*Hellenes*	4.1962	India
Deep River	USA/Italy	Liberia	*Avismere*	6.1962	Italy
Uje	Switzerland/Italy	Costa Rica (Panama)	*Avisvale*	8.1962	Italy
Santa Irene	Greece	Greece (Panama)	Ruysdael	11.1962	wrecked
*Roumeli**	UK/Greece	Lebanon (Panama)	*Ramsay*	1963	Spain
Polly	Taiwan	Taiwan	*Ocean Victory*	1963	Taiwan
Kuala Terengganu	Hong Kong	Bahamas	*Benrinnes*	1.1963	Japan
Nereo	Italy	Italy	*Ocean Vanquisher*	11.1963	Japan
Sincere Trader	Taiwan	Taiwan	*Clan Macbeth*	11.1964	Taiwan
Ekberg	Hong Kong	Panama	*Herminius*	12.1964	Japan
African Lady	Italy	Liberia	*Garryvale*	1.1965	Japan
African Baron	Italy	Liberia	*Alcyone Faith*	6.1965	Japan
*Omonia II**	Greece	Greece (Panama)	*Clan Kenneth*	7.1966	West Germany
*Susana K L**	Philippines	Liberia (Panama)	*Oakby*	8.1966	Taiwan
Alice	Hong Kong	Panama	*Clan Macbride*	10.1966	Japan
Yangos	Greece	Greece (Panama)	*Benlomond*	10.1966	Spain
Winchester Queen	UK	UK	*Winchester Queen*	11.1966	Spain
Cleo	Greece	Panama	*Charles Dickens*	1.1967	Japan
*Newgrove****	Greece	Cyprus	*Newgrove*	1.1967	Cub
*Marine Discoverer**	Hong Kong	Hong Kong	*Cape Nelson*	2.1967	Japan
Liana	Italy	Italy	*Heronspool*	2.1967	Italy
Confidenza	Italy	Italy	*Galavale*	9.1967	Italy
Amfitriti	Greece	Cyprus	*Pikepool*	10.1967	Taiwan
Golden Phoenix	Hong Kong	UK (Bahamas)	*Teespool*	1.1968	Japan
Syros	Greece	Greece (Panama)	*Raphael*	7.1968	China
Karimantan	Hong Kong	Panama	*Winchester King*	8.1968	Taiwan
Welcome	Taiwan	Panama	*Ingleby*	3.1969	Taiwan
Free Navigator	Greece	Cyprus	*Newdene*	7.1969	Italy
Defis	Italy	Cyprus	*Merchant Royal*	8.1969	Japan
Allegra	Italy	Panama	*Ocean Viking*	10.1969	Spain
Sanrocco	Switzerland/Italy	Panama	*Ocean Veteran*	11.1969	Italy
Lucrino	Italy	Italy	*Saint Edmund*	1.1970	Italy
Bialystok	Poland	Poland	*Ocean Hope*	11.1971	Spain
Andrea C	Italy	Italy	*Ocean Virtue*	12.1982	Italy
Zhan Dou 75	China	China	*Ocean Athlete*	1985	China
Zhan Dou 26	China	China	*Ocean Merchant*	1992	Untraced

* Sold to shipbreakers as a constructive total loss ** Sold to Taiwan owner and renamed for delivery voyage to shipbreakers

*** Abandoned to the Cuban government as a wreck

Ocean Glory making it abundantly clear that she is still coal-fired as she sails from Cape Town in the colours of her post-war charterer, the Clan Line. *(Roy Fenton collection)*

Liberties, both of which were sold in the 1958–61 window.

While Clan Line's Empires lasted a year or so longer than its Oceans and Liberties, fleet service and durability were much more similar in the fleet of tramp operator Ropner. This company had acquired six Empires at the end of 1945 and gone on to purchase the six Oceans it had under charter in early 1947, rounding off the rebuilding programme by buying three *Sam*-Liberty ships later in the same year. In this case, disposals began in the mid-1950s, with one *Sam* leaving in 1952, two *Sams* and one Empire in 1954, two Oceans in 1955, and one Empire in 1956. The remaining eight ships all departed the fleet in 1959-62. Two former Empires made relatively early trips to the breakers, only one of these directly from Ropner ownership, and two others just lasted into the early 1970s, while the remaining vessels (less one abandoned as a constructive total loss in 1962) were scrapped between 1966 and 1969.

Before concluding, it is interesting to look at the overall statistics for ex-*Sam* Liberty ships in post-war UK commercial service. British operators purchased 116 of these ships when their bareboat government charters expired in 1947. Five became marine losses while in British commercial service, leaving 111 in the sample for comparative purposes. These ships had been built in the second half of 1943 and the

Purchased by Clan at the end of 1947, *Ocean Glory* was renamed *Clan Macbeth*, under which name she was photographed arriving again at Cape Town in August 1951. *(Malcolm Cranfield collection)*

Sold east by Clan in early 1959, the former *Clan Macbeth* operated as *Madonna* under the Panamanian flag in the colours of the Hong Kong firm of ship managers Wheelock, Marden & Co, who operated the vessel on behalf of her new owner, V K Eddie Hsu of Keelung in Taiwan.
(C C Hsu – Eddie Steamship Co Ltd)

first half of 1944 and were thus on average a year and a half younger than the 1942-built Oceans and Empires. The ex-Liberties might also have been considered a more attractive proposition as they were built with oil-fired water-tube boilers and did not need expensive conversion from coal-burning. While these ships did prove more durable overall, averaging twenty-five years in age when they finally went to the breakers, the data for their initial stay on the UK register points in the opposite direction, the figure of fourteen years being two and three years shorter than those for the Oceans and Empires, respectively. It would be unwise to over-analyse this data, not least because the Liberties were more heavily purchased by liner companies driven by different commercial concerns from tramp owners. The closely grouped mean disposal years for the three classes of vessel (1957 for the *Sams*, 1958 for the Oceans and 1959 for the Empires) would suggest that the fairest broad conclusion would be that general trading conditions and fleet renewal trends were responsible for a general selling-off of war-built tonnage by British owners,

Hsu took over direct management of his ship in 1961, moving her to the Taiwanese flag, where she ended her career as *Sincere Trader.*
(A Duncan/Roy Fenton collection)

Cayzer, Irvine & Co Ltd – Acquisition and Disposal of War-Built Vessels

Vessel	Charter	Purchase	New Name	Disposal	Purpose
Empire Barrie		11.1945	*Clan Alpine*	11.1960	Breaking up, Japan (constructive total loss)
Empire Forest		12.1945	*Clan Allan*	8.1961	Further trading – Mullion & Co, Hong Kong
Empire Prince		1.1946	*Clan Angus*	4.1962	Breaking up, Japan
Empire Cato	4.1946	12.1947	*Clan Mackenzie*	10.1960	Breaking up, Hong Kong
Empire Pickwick	5.1946	12.1947	*Clan Mackendrick*	3.1961	Further trading – Mullion & Co, Hong Kong
Empire Lankester	8.1946	12.1947	*Clan MacKellar*	5.1961	Further trading – Mullion & Co, Hong Kong
Empire Capulet		5.1946	*Hesione*	10.1960	Breaking up, Hong Kong
Empire Falkland		5.1946	*Stirlingshire*	9.1966	Breaking up, Belgium
Empire Fawley		11.1946	*Clan Mackinlay*	11.1962	Breaking up, Hong Kong
Empire Dunnet		9.1946	*Clan Mackinnon*	5.1961	Further trading – Mullion & Co, Hong Kong
Empire Gunfleet		9.1946	*Clan Mackay*	6.1962	Further trading – Teh-Hu Stmship Co, Hong Kong
Empire Southwold		5.1946	*Hesperia/Clan Murdoch*	1.1962	Further trading – Sadikzade Rusen, Istanbul
Empire Longstone		8.1946	*Hesperides/Clan Murray*	11.1962	Breaking up, Japan
Sambrian		6.1947	*Clan Macfarlane*	4.1961	Further trading – Frinton Shipbrokers, London
Samderwent		6.1947	*Clan Macfadyen*	5.1958	Further trading – Adelphi Vergottis, London
Ocean Glory	4.1946	12.1947	*Clan Macbeth*	4.1959	Further trading – E Hsu, Taiwan
Ocean Courier	5.1946	12.1947	*Clan Macbean*	8.1960	Breaking up, Japan
Ocean Viceroy	6.1946	12.1947	*Clan Kenneth*	10.1958	Further trading – E Xenios, Piraeus
Ocean Gypsy	7.1946	12.1947	*Clan Macbride*	5.1958	Further trading – C S Koo, Hong Kong
Ocean Messenger	8.1946	12.1947	*Clan Macbrayne*	3.1961	Breaking up, Japan
Ocean Verity	9.1946	12.1947	*Clan Keith*	11.1961	Marine loss
Ocean Viscount	1.1947	12.1947	*Clan Kennedy*	8.1959	Breaking up, Japan
Ocean Vesper	5.1946*	1.1951	*Clan Macqueen/Herminius*	3.1958	Further trading – P S Li, Hong Kong
Ocean Wayfarer	7.1946*	1.1951	*Clan Macquarrie*	7.1953	Breaking up, UK (constructive total loss)
Ocean Vestal	11.1946#	2.1952	*Hellenes*	6.1958	Further trading – Malabar Stmship Co, Bombay

* chartered by Thompson Steamshipping # purchased by Thompson Steamshipping

regardless of type. In 1955, the number of war-built cargo vessels in British commercial service was down by only one from the 1950 figure for ex-Fort/Parks, and stood at 80 per cent of that figure for British ships built to private contract, 76 per cent for ex-Empires, 75 per cent for ex-Oceans and 64 per cent for ex-Liberties (the quicker sell-off of which was partially due to their higher ownership by liner companies). By 1960, the total number of war-built cargo ships had fallen to just 119, with almost-two thirds of the decline having taken place after 1955. The Canadian-built standard ships and the private contract British equivalents remained the more durable, with 44 per cent and 33 per cent respectively of the 1950 figure remaining in service. Only 22 to 26 per cent of the other three types were still with the red ensign.

Overall, an average of roughly twenty-three years of service from the Oceans should be considered a more than adequate return on an emergency wartime building venture. Even at the beginning of 1962, with the ships completing their second decade afloat, there were still thirty-five Oceans in service around the world, and nineteen of these were still

Sir R Ropner & Co Ltd – Acquisition and Disposal of War-Built Vessels

Vessel	Charter	Purchase	New Name	Disposal	Purpose
Empire Cabot		1945	*Clearpool*	1954	Further trading – Cardigan Shipping, Cardiff
Empire Lionel		1945	*Levenpool*	1962	Further trading – A Tsavliris, London
Empire Sunbeam		1945	*Swainby*	1962	Further trading – A Tsavliris, London
Empire Tide		1945	*Thirlby*	1956	Further trading – Wheelock, Marden, Hong Kong
Empire Irving		1945	*Bellerby*	1960	Further trading – Iranian Lloyd, Khorramshahr
Empire Clarion		1945	*Cedarpool*	7.1959	Breaking up, West Germany
Ocean Vengeance	4.1946	2.1947	*Ingleby*	6.1960	Further trading – Chowgule, Nassau/Goa
Ocean Valour	6.1946	2.1947	*Heronspool*	3.1955	Further trading – A Lauro, Naples
Ocean Pride	7.1946	2.1947	*Oakby*	7.1959	Further trading – Pateras Shipbrokers, London
Ocean Pilgrim	8.1946	2.1947	*Pikepool*	6.1959	Further trading – J Livanos, Piraeus
Ocean Fame	8.1946	2.1947	*Firby*	3.1955	Further trading – N G Kyriakides, London
Ocean Vanity	10.1946	2.1947	*Teespool*	1.1960	Further trading – P S Li, Hong Kong
Samlistar		6.1947	*Hurworth*	6.1954	Further trading – T. Voyazides, Piraeus
Samdart		8.1947	*Sedgepool*	8.1954	Further trading – Tabor Shipping, Nassau
Samtay		10.1947	*Rudby*	6.1952	Further trading – Transmarina S A, Panama

War-Built Tramp and Liner Cargo Vessels in British Commercial Service, 1950–65

year	Empire (no)	(%)	UK private (no)	(%)	Ocean (no)	(%)	Fort/Park* (no)	(%)	Sam/Liberty (no)	(%)	total (no)
1950	134	*35.2*	75	*18.2*	36	*8.7*	52	*12.6*	115	*27.9*	412
1951	125		70		31		59		100		385
1952	118		66		31		56		88		359
1953	116		65		30		56		83		350
1954	111		63		30		52		77		333
1955	102	*32.5*	60	*19.1*	27	*8.6*	51	*16.2*	74	*23.6*	314
1956	92		55		25		49		66		287
1957	86		50		23		33		65		257
1958	75		44		16		29		52		216
1959	52		32		11		26		40		161
1960	33	*27.7*	25	*21.0*	8	*6.7*	23	*19.3*	30	*25.2*	119
1961	18		23		5		20		23		89
1962	12		15		5		18		15		65
1963	7		10		3		16		10		46
1964	5		9		3		13		9		39
1965	5	*13.9*	7	*19.4*	3	*8.3*	14	*38.9*	7	*19.4*	36

* Excludes Canadian-owned, British-flagged vessels Source: I G Stewart, British Tramps and Their Contribution to World Shipping History

plying their trade five years later. The uneven nature of technological progress and the severe oscillations of shipping market conditions have combined at times either to stretch or abbreviate the average working life of sea-going cargo vessels, but very roughly speaking, an average lifespan of anything over twenty years could be considered more than satisfactory. It seems fair to conclude that the Oceans were as competitive as most steam tramps in the late 1940s and early 1950s. While many British owners might have wished to make an earlier move into more modern tonnage, the shipyard resources to allow this simply did not exist. After three demanding years of wartime service, the first decade of peace saw the Oceans doing a more than adequate job of filling in a shortage of shipping capacity when no other viable remedies to the problem existed. The steady stream of purchases by foreign owners in the following decade equally demonstrated that the ships remained competitive in a FOC environment.

These conclusions are supported by overall figures for the British commercially owned tramp fleet over the first two decades of peace, broken down between pre-war, war-built, and post-war tonnage. Even in 1946, war-built tonnage (at this stage largely vessels built to private order, most government-owned tonnage remaining having not yet been sold) made up 35 per cent of the fleet. This percentage increased steeply over the remainder of the decade as several hundred Government-owned British, Canadian, and American-built standard ships were sold to commercial operators. By 1951–2 these vessels accounted for 60 per cent of the fleet. The fleet peaked in size in 1950, and thereafter began to shrink, largely because older pre-war vessels were going to the breakers or being sold to foreign buyers in ever increasing numbers. Over the first five years of the period, owners struggled to acquire new tonnage from the domestic shipbuilding industry, and post-war construction only passed 10 per cent of the total fleet in 1950. In 1956, war-built tonnage still accounted for 50 per cent of the shrinking British tramp fleet, and it was only in 1958 that its share fell below that of post-war tonnage. Overall, war-built ships, the Oceans among them, remained the most important component of the British tramp fleet for roughly fifteen years after they were built.

The British Commercial Tramp Fleet, 1946–60

year	ships (no)	grt (million)	pre-war %	war-built %	post-war %
1946	391	2.25	61	35	4
1947	484	2.89	45	49	6
1948	478	2.90	40	53	7
1949	487	2.95	39	52	9
1950	569	3.60	30	59	11
1951	530	3.29	27	60	13
1952	494	3.07	24	60	16
1953	507	3.14	23	57	20
1954	508	3.13	19	55	26
1955	489	3.11	17	54	29
1956	467	2.88	16	50	34
1957	445	2.71	14	43	43
1958	417	2.65	11	40	49
1959	389	2.50	9	30	61
1960	362	2.49	7	23	70
1961	354	2.45	4	19	77
1962	343	2.38	4	15	81
1963	313	2.34	2	12	86
1964	286	2.14	1	11	88
1965	274	2.07	1	11	88

Source: I G Stewart, British Tramps and Their Contribution to World Shipping History

APPENDIX

— 1 —

OCEAN CLASS VESSEL SPECIFICATIONS

Closed shelter-deck steamship with scantlings to allow for deadweight of 10,500 tons on 26ft 10in draft, Lloyd's Summer Freeboard (draft 18in above that allowed for open shelter-deck configuration).

Length between perpendiculars	416ft 0in
Length L W line	427ft 0in
Length overall	441ft 6in
Breadth, extreme	57ft 0in
Breadth, moulded	56ft 10 ¾in
Depth moulded to upper deck	37ft 4in
Depth moulded to second deck	28ft 7in
Height of 'tween decks amidships at side	8ft 9in
Registered length	425.1ft
Registered breadth	57.0ft
Registered depth	34.85ft

Registered tonnage	Todd-California vessels	Todd-Bath vessels
Gross registered tonnage	7,174.44 tons	7,178.42 tons
Net registered tonnage	4,272.08 tons	4,279.66 tons

Designed service speed 11kts and a trial speed of 12kts, fully loaded in fair weather. Two lower masts, and one telescopic topmast of steel on port midship derrick post, arranged to clear Manchester Ship Canal bridges in ballast.

Double bottoms cellular, suitable for water ballast. Water ballast deep tank immediately aft of engine room. Fore and aft peak tanks arranged as ballast tanks. Total capacity 2,120 tons (at 35ft^3)

Eight watertight bulkheads extended to upper deck. Permanent cross bunker holding 525 tons, 45ft^3. Watertight tunnel fitted through cross bunker on centreline above tank top to make No 3 hold available as a reserve bunker.

Hatches

Five in number, three forward of the engine room and two aft

No 1	33ft 9in x 20ft 0in
No 2	35ft 0in x 20ft 0in
No 3	15ft 0in x 20ft 0in
No 4	29ft 9in x 20ft 0in
No 5	35ft 0in x 20ft 0in

Derricks

One steel 30-ton derrick to No 2 hatch
One steel 15-ton derrick to No 4 hatch
Ten steel 5-ton derricks on masts and derrick posts, two to each hatch

Cargo Capacity

Cargo spaces	Grain Capacity (ft^3)	Bale Capacity (ft^3)
No 1 hold	65,720	54,438
No 2 hold	102,240	90,678
No 3 hold	46,000	41,447
Port side frame 108 to frame 116	13,760	12,092
Starboard side frame 108 to frame 116	12,900	11,071
No 4 hold	61,820	53,772
No 5 hold	62,550	55,736
Total hold space	364,990	319,234
No 1 tween decks	39,510	38,754
No 2 tween decks	42,580	42,012
No 3 tween decks	15,610	14,739
No 4 tween decks	30,320	29,597
No 5 tween decks	20,040	20,824
Total tween decks	148,060	145,926
Total holds and tween decks	513,050	465,160

Bunkers

Bunker space	ft^3	Tons (at 45 ft^3)
Cross bunker (below second deck)	22,455	500
Bunker second deck (Including chute)	26,698	593
Pocket bunkers	418	9
Total permanent bunkers	49,571	1,102
No 3 hold including WT tunnel	44,020	978
No 3 tween decks	14,419	320
Total reserve bunkers	58,421	1,298
Total all bunkers	107,992	2,400

Machinery

Triple-expansion reciprocating steam engine

IHP	2,500
Cylinders	24 ½in – 37in – 70in
Stroke	48in
Valves	HP piston valve NP and LP matchbox valves
Boilers	Three 14ft 9in x 11ft 9in forced draft
Fuel	Coal only, hand fired
Steam	220lb/in^2 superheated to about 575° F

Machinery designed for 2,500IHP at about 76RPM. Surface condensing, condenser bolted to back columns. Air and bilge pumps by levers from LP engine crosshead.

Two independent feed pumps, 12in x 8in x 24in each ample for full power.

Michell, Kingsbury type or equal thrust block.

Four-bladed solid bronze propeller with cast iron spare.

Independent ballast and general service pumps.

25-ton evaporator supplying steam to distiller, capacity 1,500 US gallons per 24 hours.

Three boilers 14ft 9in extreme diameter x 11ft 9in extreme length.

Total heating surface about 7,140ft^2 arranged for Howden's forced draught. Working pressure 220lb/in^2 fitted with superheaters of the smoke type with clement heads 6in inside combustion chamber end of tubes. Headers fitted in smoke boxes. Designed to give a steam temperature of about 575° F when engines developing 2,500IHP. Three furnaces per boiler.

Electrical

Two steam driven generators of 15kw each at 100v DC.

Machinery Suppliers

One contract for sixty engines was placed with the General Machinery Corporation of Hamilton, Ohio, of which thirty were used to equip the ships built at Richmond. The registration papers of these vessels name the engine supplier as Hooven, Owens & Rentschler & Co of Hamilton, Ohio, but this is simply a different trade name for the same concern, the two original companies having merged in the 1920s.

These engines were identical and interchangeable with those ordered from a range of Canadian and US suppliers to equip both the Fort and Park-class ships building in Canada, and the Liberty ships building in the United States. In the event, fourteen of the engines originally destined for the last vessels building at South Portland were diverted to other ships, with substitutes being provided by three different Canadian engine builders:

Canadian Allis-Chalmers Ltd, Montreal, Quebec – Yard Nos 19, 22 & 28.

Dominion Engineering Works Ltd, Montreal, Quebec – Yard Nos 17, 18, 21, 24 & 26.

John Inglis Co Ltd, Toronto, Ontario – Yard Nos 20, 23, 25, 27, 29 & 30.

Two separate contracts for thirty sets of boilers each, those for the west coast ships being manufactured by the Western Pipe & Steel Company of Los Angeles and those for their east coast sisters by the American Locomotive Company of Schenectady, New York.

A large-scale, highly detailed marine architect's presentation model of *Ocean Traveller* produced by Gibbs & Cox – the only slight imperfection being the use of the American spelling *'Traveler'* on the ship's name boards!
(Mariners' Museum & Park)

Top: Broadside view of the complete model.

Left: Detailed view of the aft cargo-handling equipment looking forward, with the AND booms stored lying flush along the hatch sides.

Right: Detailed side view of the bridge structure with the errant name boards prominent.

APPENDIX

2

OCEAN CLASS VESSEL HISTORIES

Ocean Liberty at Cape Town in Neill & Pandelis colours with her wartime bridge armour still in place.
(John & Marion Clarkson collection)Park)

Built by Todd-California Shipbuilding Corporation (later Permanente Metals Corporation, Shipyard No.1), Richmond, California

Yard No 1
Ocean Vanguard

ON 168627
16.8.1941: Launched for the Ministry of War Transport, London (W H Seager & Co Ltd, Cardiff, managers).
27.10.1941: Delivered.
14.2.1942: Registered at Cardiff (2/1942).
13.9.1942: Torpedoed and sunk by the German submarine *U 515* about 45 miles east of Galera Point, Trinidad, in position 10°43′ north, 60°11′ west while on a voyage from Suez and Table Bay for Trinidad and New York in ballast. Of forty-five crew and six gunners, ten crew and one gunner were lost, and forty saved by the Norwegian motor ship *Braga* (1,671g/1938) and landed at Port of Spain, Trinidad.
7.10.1942: Register closed.

Yard No 2

Ocean Vigil

ON 168258

31.8.1941: Launched for the Ministry of War Transport, London (Bolton Steam Shipping Co Ltd, London, managers).

13.11.1941: Delivered.

12.2.1942: Registered at London (17/1942).

20.3.1946: Owners became the Ministry of Transport, London.

1.4.1946: Sold to the Bolton Steam Shipping Co Ltd, London.

17.5.1946: Renamed *Ramsay*.

6.1947: Converted to oil fuel.

16.2.1951: UK register closed on sale to Cia Naviera Maropan S A, Panama (Goulandris Bros (Hellas) Ltd, Piraeus, Greece) and renamed *Stork*.

1954: Transferred to Cia Maritima de Navegacion Conval, S A, Panama (Mrs. V N Goulandris/N J Goulandris Ltd, London).

1960: Sold to Derna Cia de Navegacion S A, Panama (John Livanos & Sons Ltd, London), registered at Beirut, Lebanon, and renamed *Roumeli*.

3.2.1963: Stranded while leaving dry dock at Gijon, Spain.

11.2.1963: Re-floated.

21.2.1963: Beached. Subsequently declared a compromised total loss and sold for breaking up.

Ocean Voice, seen here immediately after launch on 27 September 1941, would be deployed on north Russian convoy duty after arrival in Britain, surviving bomb damage on the outward voyage but not two torpedoes from *U 435* on the way home.
(Courtesy of San Francisco Maritime National Historical Park)

Yard No 3

Ocean Voice

ON 168708

27.9.1941: Launched for the Ministry of War Transport, London (Larrinaga Steamship Co Ltd, Liverpool, managers).

28.11.1941: Delivered.

5.3.1942: Registered at Glasgow (5/1942).

27.5.1942: Bombed by German Ju-88 aircraft of

Ocean Vigil in San Francisco Bay fresh from her sea trial on 9 November 1941.
(Richmond Museum of History)

Ocean Viking at anchor in Bedford Basin ready to sail from Halifax for Britain on 2 May 1943 in SC 129.
(John & Marion Clarkson collection)

Kampfgeschwader 30 in the Barents Sea while on a voyage from Glasgow and Reykjavik for Murmansk with military cargo as commodore ship in convoy PQ 16. Remained with convoy and arrived safely on 30.5.1942.
22.9.1942: Torpedoed and sunk by the German submarine *U 435* in the Norwegian Sea, west of Jan Mayen Island, in position 71°23′ north, 11°03′ west while on a voyage from Archangel for the UK as commodore ship in convoy QP 14 with a part cargo of 858 standards of timber and 1,121 metric tons of sulphite pulp. All fifty-eight crew and forty passengers were saved by the British minesweeper *Seagull* and the British rescue ship *Zamalek*.
19.10.1942: Register closed.

Yard No 4
Ocean Venture

No ON
27.9.1941: Launched for the Ministry of War Transport, London (Larrinaga Steamship Co Ltd, Liverpool, managers).
12.12.1941: Delivered.
8.2.42: Torpedoed and sunk by the German submarine *U 108* off Cape Hatteras, North Carolina, in position 37°05′ north, 74°46′ west while on her maiden voyage from Vancouver and Cristobal for Hampton Roads; Halifax, Nova Scotia; and the UK with a cargo of 9,115 tons of foodstuffs as well as four aircraft on deck. Of forty-three crew and two gunners, twenty-nine crew and two gunners were lost, and fourteen rescued by the American destroyer *Roe* (*DD-418*) and landed at Norfolk, Virginia.

Yard No 5
Ocean Viking

ON 168628
23.10.1941: Launched for the Ministry of War Transport, London (Bolton Steam Shipping Co Ltd, London, managers).
20.12.1941: Delivered.
1.4.1942: Registered at Cardiff (3/1942).
11.10.1943: Mined in the Mediterranean, off Taranto, in position 40°19.45′ north, 16°59.30′ east while on a voyage from Beirut for Taranto. No casualties among forty-six crew and twenty-one gunners. Made port under her own steam.
23.1.1944: Towed to Bari and scuttled as a blockship to fill a breach in the harbour breakwater.
10.9.1946: Sold to Italian salvors.
4.10.1946: UK register closed.
10.3.1947: Sailed from Bari after re-floating for repair by Cantieri Navali Riuniti, Palermo.
1947: Sold to Societa Ligure di Armamento, Genoa, Italy and renamed *Alceo*.
1963: Sold to Cia Comercial y Financiera Sudamericana S A, Panama (Cia Armatoriale Italiana S A S, Venice, Italy) and renamed *Allegra*.
15.10.1969: Arrived at Bilbao, Spain to be broken up.
7.12.1969: Breaking up started.

Ekberg unloading into lighters at Tokyo on 13 March 1960, operating under Hong Kong ownership after serving Thompson Steamshipping on charter as *Ocean Vesper* and then sailing as *Clan Macqueen* and *Herminius* after sale to the Clan Line.
(Raul Mara/W M Schell collection)

Yard No 6

Ocean Vesper

ON 168630

2.12.1941: Launched for the Ministry of War Transport, London (Kaye, Son & Co Ltd, London, managers).

16.1.1942: Delivered.

15.4.1942: Registered at Cardiff (6/1942).

15.4.1942: Management transferred to Connell & Grace Ltd, London.

20.3.1946: Owners became the Ministry of Transport, London.

29.5.1946: Chartered for five years to the Thompson Steamshipping Co Ltd, London.

29.1.1951: Sold to the Thompson Steamshipping Co Ltd, London.

20.4.1951: Sold for £184,500 to The Clan Line Steamers Ltd (Cayzer, Irvine & Co Ltd, managers), Glasgow.

1951: Re-registered at Glasgow (13/1951) and renamed *Clan Macqueen*.

7.1951: Converted to oil fuel.

3.12.1953: Transferred to the British and South American Steam Navigation Co Ltd (Houston Line Ltd, London, managers), London.

12.6.1954: Re-registered at London (128/1954).

9.7.1954: Renamed *Herminius*.

31.10.1957: Transferred to the Houston Line Ltd, London.

1.10.1958: UK register closed on sale to the Pan Norse Steamship Company S A (Wallem & Co Ltd, Hong Kong, managers), Panama (P S Li, Hong Kong) and renamed *Ekberg*.

1962: Transferred to Marine Development and Supply S A,

Ocean Valley was purchased by Alexander Shipping at the end of a three-year charter and renamed *Malmesbury*.
(World Ship Society Ltd)

Panama (P S Li, Hong Kong).
11.12.1964: Arrived at Onomichi, Japan, for breaking up by Koshin Sangyo K K.
12.12.1964: Breaking up started.
10.2.1965: Demolition complete.

Yard No 7
Ocean Valley

ON 168556
16.11.1941: Launched for the Ministry of War Transport, London (Capper, Alexander & Co, London, managers).
28.1.1942: Delivered.
8.5.1942: Registered at Manchester (3/1942).
20.3.1946: Owners became the Ministry of Transport, London.
27.6.1946: Chartered for three years to the Alexander Shipping Co Ltd, London.
26.3.1949: Sold for £110,500 less depreciation to the Alexander Shipping Co Ltd (Houlder Brothers & Co, managers), London.
2.4.1949: Re-registered at London (61/1949).
13.9.1949: Renamed *Malmesbury*.
7.3.1955: Sold for £230,000 to the Trafalgar Steamship Co Ltd (Tsavliris (Shipping) Ltd, managers), London.
9.3.1955: Renamed *Granny Suzanne*.
6.1955: Converted to oil fuel.
11.1.1958: UK register closed on transfer to the Nigean Shipping Co S A (same managers), Panama, registered at Monrovia, Liberia, and renamed *Free Enterprise*.
1959: Management transferred to Tsavliris (Hellas) Maritime Co Ltd, re-registered at Piraeus, Greece and renamed *Alexandros Tsavliris*.
6.6.1964: Transferred to the Trafalgar Steamship Co Ltd (Tsavliris (Shipping) Ltd, managers), London on a provisional certificate of British registry issued at Rotterdam and renamed *Newdene*.
1965: Transferred to the Pancristo Shipping Co S A (same managers), Panama, registered at Port-au-Prince, Haiti.
1965: Transferred to the Kantara Shipping Co Ltd (same managers), Famagusta, Cyprus, and renamed *Free Navigator*.
1.7.1969: Arrived at La Spezia, Italy in tow from Kynossoura where she had been laid up since 11.1968 to be broken up by Cantieri Navali del Golfo S p A.
12.1969: Breaking up started.

Yard No 8
Ocean Vestal

ON 168815
17.11.1941: Launched for the Ministry of War Transport, London (Kaye, Son & Co Ltd, London, managers).

A deeply laden *Ocean Vestal* photographed in 1946 at Auckland in the colours of Thompson Steamshipping.
(V H Young and L A Sawyer)

6.1.1942: Delivered.
13.4.1942: Registered at Liverpool (8/1942).
20.3.1946: Owners became the Ministry of Transport, London.
18.11.1946: Sold to the Thompson Steamshipping Co Ltd, London.
22.11.1946: Re-registered at London (425/1946).
26.11.1946: Renamed *Farningham*.
10.1949: Converted to oil fuel.
25.3.1952: Sold to The Clan Line Steamers Ltd. (Cayzer, Irvine & Co Ltd, managers), Glasgow.
1.7.1952: Transferred to the British and South American Steam Navigation Co Ltd (Houston Line Ltd, London, managers), London.
18.8.1952: Renamed *Hellenes*.
31.10.1957: Transferred to the Houston Line Ltd, London.
3.6.1958: UK register closed on sale to the Malabar Steamship Co Ltd, Bombay, India, and renamed *Janmada*.
15.4.1962: Breaking up started at Bombay, India, by Abid and Co.

Yard No 9
Ocean Vision

ON 166054
18.12.1941: Launched for the Ministry of War Transport, London (Haldin & Philipps Ltd, London, managers).
6.2.1942: Delivered.
8.5.1942: Registered at Bristol (4/1942).

Avismere in South African waters wearing the colours of Noel Purvis's Aviation and Shipping Co Ltd which had previously chartered her as *Ocean Vision*.
(Roy Fenton collection)

20.3.1946: Owners became the Ministry of Transport, London.
15.7.1946: Chartered for three years to The Aviation and Shipping Co Ltd (N W Purvis, manager), London.
15.5.1947: Sold to The Aviation and Shipping Co Ltd (N W Purvis, manager), London.
4.6.1947: Re-registered at London (188/1947).
18.8.1947: Renamed *Avismere.*
9.3.1955: UK register closed on sale to the International Navigation Corp, Monrovia, Liberia (Tidewater Commercial Co, Baltimore, Maryland [Alberto Ravano fu Pietro, Genoa, Italy]) and renamed *Deep River.*
4.1957: Converted to oil fuel.
10.6.1962: Arrived at La Spezia, Italy, to be broken up by Cantieri Navali del Golfo S p A.
12.1962: Breaking up started.

Yard No 10
Ocean Vulcan

ON 168631
14.1.1942: Launched for the Ministry of War Transport, London (Idwal Williams & Co, Cardiff, managers).
20.2.1942: Delivered.
12.5.1942: Registered at Cardiff (7/1942).
20.3.1946: Owners became the Ministry of Transport, London.
5.2.1948: Sold for £182,000 to the Lyle Shipping Co Ltd, Glasgow.

Ocean Vulcan anchored at New York on 28 October 1942 a day after completing a two-month ballast passage back from the Red Sea via South Africa. *(US Coast Guard/Mariners' Museum & Park)*

1948: Re-registered at Glasgow (12/1948) and renamed *Cape Nelson.*
1949: Converted to oil fuel by Smiths Ltd, Middlesbrough.
1.12.1959: Sold for £72,500 to the Marine Navigation Co Ltd (World-Wide Co (Shipping Managers) Ltd, managers), Hong Kong (Y K Pao).
1960: Transferred to the Sunshine Shipping Co Ltd (same managers), Hong Kong, and renamed *Happy Sunshine.*
1961: Transferred to the Ace Shipping Co Ltd, Hong Kong (Marine Navigation Co, London – World-Wide) and renamed *Marine Discoverer* (same beneficial owners).
1961: Transferred to the Lotus Shipping Co Ltd, Hong Kong (same beneficial owners).
1964: Transferred to the Vine Shipping Co Ltd Hong Kong (same beneficial owners).
23.5.1966: Beached near Chittagong, East Pakistan, after fire had broken out in her cargo of coal while on a voyage from Chinwangtao to Chittagong.
7.6.1966: Arrived at Chittagong to discharge cargo.
4.2.1967: Arrived at Hirao, Japan, to be broken up by Matsukura Kaiji K K.
3.1967: Breaking up started.
5.1967: Demolition complete.

Yard No 11
Ocean Valour

ON 167853
20.1.1942: Launched for the Ministry of War Transport, London (W A Souter & Co Ltd, Newcastle upon Tyne, managers).
28.2.1942: Delivered.

Ocean Valour after charter to Ropner's Pool Shipping Co Ltd, which would rename her *Heronspool* after exercising its purchase option.
(A Green/R A Priest – Nautical Association of Australia collection)

29.5.1942: Registered at Southampton (1/1942).
20.3.1946: Owners became the Ministry of Transport, London.
26.6.1946: Chartered for five years to the Pool Shipping Co Ltd (Sir R Ropner & Co Ltd, Darlington, managers), West Hartlepool.
26.2.1947: Sold to the Pool Shipping Co Ltd (Sir R Ropner & Co Ltd, Darlington, managers), West Hartlepool.
8.3.1947: Re-registered at West Hartlepool (1/1947).
12.4.1949: Renamed *Heronspool.*
1.3.1955: UK register closed on sale to Achille Lauro, Naples; re-engined as motor ship and renamed *Liana*.
25.2.1967: Arrived at La Spezia, Italy, to be broken up by Cantieri Navali del Golfo S p A.

Yard No 12
Ocean Venus

No ON
31.1.1942: Launched for the Ministry of War Transport, London (John Morrison & Son, Newcastle-upon-Tyne, managers).
9.3.1942: Delivered.
3.5.1942: Torpedoed and sunk by the German submarine *U 564* about 12 miles east-southeast of Cape Canaveral, Florida, in position 28° 23′ north, 80° 21′ west while on a voyage from Union Bay and Cristobal for Halifax, Nova Scotia, and the UK with 9,450 tons of general cargo including 4,000 tons of lead, 4,000 tons of lumber, 1,000 tons of canned herring and 80 tons of acetone. Of forty-three crew and four gunners, five were lost and forty-two made it ashore in ship's boats.

Yard No 13
Ocean Vigour

ON 168826
14.2.1942: Launched for the Ministry of War Transport, London (E R Management Co Ltd, Cardiff, managers).
19.3.1942: Delivered.
27.6.1942: Registered at Liverpool (19/1942).
20.3.1946: Owners became the Ministry of Transport, London.
13.12.1948: Sold for £130,000 to the British Steam Shipping Co Ltd (John Cory & Sons Ltd, managers), Cardiff.
18.12.1948: Re-registered at Cardiff (13/1948).
24.12.1948: Renamed *Ramillies.*
12.1950: Converted to oil fuel.
30.6.1954: Transferred to the Orders & Handford Steamship Co Ltd (same managers), Cardiff.
2.3.1955: Sold to the Buchanan Shipping Co Ltd (Andrew Crawford & Co Ltd, managers), Glasgow.
1955: Re-registered at Glasgow (1/1955) and renamed *Galavale.*
22.2.1957: Owning company sold to the Avenue Finance Co Ltd, London.
1957: Sold to 'Corrado' Societa di Navigazione, Genoa, Italy

Ocean Vigour at anchor in Bedford Basin on 8 June 1943 carrying a cargo of grain for Britain which she had loaded at St John, New Brunswick. *(John & Marion Clarkson collection)*

and renamed *Confidenza*.
11.1966: Laid up awaiting disposal.
9.1967: Breaking up started at La Spezia, Italy by Cantieri Navali 'Santa Maria' S p A.

Yard No 14
Ocean Vanity

ON 168721
28.2.1942: Launched for the Ministry of War Transport, London (Raeburn & Verel Ltd, Glasgow, managers).
30.3.1942: Delivered.
24.6.1942: Registered at Glasgow (19/1942).
20.3.1946: Owners became the Ministry of Transport, London.
18.10.1946: Chartered for five years to the Pool Shipping Co Ltd (Sir R. Ropner & Co Ltd, Darlington, managers), West Hartlepool.
18.2.1947: Sold to the Pool Shipping Co Ltd (Sir R. Ropner & Co Ltd, Darlington, managers), West Hartlepool.
19.3.1947: Re-registered at West Hartlepool (2/1947).
12.4.1947: Renamed *Teespool*.
9.1949: Converted to oil fuel.
25.1.1960: Sold to the Clipper Steamship Co Ltd (Wallem & Co Ltd, managers), Hong Kong (Y K Pao). Registry

Wynn alongside, Hong Kong-owned but still registered at West Hartlepool, her homeport while sailing for Ropner's Pool Shipping Co Ltd which had purchased the chartered *Ocean Vanity* and renamed her *Teespool*. *(Roy Fenton collection)*

remained at West Hartlepool.
30.2.1960: Renamed *Wynn.*
1963: Management transferred to World-Wide (Shipping) Ltd (Y K Pao).
13.7.1964: Renamed *Golden Phoenix.*
4.8.1965: Transferred to the Nassau Maritime Co Ltd, Nassau, Bahamas (same managers). Registry remained at West Hartlepool.
7.1.1968: Sailed from Muroran for breaking up at Onomichi, Japan.
31.1.1968: Breaking up started.
16.2.1968: Register closed.

Yard No 15

Ocean Vintage

ON 164856
5.3.1942: Launched for the Ministry of War Transport, London (Muir Young Ltd, London, managers).
6.4.1942: Delivered.
26.6.1942: Registered at Middlesbrough (7/1942).
22.10.1942: Torpedoed and sunk by the Japanese submarine *I-27* near Masirah Island, Gulf of Oman in position 21° 37′ north, 60° 06′ east whilst on a voyage from New York and Durban for Abadan and Bandar Shapur with 9,300 tons of general cargo. All forty-four crew and six gunners were saved.
13.11.1942: Register closed.

Yard No 16

Ocean Volunteer

ON 168560
15.3.1942: Launched for the Ministry of War Transport, London (W H Cockerline & Co Ltd, Hull, managers).
14.4.1942: Delivered.
30.7.1942: Registered at Manchester (7/1942).
20.3.1946: Owners became the Ministry of Transport, London.
31.7.1946: Chartered for three years to the Alcyone Shipping Finance Co Ltd, London.

Ben Line's *Benrinnes* (ex-*Alcyone Union*, ex-*Ocean Volunteer*) showing her hull lines to good effect.
(John & Marion Clarkson collection)

26.7.1949: Sold for £100,000 to the Alcyone Shipping Finance Co Ltd, London (Adelphi Vergottis Ltd).
23.9.1949: Re-registered at London (214/1949).
14.11.1949: Renamed *Alcyone Union*.
20.9.1950: Sold to Ben Line Steamers Ltd. (William Thomson & Co, managers), Leith.
26.9.1950: Re-registered at Leith (13/1950) and renamed *Benrinnes*.
11.1950: Converted to oil fuel.
1.1959: Sold to the Queensland Shipping Co Ltd (Great Southern Steam Ship Co Ltd, Hong Kong, managers), Nassau, Bahamas (Frank Tsao Wen-king, Hong Kong) and renamed *Twinbear*.
1962: Renamed *Kuala Terengganu*.
1.1963: Arrived at Osaka, Japan to be broken up by Amakasu Sangyo Kisen K K.

Yard No 17

Ocean Veteran

ON 167855
28.3.1942: Launched for the Ministry of War Transport, London (Counties Ship Management Co Ltd, London, managers).
23.4.1942: Delivered.
27.7.1942: Registered at Southampton (3/1942).
21.6.1943: Sold to the Belgian government (Agence Maritime Internationale S A, managers), Antwerp, Belgium and renamed *Belgian Veteran*.
23.6.1943: UK register closed.
1948: Sold to Cie Maritime Belge (Lloyd Royal) S A, Antwerp, Belgium, and renamed *Capitaine Lauwerins*.
1961: Sold to Cia de Navegacion Indomitus S A, Panama (Sebastiano Tuillier, Lugano, Switzerland), and renamed *Sanrocco*.
26.11.1969: Arrived at La Spezia, Italy, to be broken up by Cantieri Navali del Golfo S p A.

Yard No 18

Ocean Voyager

ON 168831
6.4.1942: Launched for the Ministry of War Transport, London (H Hogarth & Sons, Glasgow, managers).
30.4.1942: Delivered.
27.7.1942: Registered at Liverpool (24/1942).
19.3.1943: Bombed and sunk by German Ju-88 aircraft at anchor in Tripoli harbour, Libya, while on a voyage from Alexandria for Tripoli with a cargo of 2,500 tons of high

Sanrocco, seen here passing Rozenburg in May 1965 in the colours of the Lugano-based Italian expatriate Sebastiano Tuillier, had been sold as *Ocean Veteran* to the Belgian government in 1943 and renamed *Belgian Veteran*, and had then seen peacetime commercial service for Cie Maritime Belge as *Capitaine Lauwerins*.
(Malcolm Cranfield collection)

explosives, 3,000 tons of aviation spirit and 1,000 tons of military stores. Of forty-four crew, nine gunners and two military policemen, five crew and one military policeman were lost.
23.4.1943: Register closed.

Yard No 19
Ocean Vista

ON 169057
11.4.1942: Launched for the Ministry of War Transport, London (The Saint Line Ltd, London, managers).
8.5.1942: Delivered.
12.8.1942: Registered at Manchester (9/1942).
20.3.1946: Owners became the Ministry of Transport, London.
15.5.1946: Chartered for three years to The Saint Line Ltd, London.
15.2.1948: Sold to The Saint Line Ltd (Mitchell, Cotts & Co Ltd, managers), London.
26.2.1948: Re-registered at London (65/1948).
27.3.1948: Renamed *Saint Edmund*.

Ocean Vista served the Saint Line for sixteen years, being renamed *Saint Edmund* after purchase off charter in 1948. *(Ships in Focus)*

6.1952: Converted to oil fuel.
3.5.1962: UK register closed on sale to Achille Lauro, Naples, Italy, and renamed *Lucrino*.
14.1.1970: Arrived at La Spezia, Italy, to be broken up by Cantieri Navali 'Santa Maria' S p A.

Yard No 20
Ocean Volga

ON 168311
21.4.1942: Launched for the Ministry of War Transport, London (H M Thomson, manager).
15.5.1942: Delivered.
4.9.1942: Registered at London (90/1942).
31.7.1944: Torpedoed by German motor torpedo boats of the 6th Flotilla (*S-91*, *S-97* and *S-114*) in the English Channel, off Beachy Head while on a voyage from Juno Beach, Normandy Bridgehead for the Thames in ballast in convoy FTM 53. There were no casualties among the sixty-four crew. Arrived at London for temporary repairs on the same day, and at Middlesbrough for permanent repairs on 6.8.1944.
20.3.1946: Owners became the Ministry of Transport, London.
30.7.1946: Sold to Henry Murray Thomson, Edinburgh.

Sithonia seen here in the Mersey, spent her entire commercial career in the small tramp fleet of Henry Murray Thomson, who had also managed her during wartime service as *Ocean Volga*.
(B Fielden/Ships in Focus)

14.10.1946: Renamed *Sithonia*.
10.1946: Converted to oil fuel.
18.12.1961: Arrived at Preston to be broken up by T W Ward Ltd.
11.10.1962: Register closed.

Yard No 21
Ocean Vengeance

ON 169059
21.4.1942: Launched for the Ministry of War Transport, London (Raeburn & Verel Ltd, Glasgow, managers).
21.5.1942: Delivered.

Ropner Shipping's *Ingleby*, photographed underway in ballast at Otago, New Zealand, had first served the company on charter as *Ocean Vengeance*.
(D Wright/Roy Fenton collection)

28.8.1942: Registered at Manchester (11/1942).
20.3.1946: Owners became the Ministry of Transport, London.
22.4.1946: Chartered for five years to the Ropner Shipping Co Ltd (Sir R Ropner & Co Ltd, Darlington, managers), West Hartlepool.
23.2.1947: Sold to the Ropner Shipping Co Ltd (Sir R Ropner & Co Ltd, Darlington, managers), West Hartlepool.
12.4.1947: Re-registered at West Hartlepool (6/1947).
27.10.1947: Renamed *Ingleby*.
2.1950: Converted to oil fuel.
21.6.1960: UK register closed following sale to the Chowgule Steamships (Bahamas) Ltd (Harley, Mullion & Co Ltd, managers), Nassau, Bahamas (Chowgule & Co Ltd, Murmagao, Goa, India), and renamed *Maratha Enterprise*.
1964: Management taken over by the Fife Shipping Co Ltd (Chowgule & Co Ltd, Murmagao, Goa, India).
1966: Sold to the Welcome Shipping Corporation S A, Panama (Great Ocean Steamship Co., Taipei, Taiwan), and renamed *Welcome*.
2.3.1969: Arrived at Kaohsiung, Taiwan, for breaking up.

Yard No 22

Ocean Vagrant

ON 166057
30.4.1942: Launched for the Ministry of War Transport, London (W H Cockerline & Co Ltd, Hull, managers).
27.5.1942: Delivered.
10.9.1942: Registered at Bristol (8/1942).
20.3.1946: Owners became the Ministry of Transport, London.
16.7.1946: Chartered for three years to the Baltic Shipping Co (Newcastle upon Tyne) Ltd, Newcastle upon Tyne.
16.8.1948: Sold to the Baltic Shipping Co (Newcastle upon Tyne) Ltd, Newcastle upon Tyne.
25.8.1948: Renamed *Atlantic Vagrant*.
7.12.1949: Sold for £77,500 to the Bolton Steam Shipping Co Ltd, London.
4.4.1950: Re-registered at London (57/1950).
17.4.1950: Renamed *Raphael*.
5.1950: Converted to oil fuel.
1.1.1951: UK register closed on sale to Cia de Vapores Siram S A, Panama (Maris A Embiricos, Andros, Greece), and renamed *Siram*.
1961: Sold to Syramar Cia Naviera S A, Panama (S Krystallis), registered at Syros, Greece and renamed *Syros*.
13.7.1968: Arrived at Shanghai, China, for breaking up.

Yard No 23

Ocean Viscount

ON 165840
9.5.1942: Launched for the Ministry of War Transport, London (Bibby Brothers & Co, Liverpool, managers).
31.5.1942: Delivered.
17.9.1942: Registered at Newcastle upon Tyne (21/1942).

Ocean Vagrant ready to sail from New York on 6 August 1942 for Halifax and her maiden crossing of the Atlantic in HX 203.
(US Coast Guard/Mariners' Museum & Park)

Clan Kennedy (ex-*Ocean Viscount*) in transit through the North Sea Canal during a peacetime career spent entirely in the service of the Clan Line.
(G Bunschoten/Malcolm Cranfield collection)

20.3.1946: Owners became the Ministry of Transport, London.
9.1.1947: Chartered for five years to The Clan Line Steamers Ltd (Cayzer, Irvine & Co Ltd, managers), Glasgow.
31.12.1947: Sold for £107,949 to The Clan Line Steamers Ltd (Cayzer, Irvine & Co Ltd, managers), Glasgow.
1948: Re-registered at Glasgow (10/1948) and renamed *Clan Kennedy*.
6.1951: Converted to burn oil fuel.
7.8.1959: Sold for £43,000 less 4 per cent commission to the Eddie Steamship Co, Keelung, Taiwan, for breaking up. Renamed *Kelly* for the delivery voyage from Rotterdam to Japan.
21.3.1960: Breaking up began at Yokohama, Japan.

Yard No 24
Ocean Verity

ON 167858
14.5.1942: Launched for the Ministry of War Transport,

Ocean Verity at Cape Town in Clan Line colours before she was purchased and renamed *Clan Keith*.
(John & Marion Clarkson collection)

London (Alfred Holt & Co, Liverpool, managers).
8.6.1942: Delivered.
21.9.1942: Registered at Southampton (7/1942).
1944: Management transferred to the Glen Line Ltd, London.
20.3.1946: Owners became the Ministry of Transport, London.
23.9.1946: Chartered for three years to The Clan Line Steamers Ltd (Cayzer, Irvine & Co Ltd, managers), Glasgow.
31.12.1947: Sold for £106,270 to The Clan Line Steamers Ltd (Cayzer, Irvine & Co Ltd, managers), Glasgow.
1948: Re-registered at Glasgow (6/1948) and renamed *Clan Keith*.
4.1950: Converted to burn oil fuel.
5.11.1961: Wrecked during a gale in poor visibility on rocks off Ecueils des Sorelles, in the Mediterranean, near Cap Bon, 11 miles south of Galita Island, Tunisia, while on a voyage from Middlesbrough and Malta for Colombo with general cargo. The after-part sank the same day and the forepart the next. Of sixty-eight crew, sixty-three were lost and five picked up by the motor vessel *Durham Trader* (6,214g/1959).

Yard No 25

Ocean Viceroy

ON 168734
19.5.1942: Launched for the Ministry of War Transport, London (P Henderson & Co, Glasgow, managers).
14.6.1942: Delivered.
24.9.1942: Registered at Glasgow (32/1942).
29.3.1943: Torpedoed by the German submarine *U 662* in the North Atlantic, about 425 miles northwest of Cape Finisterre in position 46° 44′ north 16° 38′ west while on a voyage from Pepel and Freetown to Sunderland in convoy SL 126 with a cargo of 8,650 tons of iron ore. Of fifty-seven crew, five were lost. Arrived under own steam at Belfast Lough 9.4.1943 and at Glasgow on the following day.
20.3.1946: Owners became the Ministry of Transport, London.
21.6.1946: Chartered for three years to The Clan Line Steamers Ltd (Cayzer, Irvine & Co Ltd, managers), Glasgow.
31.12.1947: Sold for £104,809 to The Clan Line Steamers Ltd (Cayzer, Irvine & Co Ltd, managers), Glasgow and renamed *Clan Kenneth*.
2.1951: Converted to burn oil fuel.
8.10.1958: Sold for £105,000 to Cia Concordia de Navegacion S A, Panama (Elias Xenios), registered at Chios, Greece, and renamed *Omonia II*.
13.4.1966: Caught fire while discharging cargo at Amsterdam after arriving from Colombo. The affected hold was flooded, and the vessel towed to a safe area outside Amsterdam harbour and beached. During discharge of the remaining cargo further fires broke out but were extinguished.

Clan Line's *Clan Kenneth* had initially been chartered by the same company as *Ocean Viceroy*.
(Ships in Focus)

15.7.1966: Arrived at Hamburg, West Germany, under tow for breaking up by Eisen und Metall A G.
3.1967: Work began.

Yard No 26
Ocean Virtue

ON 169061
5.6.1942: Launched for the Ministry of War Transport, London (Prince Line Ltd, London, managers).
24.6.1942: Delivered.
1.10.1942: Registered at Manchester (13/1942).
21.7.1943: Bombed and set on fire by German aircraft while at anchor off Augusta, Sicily, with a cargo of 4,000 tons of military stores. All forty-seven crew and sixteen gunners were saved. Towed to shallow water and sank.
27.9.1943: UK register closed.
30.9.1943: Re-floated.
13.4.1944: Left in tow for Catania and subsequently used as a coal hulk.
9.8.1946: Sold 'as lies' to Giacomo Costa fu Andrea, Genoa, Italy. Converted to a passenger liner, re-engined as a motor ship (7,867g/4,637n, 8-cyl 2SCSA oil engine) and renamed *Andrea C.*
1959: Lengthened and re-engined (8,604g/5,170n, 466.8' [l o a], 7-cyl. 2SA oil engine).
1969: Transferred to Costa Armatori S p A, Genoa, Italy.
15.12.1982: Arrived at La Spezia, Italy for breaking up by Andrea Mezzario.
1.1983: Re-sold to Cantieri della Palmaria and broken up.

Yard No 27
Ocean Valentine

ON 167859
7.6.1942: Launched for the Ministry of War Transport, London (William Thomson & Co, Leith, managers).
29.6.1942: Delivered.
25.9.1942: Registered at Southampton (8/1942).
20.3.1946: Owners became the Ministry of Transport, London.
6.6.1946: Sold to Ben Line Steamers Ltd (William Thomson & Co, managers), Leith.
1946: Re-registered at Leith (7/1946) and renamed *Benlomond.*
3.1956: Sold to Sociedad Armadora del Pacifico S A,

Her brief wartime career ended by air attack off Sicily, *Ocean Virtue* was rebuilt as a passenger liner in 1946–7 and served Costa of Genoa as *Andrea C* until 1982, her career extended by two further reconstructions.
(Roy Fenton collection)

D C Mazarkis' *Yangos* in the St Lawrence River inbound from Aalborg on 15 May 1965 near the end of a career which had seen her sail as *Ocean Valentine* under wartime management by the Ben Line and then complete a decade's peacetime service under the flag of the same company as *Benlomond*. *(Simon Olsen collection)*

((Lykiardopulo & Co Ltd, London, managers), Panama (D C Mazarakis, Athens, Greece), registered at Monrovia, Liberia, and renamed *Yangos*.

1960: Re-registered at Piraeus, Greece.

16.10.1966: Sold for £41,000 and arrived at Bilbao, Spain for breaking up by Revalorizacion de Materiales S A.

Yard No 28
Ocean Vanquisher

ON 167134

13.6.1942: Launched for the Ministry of War Transport, London (H Hogarth & Sons, Glasgow, managers).

8.7.1942: Delivered.

Beached at Algiers at the end of 1942 with damage inflicted by Italian frogmen, *Ocean Vanquisher* would be salvaged and rebuilt post-war by her former enemies and enjoy a long second career as *Nereo*, in which guise she was photographed at Vancouver on 20 August 1957. *(Walter E Frost/City of Vancouver Archives CVA 447-7123)*

13.10.1942: Registered at Hull (33/1942).
12.12.1942: Damaged by explosive charge planted by a frogman from the Italian submarine *Ambra* while at anchor in the Bay of Algiers in position 36° 48′ north, 03° 04′ east during a voyage from Faslane and Greenock for Algiers with a cargo of coal and military stores. Of forty-four crew and five gunners, two crew were lost. Vessel beached in Algiers harbour.
4.2.1943: UK register closed.
7.1945: Re-floated and towed to Oran for temporary repairs.
1946: Sold to Cantieri Navali Riuniti, Palermo, Italy, for permanent repairs.
6.2.1946: Arrived at Palermo in tow.
1946: Sold to Societa Ligure di Armamento, Genoa, Italy and renamed *Nereo*.
13.11.1963: Arrived at Hirao, Japan, for breaking up by Matsukura K K.

Yard No 29
Ocean Vagabond

No ON
19.6.1942: Launched for the Ministry of War Transport, London (W H Runciman Shipping Co Ltd, Newcastle upon Tyne, managers).
11.7.1942: Provisional certificate of British registry valid for six months issued at San Francisco.
12.7.1942: Delivered.
29.9.1942: Torpedoed by the German submarine *U 513* in the North Atlantic in position 47° 31′ north, 52° 27′ west while on a voyage from Vancouver and Halifax, Nova Scotia for Loch Ewe with a cargo of wheat, lumber and sleepers, after having turned back from convoy HX 209 for St John's, Newfoundland, with engine defects. Successfully towed to St John's, Newfoundland, with no casualties among forty-four crew and four gunners. Some cargo discharged, and temporary repairs carried out.
3.1.1943: Sailed from St John's for the UK to join convoy SC 115 at sea.
10.1.1943: Torpedoed and sunk by the German submarine *U 186* in the North Atlantic in position 57° 17′ north, 20° 11′ west while straggling from convoy SC 115 on a voyage from Botwood and St John's for Hull with a cargo of wheat, lumber, sleepers and 3,165 tons of sulphite pulp. Of forty-two crew and five naval ratings, one man was lost, and the remainder saved by the British destroyer *Wanderer*.

Yard No 30
Ocean Victory

ON 168837
27.6.1942: Launched for the Ministry of War Transport, London (McCowen & Gross Ltd, London, managers).
22.7.1942: Delivered.
16.10.1942: Registered at Liverpool (31/1942).
3.8.1943: Sold to the Royal Netherlands Government

Anchored in the Delaware River on 18 August 1962 in Taiwanese colours, *Polly* had seen wartime duty first under the red ensign as *Ocean Victory* and then in Dutch government ownership as *Jan Steen* before entering peacetime commercial service for an Amsterdam owner as *Amstelveen*. *(Francis Palmer/Markus Berger collection)*

(N V Stoomvaart Maatschappij 'Nederland', managers), Amsterdam, Netherlands, and renamed *Jan Steen*.
9.8.1943: UK register closed.
1946: Sold to N V Reederij 'Amsterdam', Amsterdam, Netherlands, and renamed *Amstelveen*.
1959: Sold to the Eddie Steamship Co Ltd, Keelung, Taiwan (W H Eddie Hsu), and renamed *Polly*.
1963: Broken up at Kaohsiung, Taiwan; breaking up in progress in mid-5.1963.

Built by Todd-Bath Iron Shipbuilding Corporation (later New England Shipbuilding Corporation, East Yard), South Portland, Maine

Yard No 1
Ocean Liberty

ON 168629
20.12.1941: Launched for the Ministry of War Transport, London (Mitchell Cotts & Co Ltd, London, managers).
27.2.1942: Delivered.
13.4.1942: Registered at Cardiff (5/1942).
20.3.1946: Owners became the Ministry of Transport, London.
30.6.1946: Chartered for five years to Neill & Pandelis Ltd, London.
1.3.1948: Sold to the Ascot Shipping Co Ltd (Purvis Shipping Co Ltd, managers), London.
22.3.1948: Re-registered at London (104/1948).
16.7.1948: Renamed *Avismoat*.
30.12.1954: Transferred to The Aviation & Shipping Co Ltd, London (same managers).
14.3.1955: Sold to the Romney Steamship Co Ltd (Tsavliris (Shipping) Ltd, managers), London.
15.3.1955: Renamed *Claire T*.
5.1955: Converted to oil fuel.
11.1.1958: UK register closed on transfer to the Nigean Shipping Co S A (same managers), Panama, registered at Monrovia, Liberia, and renamed *Free Trader*.
1959: Management transferred to Tsavliris (Hellas) Maritime Co Ltd, Piraeus, Greece, and renamed *Theodoros Tsavliris*.
13.4.1964: Transferred to the Trafalgar Steamship Co Ltd (Tsavliris (Shipping) Ltd, managers), London on a provisional certificate of British registry issued at Rotterdam and renamed change *Newgrove*.
1965: Transferred back to the Nigean Shipping Co S A (same managers), Panama, registered at Port-au-Prince, Haiti.
1965: Transferred to the Kantara Shipping Co Ltd (same managers), Famagusta, Cyprus.
14.5.1966: Stranded at Corona do Cobarubias, off Puerto Padre, Cuba in position 21° 30′ north, 76° 38′ west while on a voyage from Liverpool to Manati in ballast. Declared a constructive total loss and wreck abandoned to the Cuban Government.
19.1.1967: Re-floated; towed to Antilla; subsequent fate unknown.
1969: Deleted from Lloyd's Register.

Ocean Liberty arriving at New York in ballast from Algiers in convoy GUS 11 on 26 August 1943.
(US Coast Guard/Mariners' Museum & Park)

Yard No 2
Ocean Freedom

ON 168555
20.12.1941: Launched for the Ministry of War Transport, London (J & J Denholm Ltd, Glasgow, managers).
18.3.1942: Delivered.
8.5.1942: Registered at Manchester (2/1942).
13.3.1943: Bombed and sunk by German Ju-88 aircraft of Kampfgeschwader 30 in Murmansk harbour after arriving from the UK in convoy JW 53; only 570 tons of government stores still aboard at time of loss. All forty-six crew and eighteen gunners were saved.
21.4.1943: Register closed.
1.6.1943: Re-floated and beached on west shore of Kola Inlet; subsequently broken up.

Yard No 3
Ocean Peace

ON 168558
8.2.1942: Launched for the Ministry of War Transport, London (Hain Steamship Co Ltd, London, managers).
26.5.1942: Registered at Manchester (5/1942).
12.7.1943: Bombed and set on fire by Axis aircraft while anchored off Avola Beach, Sicily, in position 36° 55′ north, 15° 13′ east having arrived from Alexandria in invasion convoy MWS 36 with a cargo of 3,000 tons of military stores including 103 vehicles, 253 cases of petrol and 432 tons of stores. All forty-six crew, twenty gunners and twelve service personnel were saved and taken aboard the landing ship *Prins Albert*. Ship blew up despite attempts by a British destroyer to sink the vessel to extinguish fires.
25.8.1943: Register closed.

Yard No 4
Ocean Justice

ON 168632
8.2.1942: Launched for the Ministry of War Transport, London (Hain Steamship Co, London, managers).
20.5.1942: Registered at Cardiff (8/1942).
6.11.1942: Torpedoed and sunk by the German submarine *U 505* east of Trinidad in position 10° 06′ north, 60° 00′ west while on a voyage from Karachi and Durban for Trinidad and New York with a cargo of 600 tons of manganese ore as ballast. Of forty-four crew, ten gunners and two survivors from the Belgian steamship *Belgian Fighter*, all were saved, either rowing ashore or being picked up by the British motor torpedo boat *MTB 343* and landed at Port of Spain, Trinidad.
16.12.1942: Register closed.

Yard No 5
Ocean Honour

ON 168822
23.3.1942: Launched for the Ministry of War Transport, London (Chellew Navigation Co Ltd, London, managers).
12.6.1942: Registered at Liverpool (15/1942).
16.9.1942: Torpedoed, shelled and sunk by the Japanese submarine *I-29* west of Socotra in the Gulf of Aden in position 12° 48′ north, 50° 50′ east while on a voyage from Liverpool and Durban for Aden and Alexandria with a cargo of 6,000 tons of motor transport and stores. Of forty-five crew and eight gunners, fifteen crew and five gunners were lost.
17.10.1942: Register closed.

Yard No 6
Ocean Faith

ON 168559
23.3.1942: Launched for the Ministry of War Transport, London (Headlam & Son, Whitby, managers).
9.5.1942: Delivered.
12.6.1942: Registered at Manchester (6/1942).
15.8.1943: Bombed by German aircraft in the North Atlantic in position 39° 05′ north, 12° 54′ west while on a voyage from Manchester and the Mersey for Syracuse, Sicily, in convoy KMS 23. There were no casualties among the fifty crew, twelve gunners and ten passengers. After temporary repairs at Gibraltar, discharged cargo at Brindisi and proceeded to Bougie for further temporary repairs.
29.11.1943: Arrived at Gibraltar for permanent repairs.
20.3.1946: Owners became the Ministry of Transport, London.
1.6.1946: Chartered for five years to Neill & Pandelis Ltd, London.
1.3.1948: Sold to the Ascot Shipping Co Ltd (Purvis Shipping Co Ltd, managers), London.
6.3.1948: Re-registered at London (76/1948).

Avisvale (ex-*Ocean Faith*), seen here at Cape Town, was one of three Oceans owned by Noel Purvis's Aviation and Shipping Co Ltd.
(V H Young and L A Sawyer)

7.3.1948: Renamed *Avisvale*.
30.12.1954: Transferred to The Aviation & Shipping Co. Ltd., London (same managers).
15.2.1955: UK register closed on sale to Cia de Navegacion San Rocco S A, Panama (Sebastiano Tuillier, Lugano, Switzerland), registered at Puerto Limon, Costa Rica, and renamed *Uje*.
9.1957: Converted to oil fuel.
1959: Re-registered at Panama.
2.8.1962: Arrived at La Spezia, Italy to be broken up by Cantieri di Portovenere S p A.
10.1962: Breaking up began.

Yard No 7
Ocean Hope

ON 166055
23.3.1942: Launched for the Ministry of War Transport,

Photographed in transit through the Kiel Canal, *Bialystok* (ex-*Ocean Hope*) sailed under the same name throughout her long career in Polish colours.
(Bertil Zandelin)

London (Haldin & Philipps Ltd, London, managers).
2.7.1942: Registered at Bristol (6/1942).
17.8.1943: Sold to the Polish Government (Gdynia-America Shipping Lines Ltd, managers), Gdynia, Poland, and renamed *Bialystok*.
20.8.1943: UK register closed.
1951: Transferred to Polskie Linie Oceaniczne, Gdynia, Poland.
1964: Transferred to Polska Zegluga Morska, Szczecin, Poland.
18.11.1971: Arrived at Bilbao, Spain to be broken up by Revalorizacion de Materiales S A.

Yard No 8

Ocean Pride

ON 168722
19.4.1942: Launched for the Ministry of War Transport, London (Sir William Reardon-Smith & Sons Ltd, Cardiff, managers).
29.5.1942: Delivered.
3.7.1942: Registered at Glasgow (20/1942).
20.3.1946: Owners became the Ministry of Transport, London.
13.7.1946: Chartered for five years to the Ropner Shipping Co Ltd (Sir R Ropner & Co Ltd, Darlington, managers), West Hartlepool.
13.2.1947: Sold to the Ropner Shipping Co Ltd (Sir R Ropner & Co Ltd, Darlington, managers), West Hartlepool.
20.3.1947: Re-registered at West Hartlepool (3/1947).
11.4.1947: Renamed *Oakby*.
31.7.1959: UK register closed on sale to the Master Shipping Co S A, Panama (Pateras Shipbrokers Ltd, London), registered at Beirut, Lebanon and renamed *Erinio*.
1963: Sold to the Penelope Steamship Co Ltd, Monrovia, Liberia (George and Peter Lygnos), and renamed *Penelope L*.
1965: Sold to Marvencedor Cia Naviera S A, Panama (Litonjua & Co, Manila, Philippines), registered at Monrovia, Liberia, and renamed *Susana K L*.
16.5.1966: Abandoned by her crew after catching fire in the boiler room while on a voyage from Yokohama to Manila in ballast; taken in tow next day for Keelung.
21.5.1966: Fire extinguished. Subsequently declared a constructive total loss.
13.8.1966: Delivered at Keelung for breaking up; broken up at Kaohsiung, Taiwan.

Purchased by Ropner Shipping after a brief spell on charter as *Ocean Pride*, *Oakby* and her five Ocean fleet mates were frequent visitors to New Zealand ports, and, in the case of this photograph at Auckland.
(R A Priest/Nautical Association of Australia collection)

Yard No 9

Ocean Might

ON 168829

19.4.1942: Launched for the Ministry of War Transport, London (Maclay & McIntyre Ltd, Glasgow, managers).
18.7.1942: Registered at Liverpool (22/1942).
2.9.1942: Torpedoed and sunk by the German submarine *U 109* in the Atlantic, southwest of Takoradi on the Gold Coast in position 00° 57′ north, 04° 11′ west after dispersal from convoy OS 37 while on a voyage from Liverpool for Table Bay and the Middle East with a cargo of 7,000 tons of military stores. Of forty-four crew and ten gunners, four were lost and fifty rowed ashore.
24.10.1942: Register closed.

Yard No 10

Ocean Courage

ON 168830

22.5.1942: Launched for the Ministry of War Transport, London (Hain Steamship Co Ltd, London), managers.
25.7.1942: Registered at Liverpool (23/1942).
15.1.1943: Torpedoed and sunk by the German submarine *U 182* in the Atlantic, about 200 miles south of the Cape Verde Islands in position 10° 52′ north, 23° 28′ west while on a voyage from Pepel and Freetown for Trinidad and the USA with a cargo of 8,956 tons of iron ore and eight bags of mail. Of forty-eight crew, eight gunners and two passengers, fifty-two were lost and six were rescued by the British motor ship *Silverwalnut* (6,770/1930) on 21.1.1943.
17.2.1943: Register closed.

Yard No 11

Ocean Fame

ON 169056

22.5.1942: Launched for the Ministry of War Transport, London (W H Seager & Co Ltd, Cardiff, managers).
22.6.1942: Delivered.
7.8.1942: Registered at Manchester (8/1942).
20.3.1946: Owners became the Ministry of Transport, London.
7.8.1946: Chartered for five years to the Ropner Shipping Co Ltd (Sir R Ropner & Co Ltd, Darlington, managers), West Hartlepool.
7.2.1947: Sold to the Ropner Shipping Co Ltd (Sir R Ropner & Co Ltd, Darlington, managers), West Hartlepool.
12.4.1947: Re-registered at West Hartlepool (5/1947).
24.4.1947: Renamed *Firby*.
30.3.1955: Sold to the N G Kyriakides Shipping Co Ltd, London.
23.4.1955: Re-registered at London (68/1955).
27.4.1955: Renamed *Irene K*.
7.1956: Converted to oil fuel.
16.12.1958: Transferred to the Winchester Shipping Co Ltd (N G Kyriakides Shipping Co Ltd, managers), London.

N G Kyriades' *Irene K* (ex-*Firby*, ex-*Ocean Fame)* photographed off South Wales in June 1964 shortly before she was renamed *Winchester Queen*. *(Des Harris/Malcolm Cranfield collection)*

16.10.1964: Renamed *Winchester Queen.*
29.11.1966: Arrived at Bilbao, Spain, to be broken up by Hierros Arbulu S A.
2.12.1966: Register closed.

Yard No 12
Ocean Strength

ON 169058
14.6.1942: Launched for the Ministry of War Transport, London (J & J Denholm Ltd, Glasgow, managers).
14.8.1942: Registered at Manchester (10/1942).
20.3.1946: Owners became the Ministry of Transport, London.
22.6.1946: Chartered for three years to Denholm Line Steamers Ltd (J & J Denholm Ltd, managers), Glasgow.
22.2.1947: Sold to Denholm Line Steamers Ltd (J & J Denholm Ltd, managers), Glasgow.
1947: Re-registered at Greenock (1/1947) and renamed *Broompark.*
2.1948: Converted to oil fuel.
3.1951: Sold for £236,135 to Andrew Crawford & Co Ltd, Glasgow
1951: Re-registered at Glasgow (11/1951) and renamed *Garryvale.*
14.5.1953: Owning company renamed the Buchanan Shipping Co Ltd (Andrew Crawford & Co Ltd, managers), Glasgow.
22.2.1957: Owning company sold to the Avenue Finance Co Ltd, London.
1957: Sold to the West Africa Navigation Ltd, Monrovia, Liberia (Salvatores & Racah, Genoa, Italy) and renamed *African Lady.*
1958: Transferred to the General Navigation Ltd of Monrovia, Monrovia, Liberia (same beneficial owners).
1961: Managing company renamed Salvatores & C.
18.1.1965: Arrived at Osaka, Japan for breaking up by Amakasu Sangyo K K.
5.2.1965: Breaking up started.

Garryvale, photographed from the Sydney Harbour Bridge on 17 October 1954, had sailed for another Glasgow owner, first on charter as *Ocean Strength*, and then after purchase as *Broompark*, before her sale to Andrew Crawford in 1951.
(D Finch/R A Priest/Nautical Association of Australia collection)

Ocean Trader alongside a bomb-damaged warehouse in a wartime UK port.
(World Ship Society Ltd)

Yard No 13
Ocean Trader

ON 168834
14.6.1942: Launched for the Ministry of War Transport, London (Glen Line Ltd, London, managers).
28.8.1942: Registered at Liverpool (27/1942).
20.3.1946: Owners became the Ministry of Transport, London.
30.4.1947: Sold to the Drake Shipping Co Ltd (Lykiardopulo & Co Ltd, managers), London.
5.5.1947: Re-registered at London (134/1947).
6.5.1947: Renamed *Merchant Royal.*
1.1950: Converted to oil fuel.
5.10.1951: UK register closed on transfer to Cia Armadora Transoceanica S A, Panama (Lykiardopulo & Co Ltd, London), and renamed *Oceana.*
1960: Transferred to Cia Armadora Sabinal S A, Panama (same beneficial owners), registered at Piraeus, Greece and renamed *Okeanis.*
1966: Sold to Salinamar S A, Panama (Fratelli Consulich S p A, Trieste, Italy), and renamed *Fides.*
1968: Transferred to Marsalina Shipping Co Ltd, Famagusta, Cyprus (same beneficial owners), and renamed *Defis.*
20.8.1969: Arrived at Osaka, Japan, for breaking up by Amakasu Sangyo K K at Sakaide.

Yard No 14
Ocean Wanderer

ON 168836
14.6.1942: Launched for the Ministry of War Transport, London (Donaldson Bros & Black Ltd, Glasgow, managers).
21.7.1942: Delivered.
9.9.1942: Registered at Liverpool (29/1942).
20.3.1946: Owners became the Ministry of Transport, London.
28.8.1946: Chartered to the Bolton Steam Shipping Co Ltd, London.
27.11.1947: Sold to the Bolton Steam Shipping Co Ltd, London.
9.1.1948: Re-registered at London (10/1948).
20.2.1948: Renamed *Ruysdael.*
2.1948: Converted to oil fuel.
24.9.1951: UK register closed on sale to Kronos Cia Naviera S A, Panama (Ch & E Pateras Ltd, Athens, Greece), registered at Puerto Limon, Costa Rica, and renamed *Santa Irene.*
1959: Re-registered at Piraeus, Greece.
2.11.1962: Grounded on Los Cabezos Shoal, four miles west of Tarifa, Spain, whilst on a voyage from Gdansk for Venice with a cargo of coal.
9.11.1962: Broke in two and declared a constructive total loss.

Top opposite: Bolton Steam Shipping's *Ruysdael* (ex- *Ocean Wanderer*) photographed at Auckland, New Zealand, on 17 February 1951, just months before her early sale off the UK register.
(V H Young and L A Sawyer)

Yard No 15

Ocean Pilgrim

ON 168635

28.6.1942: Launched for the Ministry of War Transport, London (Dene Shipping Co Ltd, London, managers).
27.7.1942: Delivered.
1.10.1942: Registered at Cardiff (11/1942).
20.3.1946: Owners became the Ministry of Transport, London.
5.8.1946: Chartered for five years to the Pool Shipping Co Ltd (Sir R Ropner & Co Ltd, Darlington, managers), West Hartlepool.
6.2.1947: Sold to the Pool Shipping Co Ltd (Sir R Ropner & Co Ltd, Darlington, managers), West Hartlepool.
12.4.1947: Re-registered at West Hartlepool (4/1947).

Ropner's *Pikepool* (ex-*Ocean Pilgrim*) underway in ballast in the English Channel. ***(Fotoflite incorporating Skyfotos)***

20.8.1947: Re-registered at West Hartlepool (8/1947) on remeasurement of tonnage.
20.8.1947: Renamed *Pikepool.*
8.1950: Converted to oil fuel.
9.6.1959: UK register closed on sale to the Nevada Co Ltd, Panama (John Livanos & Sons), registered at Piraeus, Greece, and renamed *Marigo* (subsequently re-registered at Chios, Greece).
1966: Transferred to the Amfitriti Shipping Co Ltd, Famagusta, Cyprus (same beneficial owners) and renamed *Amfitriti.*
4.10.1967: Arrived at Kaohsiung, Taiwan, for breaking up: broken up in 1st quarter 1968.

Yard No 16

Ocean Merchant

ON 168634
28.6.1942: Launched for the Ministry of War Transport, London (Morel Ltd, Cardiff, managers).
31.7.1942: Delivered.
22.9.1942: Registered at Cardiff (10/1942).
24.3.1943: Sold to the Royal Netherlands government (Koninklijke Nederlandsche Stoomboot Maatschappij, managers) and renamed *Jan Lievens.*
26.3.1943: UK register closed.
1946: Sold to N V Reederij 'Amsterdam', Amsterdam, Netherlands and renamed *Amstelstad.*
1959: Sold to Wallem & Co Ltd, Hong Kong and renamed *Dunn.*
1959: Sold to the People's Republic of China and renamed *Ho Ping 26.*
1967: Owner restyled the Bureau of Maritime Transport Administration, Shanghai Branch, Shanghai, China, and renamed *Zhan Dou 26.*
1992: Deleted from Lloyd's Register (believed still in service in late 1970s).

Amstelstad photographed dockside at Vancouver on 27 March 1954 had seen wartime service first as *Ocean Merchant* and then as *Jan Lievens.* *(Walter E Frost/City of Vancouver Archives CVA 447-3123.2)*

At anchor at Montevideo near the end of her long career in the fleet of N G Kyriakides, *Winchester King* had survived wartime torpedo damage as *Ocean Rider*, and had first served the same owner under the name *Nicholas K.* *(David Edge)*

Yard No 17

Ocean Rider

ON 168729

19.7.1942: Launched for the Ministry of War Transport, London (Larrinaga Steamship Co Ltd, Liverpool, managers).

10.8.1942: Delivered.

15.9.1942: Registered at Glasgow (27/1942).

21.1.1943: Torpedoed by an Italian S 79 aircraft of 132 Gruppo in the Mediterranean, four-and-a-half miles west of Cape Caxine, Algeria while on a voyage from the Clyde for Bone with a cargo of 4,000 tons of military stores and gasoline in convoy KMS 7. There were no casualties among the forty-seven crew and nine gunners. Arrived at Algiers on the same day. Permanently repaired at Liverpool.

20.3.1946: Owners became the Ministry of Transport, London.

22.11.1946: Sold to the N G Kyriakides Shipping Co Ltd, London.

7.1.1947: Re-registered at London (7/1947).

23.6.1947: Renamed *Nicholas K.*

11.1949: Converted to oil fuel.

17.2.1959: Transferred to the Winchester Shipping Co Ltd (N G Kyriakides Shipping Co Ltd, managers), London.

11.1959: Converted to burn oil fuel.

25.9.1964: Renamed *Winchester King.*

23.12.1966: UK register closed on sale to Intertrader Shipping Co S A, Panama (Intercontinental Shipping Co Ltd, Hong Kong) and renamed *Pacific Trader.*

4.1968: Renamed *Karimantan.*

25.8.1968: Arrived at Kaohsiung, Taiwan, for breaking up.

Yard No 18

Ocean Athlete

ON 166058

19.7.1942: Launched for the Ministry of War Transport, London (C T Bowring & Co Ltd, Liverpool, managers).

15.8.1942: Delivered.

23.9.1942: Registered at Bristol (9/1942).

10.4.1943: Sold to the Royal Netherlands government (Rotterdamsche Lloyd (Ruys & Zonen), managers) and renamed *Govert Flinck.*

6.9.1946: Sold to N V Rotterdamsche Lloyd (Ruys & Zonen, managers), Rotterdam.

1947: Converted to oil fuel and renamed *Ternate.*

1959: Sold to the Dah Lien Shipping Co Ltd (Oversea United Shipping & Trading Co Ltd, managers for PRC), Hong Kong, and renamed *Kasert.*

Above: An early post-war photograph of *Govert Flinck* alongside at Cape Town while still in the service of the Netherlands government, which had purchased her as *Ocean Athlete* in 1943.
(John & Marion Clarkson collection)

Below: *Ocean Wayfarer* at Sydney in the colours of her charterer, Thompson Steamshipping.
(D Finch/R A Priest/Nautical Association of Australia collection)

1960: Transferred to the People's Republic of China and renamed *Ho Ping 75*.
1967: Owner restyled the Bureau of Maritime Transport Administration, Shanghai Branch, Shanghai, China, and renamed *Zhan Dou 75*.
1985: Reported to have been broken up in China.

Yard No 19

Ocean Wayfarer

ON 168636
16.8.1942: Launched for the Ministry of War Transport, London (Thompson Steamshipping Co Ltd, London, managers).
1.9.1942: Delivered.
13.10.1942: Registered at Cardiff (12/1942).
20.3.1946: Owners became the Ministry of Transport, London.
15.7.1946: Chartered for five years to the Thompson Steamshipping Co Ltd, London.
27.1.1951: Sold to the Thompson Steamshipping Co Ltd, London.
2.2.1951: Sold for £189,500 to The Clan Line Steamers Ltd (Cayzer, Irvine & Co Ltd, managers), London.
23.2.1951: Re-registered at Glasgow (5/1951).
5.4.1951: Renamed *Clan Macquarrie*.
4.1951: Converted to oil fuel.
31.1.1953: Grounded during a gale ten miles west of the Butt of Lewis while on a voyage from Dundee to Glasgow in ballast.
16.3.1953: Re-floated and taken to Stornoway.
22.3.1953: Arrived on the Clyde for inspection. Subsequently declared a constructive total loss.
2.4.1953: Towed to the Holy Loch and laid up.
7.1953: Sold for £50,000 by the Salvage Association to Sea Tankers Inc, Monrovia, Liberia.
29.10.1953: Towed to Troon for breaking up by the West of Scotland Shipbreaking Co Ltd.
21.11.1953: Register closed.

Yard No 20

Ocean Stranger

ON 169063
16.8.1942: Launched for the Ministry of War Transport, London (Glen & Co Ltd, Glasgow, managers).

Photographed loading lumber at Vancouver on 3 December 1958, *African Baron* had been built as *Ocean Stranger* and had served Adelphi Vergottis as *Alcyone Fortune*, *Calygera*, and *Alcyone Faith* before sale to Italian FOC operators in 1956.
(Walter E Frost/City of Vancouver Archives CVA 447-2979)

5.9.1942: Delivered.
22.10.1942: Registered at Manchester (15/1942).
20.3.1946: Owners became the Ministry of Transport, London.
14.9.1946: Chartered for three years to the Alcyone Shipping Finance Co. Ltd, London.
14.5.1948: Sold to the Alcyone Shipping Finance Co. Ltd, London (Adelphi Vergottis Ltd).
22.5.1948: Re-registered at London (152/1948).
20.7.1948: Renamed *Alcyone Fortune*.
14.12.1950: Owning company restyled the Alcyone Shipping Co. Ltd, London.
9.6.1951: UK register closed on transfer to Cia Maritima Calivergo S A, Panama (same beneficial owners) and renamed *Calygera*.
7.1951: Converted to oil fuel.
5.1954: Reverted to Alcyone Shipping Co Ltd, London, and renamed *Alcyone Faith*.
3.6.1954: Restored to the UK register at London (124/1954).
10.7.1956: Register closed on sale to the West Africa Navigation Ltd, Monrovia, Liberia (Salvatores & Racah, Genoa, Italy), and renamed *African Baron*.
1961: Managing company renamed Salvatores & C.
12.6.1965: Arrived at Hirao, Japan, to be broken up by Matsukura Shoten K K.
10.7.1965: Breaking up started.

Yard No 21

Ocean Traveller

ON 168838
16.8.1942: Launched for the Ministry of War Transport, London (Lyle Shipping Co Ltd, Glasgow, managers).
12.9.1942: Delivered.
29.10.1942: Registered at Liverpool (32/1942).
20.3.1946: Owners became the Ministry of Transport, London.
21.3.1946: Chartered for five years to the Lyle Shipping Co Ltd, Glasgow.
21.2.1947: Sold for £115,500 less depreciation (calculated at the rate of 5 per cent per annum from the date of the time charter) to the Lyle Shipping Co Ltd, Glasgow.

Lyle Shipping's *Cape Corso* had earlier served the same company on charter under her original name, *Ocean Traveller*.
(Roy Fenton collection)

1947: Re-registered at Glasgow (6/1947) and renamed *Cape Corso*.
1949: Converted to oil fuel by Smiths Ltd, Middlesbrough.
12.6.1959: Sold for £57,500 to Hong Kong buyers to be broken up.
7.9.1959: Arrived at Hong Kong to be broken up by Teh An & Co.

Yard No 22
Ocean Seaman

ON 168839
16.8.1942: Launched for the Ministry of War Transport, London (Frank C Strick & Co Ltd, London, managers).
17.9.1942: Delivered.
29.10.1942: Registered at Liverpool (33/1942).
15.3.1943: Torpedoed by the German submarine *U 380* in the Mediterranean, about sixty miles west of Algiers in position 35° 55′ north, 01° 59′ east while on a voyage from Philippeville and Algiers for Gibraltar and Liverpool in ballast in convoy ET 14. There were no casualties among the forty-nine crew and ten gunners. Taken in tow by the American destroyer *Paul Jones (DD*-230) and beached the next day off Algiers.
13.5.1943: Register closed.
1945: Vessel given up as a total loss and subsequently broken up in situ.

Yard No 23
Ocean Gallant

ON 169064
16.8.1942: Launched for the Ministry of War Transport, London (Turnbull Scott & Co, London, managers).
4.11.1942: Registered at Manchester (16/1942).
20.3.1946: Owners became the Ministry of Transport.
21.8.1946: Sold to Edward G Thomson, Edinburgh.
1946: Re-registered at Leith (14/1946).
1946: Transferred to Ben Line Steamers Ltd (William Thomson & Co, managers), Leith and renamed *Bennevis*.
5.1947: Converted to oil fuel.
4.2.1959: Re-registered at London (12/1959).
16.2.1959: Sold to the Rodney Steamship Co Ltd (Anglo-Danubian Transport Co Ltd, managers), London.
18.2.1959: Renamed *Charles Dickens*.
23.5.1961: Transferred to the Chine Shipping Co Ltd, (same managers), London.
14.10.1962: Arrived at Cardiff and laid up.
9.11.1962: UK register closed on sale to Pedoulas Cia Naviera S A (L Haji Ioannou, London, managers), Panama and renamed *Cleo*.
21.11.1962: Sailed from Cardiff.
7.1.1967: Arrived at Osaka, Japan, for breaking up.
15.1.1967: Demolition started at Sakai, Japan.

Ocean Gallant alongside at Liverpool on 3 May 1943 before loading military stores for the last of three consecutive trips in support of the campaign in North Africa.
(© National Maritime Museum, Greenwich, London)

Ocean Angel along the pier-side at Auckland in Alcyone Shipping colours. *(V H Young and L A Sawyer)*

Angel (registry remained at Glasgow).
1951: Owners became the Alcyone Shipping Co Ltd, London.
4.1951: Converted to oil fuel.
1956: Sold for £430,000 to Cia de Navegacion San Augustin S A, Panama (Tidewater Commercial Company, Baltimore, Maryland [Alberto Ravano fu Pietro, Genoa, Italy]), registered at Monrovia, Liberia, and renamed *Continental.*
9.7.1960: Arrived at Kaohsiung, Taiwan for breaking up.
6.9.1960: Breaking up started.

Yard No 27
Ocean Hunter

ON 169639
27.9.1942: Launched for the Ministry of War Transport, London (J. Robinson & Sons, North Shields, manager).
1.12.1942: Registered at Cardiff (15/1942).
10.1.1944: Torpedoed and sunk by German aircraft in the Mediterranean in position 36° 03′ north, 00° 15′ west while on a voyage from New York and Gibraltar for Augusta, Brindisi, and Malta in convoy KMS 37 with a cargo of 3,500 tons of military stores and 1,500 tons of general cargo. All forty-seven crew and eight gunners were rescued by the British corvette *Bryony* and the coastal transport *FT 6.*
15.2.1944: Register closed.

Yard No 28

Ocean Crusader

No ON

18.10.1942: Launched for the Ministry of War Transport, London (Dodd, Thomson & Co Ltd, London, managers).

31.10.1942: Provisional certificate of British registry valid for six months issued at Boston.

26.11.1942: Torpedoed and sunk by the German submarine *U 262* in the North Atlantic, about 330 miles north east of St John's, Newfoundland, in position 50° 30′ north, 45° 30′ west having straggled from convoy HX 216 in heavy weather and apparently turned back to Canada with weather damage while on a voyage from Portland, Maine, and New York for Avonmouth with 8,891 tons of general cargo . All forty-five crew and five gunners lost.

Yard No 29

Ocean Gypsy

ON 169067

18.10.1942: Launched for the Ministry of War Transport, London (J & C Harrison Ltd, London, managers).

7.11.1942: Delivered.

1.11.1943: Registered at Manchester (3/1943).

20.3.1946: Owners became Ministry of Transport.

28.7.1946: Chartered for five years to The Clan Line Steamers Ltd (Cayzer, Irvine & Co Ltd, managers), Glasgow.

31.12.1947: Sold for £108,185 to The Clan Line Steamers Ltd (Cayzer, Irvine & Co Ltd, managers), Glasgow.

1948: Re-registered at Glasgow (11/1948) and renamed *Clan Macbride*.

2.1950: Converted to burn oil fuel.

22.5.1958: Sold for £110,000 to the Panamanian Oriental Steamship Corp (Wheelock, Marden & Co Ltd, Hong Kong, managers), Panama (C S Koo, Hong Kong), and renamed *Alice*.

1960: Transferred to the Valles Steamship Co Ltd, Panama (C S Koo, Hong Kong).

7.10.1966: Arrived at Hirao, Japan, for breaking up by Matsukura Kaiji K K.

13.10.1966: Breaking up started.

Clan Macbride (ex-*Ocean Gypsy*) at Cape Town on Clan Line service with railway carriages on deck.
(Ships in Focus)

Ocean Glory on the Mersey, Birkenhead, under charter to the Clan Line. *(John & Marion Clarkson collection)*

Yard No 30

Ocean Glory

ON 169176

18.10.1942: Launched for the Ministry of War Transport, London (J & C Harrison Ltd, London, managers).

18.11.1942: Delivered.

13.12.1943: Registered at Newcastle upon Tyne (16/1943).

20.3.1946: Owners became Ministry of Transport.

10.4.1946: Chartered for five years to The Clan Line Steamers Ltd (Cayzer, Irvine & Co Ltd, managers), Glasgow.

31.12.1947: Sold for £107,343 to The Clan Line Steamers Ltd (Cayzer, Irvine & Co Ltd, managers), Glasgow.

1948: Re-registered at Glasgow (9/1948) and renamed *Clan Macbeth*.

7.1950: Converted to burn oil fuel.

4.4.1959: Sold for £70,000 to the Panamanian Oriental Steamship Corp (Wheelock, Marden & Co Ltd, Hong Kong, managers), Panama (V K Eddie Hsu, Keelung, Taiwan), and renamed *Madonna*.

1961: Transferred to the Sincere Navigation Corp, Keelung, Taiwan (V K Eddie Hsu), and renamed *Sincere Trader*.

15.10.1964: Left Osaka, Japan for breaking up at Kaohsiung, Taiwan.

11.1964: Breaking up started by the China National Machinery Import and Export Corp.

APPENDIX 3

VALOUR AND STRENGTH IN THE FIRING LINE: TWO OCEANS AT WAR

The Oceans, like their modern, war-built Empire, Fort, Park and Liberty cousins, spent much of their careers in what might be termed frontline combat roles. Three vessels went straight to Russian convoy duty, while many of the other early arrivals were deployed on to the long supply route around Africa in support of the Eighth Army's campaign in the Western Desert. Most of the ships reaching Britain from August 1942 went straight to support Operation Torch, the invasion of French North Africa, and remained in theatre, operating in convoys carrying supplies from the UK for the ensuing campaign against Axis forces in Tunisia. This deployment was succeeded by direct involvement in Operation Husky, the July 1943 invasion of Sicily, following which most surviving vessels remained on Mediterranean duty, supporting the slow advance of Allied armies up the Italian peninsula. Elsewhere, the winter of 1943–4 saw a redeployment of some ships back north to the Kola Run through the Barents Sea, succeeded by summer commitments first to the campaign in northern France following the successful Normandy landings and then to Operation Dragoon, the invasion of the Mediterranean coast of Provence. Finally, the last year of the war saw a gradual transfer of ships to the Indian Ocean in support of the reconquest of Burma and Malaya from the Japanese. The wartime careers of two representative vessels, *Ocean Valour*, the eleventh west coast ship, and *Ocean Strength*, the twelfth of her east coast sisters, provide a good cross section of this range of frontline deployments.

Ocean Valour, March 1942 to August 1945

Ocean Valour crossed the Atlantic in HX 188 in May 1942, finishing her voyage at Southampton. She then followed most of her sisters onto the Middle East supply route but was forced to interrupt her journey around Africa when boiler problems necessitated a month-long stay at Cape Town for repairs, delaying her arrival in Egypt until October. After unloading at Red Sea ports, *Ocean Valour* first sailed south to pick up a part cargo in South Africa and then crossed the South Atlantic to load bauxite at Trinidad, sailing from Port of Spain for New York on New Year's Day 1943. From there she re-crossed the Atlantic with a military cargo for Allied forces in North Africa, sailing in UGS 5, a largely American convoy escorted to Casablanca by no fewer than seven USN destroyers. *Ocean Valour* returned to the UK via Gibraltar in March, and after repairs on the Tyne, and a departure aborted because of a bunker fire, sailed from the Clyde with a military cargo for Algerian ports in June, after which she was sent to load a mixed West African cargo of iron ore and bauxite for the UK, arriving back on the Mersey in mid-October.

After an extended dockyard stay for repairs and refit, *Ocean Valour* exchanged the tropical heat of the Gold Coast for the sub-zero temperatures of the Arctic winter, sailing from Loch Ewe in JW 55B for the Kola Inlet on 20 December, where her crew endured extended exposure to the meagre comforts of wartime Murmansk, before returning to the UK and another bout of repairs in February 1944. She next cleared the Mersey in mid-March, bound for Italy with a cargo for the Allied armies locked in the grim struggle to break through the Gustav Line and reach Rome. *Ocean Valour*'s arrival in theatre marked the start of a year-long commitment to the Mediterranean military motor transport service, a deployment interrupted only by an extended mid-summer stay at Suez repairing damage caused by a serious cargo fire. She finally left the Mediterranean in April 1945, sailing south through the Suez Canal for the Persian Gulf and deployment to Indian ports. VE Day on 8 May saw a war-weary ship arriving at Abadan for another set of repairs. These would prove to be a prelude to an extended stay in dockyard hands at Bombay, from which *Ocean Valour* would only arrive back in the Gulf hours before the dawn of VJ-Day on 15 August.

Departure (Convoy)	Date	Arrival	Date
San Francisco, California	6.3.1942	Union Bay, British Columbia	10.3.1942
Union Bay, BC	11.3.1942	New Westminster, BC	11.3.1942
New Westminster, BC	15.3.1942	Seattle, Washington	15.3.1942
Seattle, Washington	20.3.1942	Los Angeles, California	25.3.1942
Los Angeles, California	28.3.1942	Balboa, Panama Canal	9.4.1942
Cristobal, Panama Canal	10.4.1942	Hampton Roads, Virginia	19.4.1942
Hampton Roads, Virginia	22.4.1942	New York	23.4.1942
New York	24.4.1942	Halifax, Nova Scotia	26.4.1942
Halifax, Nova Scotia (HX 188)	3.5.1942	Liverpool	15.5.1942
Liverpool	17.5.1942	Southampton	24.5.1942
Southampton	31.5.1942	Swansea	2.6.1942
Swansea (OS 32)	18.6.1942	Freetown (dispersed from convoy)	8.7.1942
Dispersed	8.7.1942	Table Bay (boiler repairs)	24.7.1942
Table Bay	30.8.1942	Durban	4.9.1942
Durban	11.9.1942	Aden	25.9.1942
Aden	26.9.1942	Suez	3.10.1942
Suez	3.10.1942	Fanara, Red Sea	5.10.1942
Fanara	12.10.1942	Suez	14.10.1942
Suez	15.10.1942	Aden	20.10.1942
Aden	26.10.1942	Durban	9.11.1942
Durban	23.11.1942	Table Bay	27.11.1942
Table Bay	4.12.1942	Trinidad	26.12.1942
Trinidad (TAG 33)	1.1.1943	Guantanamo, Cuba	5.1.1943
Guantanamo, Cuba (GN 33)	5.1.1943	New York	13.1.1943
New York (UGS 5)	7.2.1943	Casablanca	25.2.1943
Casablanca	9.3.1943	Gibraltar	11.3.1943
Gibraltar (XK 3)	16.3.1943	Loch Ewe	27.3.1943
Loch Ewe	28.3.1943	Methil	30.3.1943
Methil	30.3.1943	London	1.4.1943
London	8.4.1943	Tyne (repairs)	10.4.1943
Tyne	29.4.1943	Methil	30.4.1943
Methil	2.5.1943	Oban	5.5.1943
Oban (OS 47)	6.5.1943	Belfast (bunker fire)	8.5.1943
Belfast	14.5.1943	Clyde	15.5.1943
Clyde (OS 48)	20.5.1943	Gibraltar (convoy split)	31.5.1943
Gibraltar (KMS 15)	1.6.1943	Algiers	4.6.1943
Algiers	13.6.1943	Oran	15.6.1943
Oran	15.6.1943	Gibraltar	17.6.1943
Gibraltar (OS 50)	27.6.1943	Freetown	8.7.1943
Freetown (OSS 52)	7.8.1943	Takoradi	11.8.1943
Takoradi (TL 21)	20.8.1943	Lagos	22.8.1943
Lagos	22.8.1943	Calabar	24.8.1943
Calabar	29.8.1943	Lagos	1.9.1943
Lagos (LTS 1)	8.9.1943	Accra	9.9.1943
Accra	15.9.1943	Takoradi	16.9.1943
Takoradi	16.9.1943	Freetown	20.9.1943
Freetown (SL 137)	23.9.1943	Liverpool (repairs and refit)	17.10.1943
Liverpool	15.12.1943	Loch Ewe	17.12.1943
Loch Ewe (JW 55B)	20.12.1943	Kola Inlet	30.12.1943
Kola Inlet (RA 56)	3.2.1944	Loch Ewe	11.2.1944
Loch Ewe	11.2.1944	Liverpool (repairs)	12.2.1944
Liverpool (OS 71)	14.3.1944	Gibraltar	27.3.1944
Gibraltar (KMS 45)	27.3.1944	Brindisi	4.4.1944
Brindisi	14.4.1944	Augusta	16.4.1944

Augusta	22.4.1944	Alexandria	26.4.1944
Alexandria	30.4.1944	Taranto	7.5.1944
Taranto	14.5.1944	Augusta	16.5.1944
Augusta	19.5.1944	Bizerta	21.5.1944
Bizerta	24.5.1944	Port Said	30.5.1944
Port Said	1.6.1944	Suez (cargo fire – repairs)	2.6.1944
Suez	1.8.1944	Alexandria	3.8.1944
Alexandria	4.8.1944	Ancona	12.8.1944
Ancona	22.8.1944	Brindisi	25.8.1944
Brindisi	27.8.1944	Augusta	29.8.1944
Augusta	3.9.1944	Alexandria	7.9.1944
Alexandria	13.9.1944	Augusta	17.9.1944
Augusta	19.9.1944	Naples	20.9.1944
Naples	21.9.1944	Toulon	29.9.1944
Toulon	13.10.1944	Port de Bouc	5.11.1944
Port de Bouc	4.11.1944	Alexandria	14.11.1944
Alexandria	25.11.1944	Augusta	29.11.1944
Augusta	4.12.1944	Brindisi	6.12.1944
Brindisi	23.12.1944	Haifa	29.12.1944
Haifa	5.1.1945	Port Said	6.1.1945
Port Said	8.1.1945	Marseille	18.1.1945
Marseille	1.2.1945	Alexandria	7.2.1945
Alexandria	8.2.1945	Suez	9.2.1945
Suez	22.2.1945	Port Said	22.2.1945
Port Said	24.2.1945	Marseille (repairs)	6.3.1945
Marseille	28.3.1945	Port Said	4.4.1945
Port Said	5.4.1945	Suez (repairs)	6.4.1945
Suez	17.4.1945	Abadan	1.5.1945
Abadan	1.5.1945	Basra	2.5.1945
Basra	8.5.1945	Abadan (repairs)	8.5.1945
Abadan	23.5.1945	Bombay (repairs & reconditioning)	30.5.1945
Bombay	8.8.1945	Abadan	14.8.1945
Abadan	23.8.1945	Karachi	28.8.1945

Ocean Strength, July 1942 to August 1945

Ocean Strength participated in no fewer than five major operations, comprising three invasions and two Arctic convoys. Having completed her transatlantic delivery voyage, she underwent six weeks of repairs (a common product of wartime building conditions, North Atlantic weather damage and overstretched UK dockyards) before sailing in KMS 2, the first major follow-up convoy for the North African invasion in October–November 1942. Returning home, she next sailed south around the Cape of Good Hope for the Middle East, arriving in Egyptian waters in March 1943. After a round trip to Tripoli in Libya, *Ocean Strength* participated in the invasion of Sicily in July, deploying to the same beachhead (Acid South) as six of her sisters, one of which, *Ocean Peace*, would be lost there. She remained in the Mediterranean until late September, when she sailed for the UK and deployment on the north Russian convoy route. She became the second and final member of her class to complete two round-trip convoy cycles in this demanding theatre, sailing outwards with JW 54B in November 1943; homewards with RA 55A in December 1943; outwards again with JW 57 in February 1944; and finally homewards with RA 58 in April 1944, after which she was refitted for service in support of the Normandy invasion. *Ocean Strength* made her first trip to Juno beachhead on 10–12 June 1944, and between then and 13 August, she completed no fewer than seven round trips to and from Seine Bay. The ship then participated in three North Atlantic convoy cycles, VE Day finding her at St John, New Brunswick, preparing for the homeward leg of the last of these, HX 357. After another round trip to Canada sailing as an independent, *Ocean Strength* was taken in hand for repairs at Bristol, from where she would sail for Germany two weeks after VJ Day.

Departure	Date	Arrival	Date
Portland, Maine (BX 29C)	20.7.1942	Halifax, Nova Scotia	22.7.1942
Halifax (HX 200)	27.7.1942	Liverpool	7.8.1942
Loch Ewe (KMS 2)	25.10.1942	Algiers	12.11.1942
Algiers (MKS 2)	23.11.1942	Belfast Lough	7.12.1942
Clyde ON 157)	27.12.1942	Belfast	30.12.1942
Belfast (KX 8)	2.1.1943	Dispersed , 05.47N 15.23W	21.1.1943
Dispersed	21.1.1943	Table Bay	5.2.1943
Table Bay	6.2.1943	Durban	10.2.1943
Durban	20.2.1943	Mombasa	2.3.1943
Mombasa	7.3.1943	Suez	21.3.1943
Port Said	14.4.1943	Alexandria	15.4.1943
Alexandria	17.4.1943	Tripoli, Libya	22.4.1943
Tripoli	8.5.1943	Alexandria	12.5.1943
Alexandria (MWS 36)	3.7.1943	Sicily, Acid South Beachhead	10.7.1943
Sicily, Acid South Beachhead	12.7.1943	Tripoli	14.7.1943
Tripoli	15.7.1943	Port Said	23.7.1943
Port Said	8.8.1943	Alexandria	9.8.1943
Alexandria	10.8.1943	Bone, Algeria	17.8.1943
Bone (MKS 25)	20.9.1943	Gibraltar	25.9.1943
Gibraltar (MKS 25G)	25.9.1943	Clyde	8.10.1943
Clyde (JW 54B)	20.11.1943	Kola Inlet	2.12.1943
Kola Inlet (RA 55A)	23.12.1943	Loch Ewe	1.1.1944
Loch Ewe (JW 57)	20.2.1944	Kola Inlet	28.2.1944
Kola Inlet (RA 58)	7.4.1944	Loch Ewe	14.4.1944
London (ETM 6)	10.6.1944	Normandy, Gold Beachhead	12.6.1944
Seine Bay (FTM 9)	16.6.1944	Southend	17.6.1944
Southend (ETM 15)	23.6.1944	Seine Bay	24.6.1944
Seine Bay (FTM 20)	27.6.1944	Southend	28.6.1944
Southend (ETM 22)	30.6.1944	Seine Bay	1.7.1944
Seine Bay (FTM 26)	3.7.1944	Southend	4.7.1944
Southend (ETM 30)	8.7.1944	Seine Bay	9.7.1944
Seine Bay (FTM 36)	13.7.1944	Southend	14.7.1944
Southend (ETM 39)	17.7.1944	Seine Bay	18.7.1944
Seine Bay (FTM 43)	20.7.1944	Southend	21.7.1944
Southend (ETM 48)	28.7.1944	Seine Bay	29.7.1944
Seine Bay (FTM 54)	1.8.1944	Southend	2.8.1944
Southend (ETM 59)	10.8.1944	Seine Bay	11.8.1944
Seine Bay (FTM 67)	13.8.1944	Solent	13.8.1944
Solent	14.8.1944	Milford Haven	16.8.1944
Clyde (ON 250)	24.8.1944	New York	7.9.1944
Halifax (SC 159)	18.10.1944	Loch Ewe	2.11.1944
Southend (ON 275)	28.12.1944	Halifax	11.1.1945
Halifax	23.1.1945	New York	27.1.1945
New York (HX 340)	23.2.1945	Liverpool	10.3.1945
Belfast Lough (ON 294)	2.4.1945	Halifax	18.4.1945
Halifax	20.4.1945	St. John, New Brunswick	22.4.1945
St. John	9.5.1945	Halifax	11.5.1945
Halifax (HX 357)	21.5.1945	Immingham	5.6.1945
Immingham	21.6.1945	Sorel, Quebec	7.7.1945
Sorel	14.7.1945	Avonmouth	27.7.1945
Avonmouth	31.8.1945	Bremerhaven, Germany	4.9.1945

APPENDIX

— 4 —

MANNING THE OCEANS

The crews that manned the Oceans in wartime were overwhelmingly British in composition. That for *Ocean Vanguard*, the first of her class to sail, counted only three non-UK nationals in her complement, the Bosun hailing from New Zealand, one seaman from Ireland, and a fireman from Malta. The master and chief engineer were long-term employees of the managing company, W H Seager & Co, and in this case joined directly from one of this firm's own ships after her loss in the North Sea. Many of the others, some of them survivors from recently sunk vessels, were assigned from the Montreal Shipping Pool. This group included the second and third officers, rescued with all their crewmates when *Empire Mallard* was sunk in a convoy collision while transiting the Belle Isle Strait on 26 September 1941. (By an unusual coincidence, this 1918-vintage ship, an early war acquisitions from the US Maritime Commission, had originally been ordered by Britain's First World War government from the Tacoma, Washington, yard of the same Todd Corporation which had just built *Ocean Vanguard* for its Second World War successor). The remainder of the crew were ferried over from the UK, the crew agreement suggesting that they had previously served in a fair cross section of the British flagged merchant marine. DEMS gunners were provided by the Navy and did not appear on the crew agreement, but it is unlikely that more than two were provided to handle a three-inch deck gun, such machine guns as were carried at this stage being left to the ship's crew to man.

Four of the crew, including the chief engineer and the bosun were in their fifties, and five, including the master and chief officer, were in their forties. There were five teenagers, and the bulk of the other men were in their twenties or early thirties. A relatively high percentage of the crew hailed from South Wales, but it is unlikely that this was in any way a product of the identity of the managers (Seager was based in Cardiff), as most sailors signed agreements on a voyage-by-voyage basis, with very few returning to the same ship. Most of the ship's complement signed the crew agreement itself shortly before the vessel sailed and would stay on the articles until they were discharged as a group when the voyage ended, as in the case of *Ocean Vanguard* on 16 February 1942 at Cardiff. On extended voyages, there were usually a small number of crew additions or replacements. In this case, the unfortunately named steward, P Bloodworth, was discharged to hospital before the ship left the northwest Pacific coast, and a replacement was signed on in British Columbia. Additional deck hands were signed on at San Pedro, California, and Kingston, Jamaica, with one of the latter also falling ill and being replaced at Halifax, Nova Scotia.

The First Crew of Ocean Vanguard

Crew Agreement signed at San Francisco, 26 October 1941 Crew discharged at Cardiff, 16 February 1942

Name	Rank	Age	Born	Home	Last Ship	Joined
W L Brett	Master	40	Liverpool	Cardiff	*Salvus*	12.5.1941
G C Dorman	First Officer	44	Port Talbot	Port Talbot	*Harpasa*	12.8.1941
H W Calvert	Second Officer	24	Stockton	Norton-on-Tees	*Empire Mallard*	11.10.1941
D Johnston	Third Officer	20	Glasgow	Glasgow	*Empire Mallard*	11.10.1941
J Ritchie	Chief Engineer	58	Leith	Barry	*Salvus*	12.5.1941
T Dorman	Second Engineer	43	South Wales	South Wales	*Artemisia*	12.5.1941
E W Hughes	Third Engineer	32	South Wales	South Wales	*Nailsea Lass*	12.5.1941
T T Greenaway	Fourth Engineer	37	Liverpool	Falmouth	*Canadian Star*	23.10.1941
I Howard	First WT Officer	43	Wandle	Rochdale	*Palacio*	12.5.1941

R W Cheary	Second WT Officer	17	Birkenhead	Birkenhead	*Treverbyn*	12.5.1941
A L Hannah	Third WT Officer	24	Glasgow	Glasgow	*Holmbury*	12.5.1941
N E Bush	Carpenter	34	Cardiff	Cardiff	*Adula*	23.10.1941
F L Hotche	Bosun	57	Auckland NZ	Cardiff	*Maycrest*	12.5.1941
S M Richards	Able Seaman	28	St Austell	St Austell	*Nivernais*	23.10.1941
L Keat	Able Seaman	38	Port Isaac	Port Isaac	*Nivernais*	23.10.1941
W A Tiltman	Able Seaman	32	Teignmouth	Teignmouth	*Nivernais*	23.10.1941
M J Fitzgerald	Able Seaman	24	Wicklow, Ireland	Wicklow	*Adula*	23.10.1941
N Eustis	Able Seaman	36	Cornwall	Cornwall	*Olympus*	23.10.1941
C J Shears	Able Seaman	48	London	Penzance	*Satellite*	23.10.1941
S C Thomas	Able Seaman	29	Port Isaac	Port Isaac	*Stanlake*	23.10.1941
E Keefer	Ordinary Seaman	32	Westham	London	*Darina*	23.10.194
A Withers	Ordinary Seaman	20	Newport	Newport	*Barrgrove*	23.10.1941
H Fowle	Ordinary Seaman	19	Bargoed	Newport	*King William*	23.10.1941
D J Bronton	Cook	30	Port Talbot	Manchester	*Corbias*	23.10.1941
L J Broome	Second Cook	18	Newport	Newport	*Empire Gull*	23.10.1941
P Bloodworth*	Steward	58	Gloucester	Barry Dock	*Tunisia*	12.5.1941
J Morrell	Assistant Steward	21	Grangemouth	Grangemouth	*Socony*	23.10.1941
A Thomson	Assistant Steward	20	Grangemouth	Grangemouth	*Socony*	23.10.1941
T Rowlands	Cabin Boy	18	Newport	Newport	*Storness*	23.10.1941
H Simms	Donkeyman	36	Liverpool	Liverpool	*Pasteur*	23.10.1941
G Major	Greaser	26	Liverpool	Liverpool	*Pasteur*	23.10.1941
J W Keown	Greaser	55	Liverpool	Liverpool	*Kent*	23.10.1941
G Jones	Fireman	28	Swansea	Newport	*Svint*	23.10.1941
A Andrews	Fireman	26	S. Shields	Newport	*Holmbury*	23.10.1941
C G Jeffries	Fireman	29	Crosskeys, Mon	South Wales	*Capeto*	23.10.1941
C Farrugio	Fireman	21	Malta	London	*Empire Resistance*	23.10.1941
E Ford	Fireman	20	Abertillery	Newport	*Kaley*	23.10.1941
F Sidney	Fireman	24	Newport	Newport	*PLM 13*	23.10.1941
P Watkins	Fireman	26	Newport	Newport	*Storness*	23.10.1941
W H Pumford*	Fireman	26	Newport	Newport	*City of Cairo*	23.10.1941
R H George	Fireman	32	Penzance	Penzance	*Warden*	23.10.1941
P McCarron	Fireman	21	Motherwell	Leith	*Loire*	23.10.1941
D Wilson	Fireman	19	Glasgow	Bathgate	*Capeto*	23.10.1941
T H Matthews	Fireman	28	Swansea	Swansea	*Empire Gull*	23.10.1941
Joined at New Westminster, British Columbia						
C Hobbs	Steward	56	Devonport	Newport	*Empire Kudu*	1.11.1941
Joined at San Francisco, California						
H R Saunders	Greaser	27	London	London	*Inversuis*	13.11.1941
Joined at San Pedro, California						
G Sanderson	Deck Hand	26	Huddersfield	Huddersfield	*Royal Ulsterman*	24.11.1941
J Bailey	Deck Hand	27	Darwen	Darwen	*Turquoise*	24.11.1941
Joined at Kingston, Jamaica						
R Cooke*	Deck Hand	28	Co Donegal	Greenock	*Clan Macarthur*	15.12.1941
G Coates	Deck Hand	30	Co Durham	Co Durham	*Clan Macarthur*	15.12.1941
Joined at Halifax, Nova Scotia						
W Best	Deck Hand	21	London	London	*Katvaldis*	30.12.1941

* Discharged due to illness

APPENDIX

— 5 —

THE COST OF WAR

A total of 196 men were killed while serving on the Oceans during the Second World War, of whom 183 died when their ships were sunk. The latter figure represented a casualty rate of 17 per cent of the total crew and passengers embarked at the time of the attack. While comprehensive data for the British merchant marine does not exist, partial figures suggest that the Ocean casualty rate was significantly below that for the entire service. A range of factors were at play here. As already noted, the ships themselves were robust by industry standards and well equipped with safety equipment. In addition, general crew survivability in 1942–5, when the Oceans were in service, was significantly higher than it had been in the first half of the war, due not only to better survival training and equipment, but also to increases in escort and rescue provision. Personnel losses were also kept down by the circumstances in which most vessels were lost. Five vessels were sunk in port or anchorage, and three more during daylight attacks on well-escorted convoys, while most of the losses in distant theatres took place in busy coastal waters. Five of the seven vessels lost in the rescue-friendly Mediterranean suffered no personnel losses, and the remaining two, only eight between them. Indeed, the bulk of the losses were accounted for by four casualties, of which two, *Ocean Venture* (thirty-one killed) and *Ocean Honour* (twenty killed) lost men due to weather and/or explosions. The two largest fatality totals, those of *Ocean Crusader* (fifty killed) and *Ocean Courage* (fifty-two killed), were each the product of one of the more common causes of total or near-total crew loss: the first sunk while sailing alone after losing her convoy in bad weather in the North Atlantic, and the second dragged under at night by her cargo of iron ore within two minutes of being torpedoed.

Personnel Casualties

Vessel	Date	Location of Loss (Damage)	Cause	Crew/Lost
Ocean Venture	8.2.1942	US east coast, off Cape Hatteras	submarine	45/31
Ocean Venus	3.5.1942	US east coast, off Cape Canaveral	submarine	47/5
*Ocean Voice**	27.5.1942	(Arctic, Barents Sea)	aircraft	-/0
Ocean Might	2.9.1942	Gold Coast, off Takoradi	submarine	54/4
Ocean Vanguard	13.9.1942	Off Trinidad, east of Galera Point	submarine	51/11
Ocean Honour	16.9.1942	Gulf of Aden, west of Socotra	submarine	53/20
Ocean Voice	22.9.1942	Norwegian Sea, west of Jan Mayen Isle	submarine	98**/0
*Ocean Vagabond**	29.9.1942	(North Atlantic)	submarine	48/0
Ocean Vintage	22.10.1942	Gulf of Oman, off Masirah Island	submarine	50/0
Ocean Justice	6.11.1942	East of Trinidad	submarine	56/0
*Ocean Vista**	21.11.1942	(Mediterranean, Bougie harbour)	aircraft	-/2
Ocean Crusader	26.11.1942	North Atlantic	submarine	50/50
Ocean Vanquisher	12.12.1942	Mediterranean, Bay of Algiers	limpet mine	49/2
Ocean Vagabond	12.1.1943	North Atlantic	submarine	47/1
Ocean Courage	15.1.1943	Atlantic, south of Cape Verde Isles	submarine	58/52
*Ocean Rider**	21.1.1943	(Mediterranean, west of Cape Caxine)	aircraft	56/0
Ocean Freedom	13.3.1943	Arctic, Murmansk harbour	aircraft	64/0
Ocean Seaman	15.3.1943	Mediterranean, northwest of Algiers	submarine	59/0
Ocean Voyager	19.3.1943	Mediterranean, Tripoli harbour	aircraft	55/6
*Ocean Viceroy**	29.3.1943	(Northeast Atlantic)	submarine	57/5
Ocean Peace	12.7.1943	Mediterranean, off Avola, Sicily	aircraft	78/0

BIBLIOGRAPHY

Archive Material

The National Archives, Kew

ADM 1	Admiralty: Correspondence & Papers
ADM 116	Admiralty: Record Office: Cases
ADM 199	Admiralty: War History, Cases & Papers, Second World War
ADM 237	Admiralty: Naval Staff: Operations Division: Convoy Records, Second World War
AVIA 38/117	British Shipbuilding Mission to the U.S.A., 1940–1.
BT 31	Files of Dissolved Companies
BT 110	British Merchant Ships - Closed Registers
BT 347	Daily Casualty Lists for Merchant Ships, 1942–4
BT 380	Crew Agreements & Official Log Books - Provisional Registers, 1941–2
BT 389	Vessel Movement Cards, 1939–45
CAB 65	War Cabinet Minutes
CAB 66	War Cabinet Memoranda
CUST 130	London Custom House Registers (London Registers of Merchant Ships)
MT 9	Board of Trade, Ministry of Transport & Successors: Marine Files
MT 40	Sea Transport: Correspondence & Papers
MT 45	Ministry of Transport Establishments & Organisation: Correspondence & Papers
MT 59	Shipping Control & Operations: Correspondence & Papers
PREM 3/381	Prime Minister's Office: Operational Correspondence

The National Records of Scotland, Register House, Edinburgh

BT 2 Files of Dissolved Companies

The National Maritime Museum – Caird Library, Greenwich

Clan Line Board Minutes

Glasgow City Archives – Mitchell Library, Glasgow

Lyle Shipping Company Ltd Board Minutes

Glasgow University Archives, Glasgow

Ben Line Archives

Glamorgan Archives, Cardiff

Cardiff Registers of Merchant Ships

Manchester Archives & Local Studies, Manchester Central Library

Manchester Registers of Merchant Ships

National Museums & Galleries on Merseyside – Maritimes Archives & Library

Liverpool Registers of Merchant Ships

Teesside Archives, Middlesbrough

West Hartlepool Registers of Merchant Ships

Books and Articles

Behrens, C B A: *Merchant Shipping and the Demands of War*, HMSO (London 1955)

Bennett, G H and Bennett R: *Survivors: British Merchant Seamen in the Second World War*, Hambledown (London 1999)

Buxton, Ian, Fenton, Roy and Murphy, Hew: 'Measuring Britain's Merchant Shipbuilding Output in the Twentieth Century', *Mariner's Mirror*, 2015

Clarkson, John, Fenton, Roy and Munro, Archie: *Clan Line: Illustrated Fleet History*, Ships in Focus (Preston 2007)

Crawford, John O: *The 'Vales' of Glasgow: Andrew Crawford & Co. Ltd., 1895–1955*, Andrew Crawford & Co Ltd, (Glasgow 1955)

Dear, Ian: *The Ropner Story*, Hutchinson Benham (London 1986)

Elphick, Peter: *Liberty: The Ships that Won the War*, Chatham (London 2001)

Fenton, Roy: *Tramp Ships: An Illustrated History*, Seaforth (Barnsley 2013)

Gray, Leonard: *The Ropner Fleet, 1874–1974*, World Ship Society (Kendal 1975)

Hague, Arnold: *The Allied Convoy System 1939–1945: Its Organisation, Defence and Operation*, Chatham (London 2000)

Heal, S C: *A Great Fleet of Ships: the Canadian Forts and Parks*, Vanwell (St Catharines, Ontario 1999)

Hennessy, Elizabeth: *The Bolton Group, 1874–1982*, Publications for Companies (Stevenage 1983)

Howarth, Stephen and Law, Derek (eds): *The Battle of the Atlantic, 1939–1945: The 50th Anniversary International Naval Conference*, Greenhill (London 1994)

Johnman, Lewis and Murphy, Hugh: *Scott Lithgow: Déjà Vu All Over Again! The Rise and Fall of a Shipbuilding Company*, International Maritime Economic History Association (St John's, Newfoundland 2005)

Lane, Frederic C with Coll, Blanche D, Fischer Gerald J and Tyler, David B: *Ships for Victory: A History of Shipbuilding under the US Maritime Commission in World War II*, Johns Hopkins (Baltimore 1951)

Lane, Tony: *The Merchant Seamen's War*, Manchester University Press (Manchester 1990)

Mallmann Showell, Jak P, *U-Boat Command and the Battle of the Atlantic*, Conway (London 1989)

Mitchell, W H and Sawyer, L A: *The Oceans, the Forts, and the Parks: Merchant Shipbuilding for British Account in North America during World War II*. Sea Breezes (Liverpool 1966)

Mitchell, W H and Sawyer, L A: *The Empire Ships: A Record of British-Built and Acquired Merchant Ships during the Second World War*, Second Edition, Lloyd's of London (London 1990)

Moss, Michael and Hume, John R: *Shipbuilders to the World: 125 Years of Harland and Wolff, Belfast, 1861–1986*, The Blackstaff Press (Belfast 1986)

O'Hara, Vincent P: *Torch: North Africa and the Allied Path to Victory*, Naval Institute Press (Annapolis MD 2015)

Orbell, John: *From Cape to Cape: The History of Lyle Shipping Company*, Paul Harris (Edinburgh 1978)

Parker, George H: *Astern Business: 75 Years of UK Shipbuilding*, World Ship Society (Kendal 1996)

Paterson, Lawrence: *Schnellboote: A Complete Operational History*, Seaforth (Barnsley 2015)

Reid, J M: *James Lithgow: Master of Work*, Hutchinson (London 1964)

Robins, Nick: *Wartime Standard Ships*, Seaforth (Barnsley 2017)

Rohwer, Jürgen: *Axis Submarine Successes*, Patrick Stephens (Cambridge 1983)

Rohwer, Jürgen and Gerhard Hummelchen: *Chronology of the War at Sea 1939–1945: The Naval History of World War Two*, Second Edition, Greenhill Books (London 1992)

Ruegg, Bob and Hague, Arnold: *Convoys to Russia: Allied Convoys and Naval Surface Operations in Arctic Waters, 1941–1945*, World Ship Society (Kendal 1992)

Runyon, Timothy J and Copes, Jan M (eds): *To Die Gallantly: The Battle of the Atlantic*, Westview Press (Boulder, Col 1994)

Sawyer, L A and Mitchell, W H: *From America to United States: The History of the Merchant Ship Types Built in the United States of America under the Long-Range Programme of the Maritime Commission*, World Ship Society (Kendal), Part One, 1979, Part Two, 1981, Part Three, 1984, Part Four, 1986

Sawyer, L A and Mitchell, W H: *The Liberty Ships: The History of the 'Emergency' Type Cargo Ships Constructed in the United States during the Second World War*, Second Edition, Lloyd's of London (London 1985)

Shores, Christopher and Massimello, Giovanni, with Guest, Russell, Olynyk, Frank and Bock, Winfried: *A History of the Mediterranean Air War, 1940–1945, Volume Three: Tunisia and the End in Africa, November 1942–May 1943*, Grub Street (London 2016)

Shores, Christopher and Massimello, Giovanni, with Guest, Russell, Olynyk, Frank, Bock, Winfried & Thomas, Andy, *A History of the Mediterranean Air War, 1940–1945, Volume Four: Sicily and Italy to the Fall of Rome, 14 May 1943–5 June 1944*. Grub Street (London 2018)

Slader, John: *The Fourth Service: Merchantmen at War, 1939–1945*, Robert Hale (London 1994)

Somner, Graeme: *Ben Line*, Ships in Focus (Preston 2009)

Stewart, I G: *British Tramps and their Peacetime Contribution to World Shipping History*, Ian Stewart (Rockingham Beach 1997)

Sturmey, S G: *British Shipping and World Competition*, Athlone Press (London 1962)

Tarrant, V E: *The U-Boat Offensive 1914–1945*, Arms & Armour Press (London 1989)

Tarrant, V E: *The Last Year of the Kriegsmarine*, Arms & Armour Press (London 1994)

Terraine, John: *Business in Great Waters: The U-Boat Wars*, Leo Cooper (London 1989)

Thomas, P N: *British Ocean Tramps, Volume One: Builders and Cargoes; Volume Two: Owners and Their Ships*, Waine Research Publications (Wolverhampton 1992)

Winser, John de S: *The D-Day Ships: Neptune: The Greatest Amphibious Operation in History*, World Ship Society (Kendal 1994)

Winser, John de S: *British Invasion Fleets: The Mediterranean and Beyond, 1942–1945*, Kendall, World Ship Society, 2002

Woodman, Richard: *The Arctic Convoys, 1941–1945*, John Murray (London 1994)

Woodman, Richard: *The Real Cruel Sea: The Merchant Navy in the Battle of the Atlantic, 1939–1943*, John Murray (London 2004)

Other Reference Material

Schell, William A, with Haworth, Rodger, continuing work begun by Starke, Tony,
Register of Merchant Ships Completed in 1940–1941
Register of Merchant Ships Completed in the USA, 1942–1945: Part II – Maritime Commission Designs and Private Orders
World Ship Society (Kendal) electronic publication

Websites

www.combinedfleet.com Japanese submarines: Tabular Records of Movements (TROMs).

www.convoyweb.org.uk Allied convoy composition and sailing records.

www.naval-history.net British warship and convoy operations.

www.shipbuildinghistory.com US emergency merchant ship construction and shipyard history.

www.uboat.net U-boat operations including patrol, Allied ships sunk and U-boat loss information.

INDEX

Warships are identified by their navy in upper case letters:
Canada/Royal Canadian Navy – RCN
Germany/Kriegsmarine – KM
Italy/ Regia Marina – RM
Japan/ Imperial Japanese Navy – IJN
Norway/Royal Norwegian Navy – RNN
UK/Royal Navy – RN; Royal Fleet Auxiliary – RFA
USA/United States Navy – USN

Merchantmen are identified by their country of register in lower case letters:
Bahamas – ba
Belgium – be
China – ch
Costa Rica – cr
Cyprus – cy
France – fr
Greece – gr
Hong Kong – hk
India – in
Israel – is
Italy – it
Lebanon – le
Liberia – li
Netherlands – du
Norway – nw
Panama – pa
Poland – po
Taiwan - ta
USA – am
USSR – ru